MUHLENBERG LIB

S0-ADL-419

This provocative case study of Princeton, New Jersey takes to task the notion that the inner city is the sole source of housing problems. Like many other "affluent suburbs" (Route 128 near Boston, Palo Alto on the West Coast, the environs of Washington, D.C.) whose inhabitants have attempted to insulate themselves from the poor and the ordinary, Princeton is going to become an even more exclusive and expensive residential enclave. Its inhabitants are already in the upper quarter of American income levels, educational achievements and life-styles. But while such areas have prestigeous housing and a substantial tax base, problems are developing. Present residents are being forced out—the poor, the old, even municipal workers—and the community is unable to provide facilities for medium income employees of new firms flocking to the area because of its desirability.

The authors have produced an impressive statistical survey of Princeton and its environs. Packed with maps, tables and charts, this volume presents the economic facts upon which realistic future housing policy in communities like Princeton must be based. It also raises profound questions about the responsibility of local officials to the people whom they serve.

Robert William Burchell is a research assistant at Rutgers University and coauthor of *Housing Costs and Housing Restraints: Newark, N. J.* and *Leisure Market Studies I: Marina Development.*

Lynne Beyer Sagalyn is a research assistant at Rutgers University. Her areas of interest include housing and education planning. This is her first publication.

George S. Sternlieb is director of the Center for Urban Policy Studies and professor of urban and regional planning at Rutgers University, New Brunswick. He has been a member of President Nixon's Task Force on Housing and a consultant to the Urban Institute and the Department of Housing and Urban Development. He has frequently testified before Congressional committees and subcommittees. Among his recent publications are *Leisure Market Studies: I The Shore User,* and *II Marina Development, The Tenement Landlord,* and *The Urban Housing Dilemma.*

THE AFFLUENT SUBURB

THE AFFLUENT SUBURB:

PRINCETON

GEORGE STERNLIEB
ROBERT W. BURCHELL
LYNNE SAGALYN
with
RICHARD M. GORDON

331.83
5839a

Published by
*trans*action *books*
New Brunswick, New Jersey
Distributed by E.P. Dutton & Co.

Copyright© 1971 by Transaction Inc.
New Brunswick, New Jersey

All rights reserved. No part of this publication may be
reproduced or transmitted in any form or by any means,
electronic or mechanical, including photocopy, recording,
or any information storage and retrieval system, without
permission in writing from the publisher.

Printed in the United States of America
Library of Congress Catalog Number: LC-75-164979
ISBN 0-87855-006-2

This volume was prepared for the Regional Planning Board of Princeton, New Jersey
by the Center for Urban Policy Research
Rutgers — the State University of New Jersey,
New Brunswick, New Jersey

CONTENTS

LIST OF EXHIBITS

ACKNOWLEDGEMENTS

This study would have been impossible without the wholehearted co-operation of the Regional Planning Board of Princeton and the municipal staffs of both Princeton Borough and Princeton Township.

The Planning Board, under the direction of Mr. Hans K. Sander, made necessary decisions and otherwise performed its portion of the contract speedily and efficiently. The Board's secretary, Mrs. Eleanor Clausen, laboriously isolated all previous studies bearing on this report and maintained them in a convenient place for our use and re-use.

Both municipal staffs also made their records available and lent their experience in specific calculations derived from them. Special mention in this vein should go to the Borough Engineering Department and the Township Tax Department.

Without the diligent performance of the clerical staff of the Rutgers Center for Urban Policy Research, this document would never have met its deadline. Mrs. Dolores Rudolph, Mrs. Joan Frantz and Mrs. Evelyn Weil went through the typing chores of several drafts and the pressures of time restrictions in a thoroughly effective fashion.

Finally, we must mention the efforts of our proofreader, Miss Karla Cohn, and our computer specialist, Mr. William Dolphin. Whatever legibility and numerical consistency this document contains is due largely to their labors.

PREFACE

In the summer of 1970, The Rutgers Center for Urban Policy Research conducted a study of the Princeton housing market for the Regional Planning Board of Princeton. This report contains the results of that study which was specifically designed to provide officials and residents with fundamental information on the workings of the local market. As will be evident to the reader, the statistics of housing supply and demand outline the forms and stresses of the residential market; the Planning Board and the citizens themselves must determine whether the local market reflects the kind of community that they desire both now and in the future.

This is a report on housing in an affluent suburb. While housing problems in the absolute sense are most significant in the core areas of our country, they are far from unique to them.The city described here, Princeton, New Jersey, has its counterparts in many sections of the United States. It has more in common perhaps with the band of suburban development peripheral to Massachusetts' "Electronic Highway" (Route 128) or to some of the newer fortresses of technocracy outside of Washington and their equivalents on the West Coast, than it does with the balance of the state in which it happens to be located.

What are these elements? Typically they are composed of a population which is substantially in the upper quartile of American income levels, educational achievements and styles of life. Why should there be any question of a housing problem? The answer is several fold: The very desirability of the place in question, the quality of its schools and of its whole style of life, make it a major focal point of home seekers anxious to share in its amenities.

The growth of industry peripheral to the community, in part cause and in part consequence of the desirability of the locale, engenders additional housing demand. The result is frequently to outprice the earlier inhabitants who have contributed to the very desirability of the municipality in question. These problems are compounded by the stresses inherent within the very prosperity of the community.

As housing costs go up, the capacity of the community to provide shelter at reasonable prices for municipal workers and other moderately incomed groups is reduced. What is the attitude of the schoolteacher or the policeman as well as other municipal employees toward the inhabitants and their own role in a community whose housing they simply can't afford? What responsibility, if any, does a community have for providing facilities for those whose services are essential to it?

Indeed, given the shifting priorities of our society, is there a responsibility to those whose incomes are even lower? What should Princeton do, for example, about the poor of New Jersey? In a state where the number of people on welfare is approximately one out of every 20, should suburban municipalities make any provision for them? And how about the elderly whose income levels cannot support the increased cost of Princeton's housing but who have spent the bulk of their lives there? Should the city make provision for these members of its society? And how can all of these elements be blended in such a fashion as to maintain the very charm and desirability of the municipality which has produced some of these stresses?

The development of the interstate highways system in conjunction with equivalent toll facilities has given a new character to "bedroom" suburbs. While the Princeton case is accentuated, it is in no way unique in serving as the locus of major industrial and commerical development.

Thus the affluent suburb has the best of both worlds: exclusive housing and a very substantial tax base. But there are strains incumbent upon this conjunction. Where are the employees of the new firms that string along the highways peripheral to the community to live? Where are they to shop? How significant to potential employees is the lack of housing within the prime community of the area? To what degree does this lack of housing significantly hinder economic growth? These are significant questions which must be answered.

Over and above them however is the problem of what, if any, responsibility the community has to house people whose employment is within its confines? And how many of them are there, both now and in the future?

As mentioned previously, policy making is the responsibility of local officials. Our effort here is to provide the factual parameters, to produce some of the building blocks of data essential for decision-making in the several spheres.

A number of different methods were utilized in the development of the findings:

DEMAND

1. *A Broad Based Sampling of Community Attitudes and Housing*
   This was based on a probability sample of 501 interviews with members of the Princeton populace.
2. *The Underhoused*
   This part of the study involved door-to-door interviews of 100 household heads in specifically designated areas of the community.
3. *Municipal Employee Attitudes*
   Seventy permanent Borough and Township employees were interviewed in depth in order to determine their attitudes toward housing and the local community.
4. *Future Employment Trends*
   Five categories of industry were developed to establish this. Interviews were conducted with 50 firms in the greater Princeton area.

SUPPLY

5. *A Land and Housing Inventory*
   A survey of housing supply from 1960 to 1970 and existing vacant land in 1970 for both the Borough and Township of Princeton was undertaken.
6. *A Profile of the Newcomers to the Community*
   Fifty recent home buyers and 50 recent renters were interviewed to secure a portrait of the successful entrants into the community. Their attributes reflect the realities of the market.

(See the Methodology in Appendix I.)

I

PRINCETON:

ITS PEOPLE AND THEIR HOUSING

This section describes the socioeconomic characteristics of Princeton's present population. The information contained here is drawn from a telephone survey of 501 households in the Township and the Borough and as such represents a probability sample of approximately 7.5 percent of the total population. For convenience, the sample is referred to as the Present Residents Survey (PRS).

While the results of the survey show that residents of the Township and the Borough are characterized by considerable differences, it should be emphasized at the outset that, as a group, Princeton residents are particularly proud of the community and show a strong loyalty to the area.

While the changes in the housing market described in subsequent chapters will undoubtedly have some effect on the residents of Princeton, this is a description of Princeton in 1970, its people and their housing.

Chapter I
THE AFFLUENT SUBURB

The chapter which follows details the socioeconomic characteristics and housing desires of present Princeton residents. It is an attempt to view the community as a unit. Most statistics utilized have been derived from the PRS and further amplified by data available from the United States Census. [1]

Within this study there has been an effort to insure that the data is statistically as well as geographically representative. In the former case a population projection was attempted based upon the sample distribution of the PRS. Exhibit I-1 indicates its comparability to preliminary population estimates available from the 1970 Census. The methodology for this projection, and a specific listing of the sub-populations which are included, appear in Appendix II.

To insure geographic representativeness, the Harvard University SYMAP Program (a computerized map-producing program) was employed to display visually data points and key variables. [2] Exhibit I-2 shows the distribution of the 501 data points. Areas appearing deficiently sampled were checked and in all cases found to be concentrations of vacant land. A brief description of the SYMAP program and its specific utilization here will be found in Appendix II.

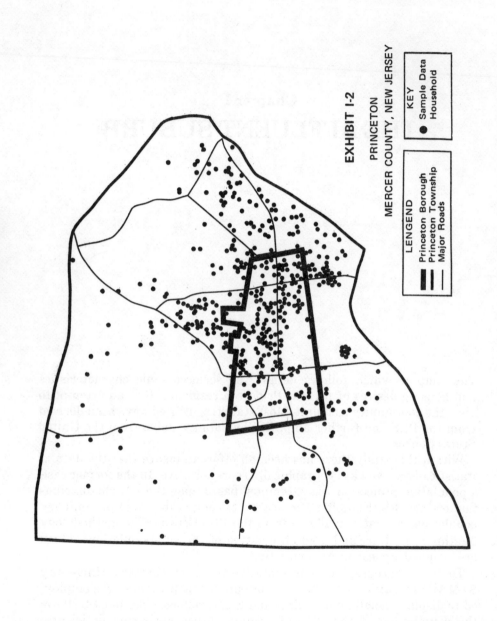

EXHIBIT I-2

PRINCETON
MERCER COUNTY, NEW JERSEY

LENGEND
Princeton Borough
Princeton Township
Major Roads

KEY
Sample Data
● Household

COMMUNITY DATA

SETTING

Princeton is located in the west central portion of New Jersey between the cities of New Brunswick and Trenton. In a regional context, it is midway between New York City and Philadelphia and is positioned within the Boston-to-Washington transportation corridor (Exhibit I-3).

Princeton is a residential and educational/research center with a land area of approximately 18 square miles in which 25,000 to 26,000 people reside. The Borough, which is completely surrounded by the Township (Exhibit I-4), is smaller in area and in population. It occupies 1.76 square miles, and houses just over 12,300 people, 4,500 of whom are students. The Township is over nine times as large as the Borough (16.25 square miles) and has a population 12 percent greater. The Township's total population is 13,651, of which 12,700 comprise its permanent non-student segment.

GOVERNMENTAL JURISDICTION

Throughout their history both Borough and Township have maintained separate territorial jurisdictions and distinct forms of municipal government. The Borough operates under the "weak" mayor-council plan in which a directly elected mayor and council share administrative power and responsibility. The Township functions under

EXHIBIT I-1

RECENT POPULATION ESTIMATES PRIOR TO THE 1970 CENSUS

			POPULATION ESTIMATES			
MUNICI-PALITY	1960 U.S. Census (Actual)	Princeton Chmbr. of Commerce 1968	N.J. Taxpayers Assoc. 1968	N.J. Dept. of Labor Industry 1969	Rutgers CUPR 1970	1970 U.S. Census (Preliminary)
Borough	11,890	13,000	12,990	13,000	11,920	12,311
Township	10,411	15,000	13,510	13,760	13,500	13,651

Source: Princeton Housing Study — 1970
Center for Urban Policy Research

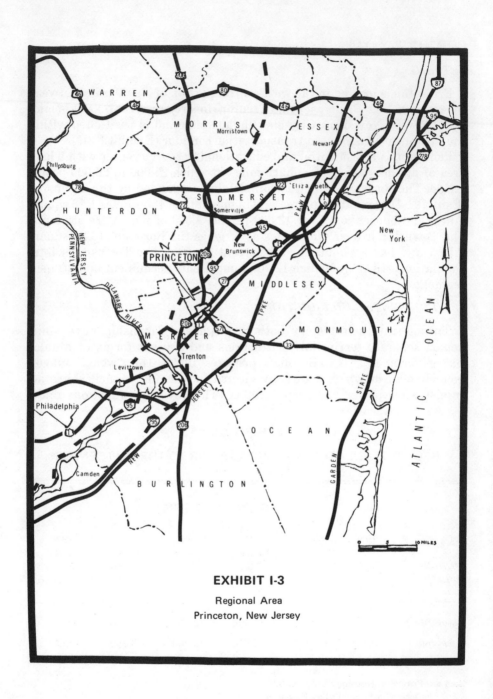

EXHIBIT I-3

Regional Area
Princeton, New Jersey

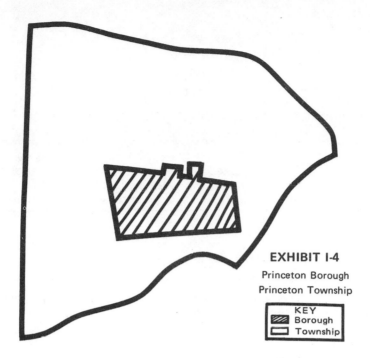

EXHIBIT I-4

Princeton Borough
Princeton Township

KEY
Borough
Township

a form of the commission plan wherein members of a township committee (including a committee-designated mayor) collectively share governmental responsibility and individually supervise operational departments. Since in both cases, senior elected officials perform governmental duties on a part-time basis, each municipality employs an administrator and a full-time staff to supervise daily municipal operations.

Although consolidation has been attempted in the past, on at least one occasion it has been rejected at the polls. Nevertheless, many community services are operated jointly, including the Free Public Library, the Princeton Regional Planning Commission, the Princeton Regional School System, the Joint Recreation Board, the Civil Rights Commission, the Sewer Operating Committee, the Joint Civil Defense Council and the Borough Volunteer Fire Department.

POPULATION

When the population growth of Princeton Borough and Township are compared, a disparity between central and peripheral development is evident. The Borough, developed to over 90 perent of its zoned capacity, has been fluctuating at this percentage for approximately 20 years. If downtown parking is "bridged over" or rearranged, and if two larger tracts in the Borough, residential zones permitting both one- and two-family dwellings, are subsequently developed, the remaining residential capacity should be reached soon after 1980.

THE AFFLUENT SUBURB

EXHIBIT I-5

PRINCETON POPULATION STATISTICS 1950-1970

YEAR	TOTAL POPULATION Borough/Township		TOTAL HOUSEHOLDS Borough/Township		POPULATION IN HOUSEHOLDS Borough/Township		MEAN HOUSEHOLD SIZE Borough/Township	
1950	12,230	5,407	2,578	—	8,107	—	3.14	—
1960	11,890	10,411	2,866	2,929	8,145	10,147	2.84	3.46
1970	12,311	13,651	2,918^e	3,919^e	8,200^e	13,100^e	2.81^e	3.34^e

Source: U. S. Censuses 1960 and 1970. Estimates (e) obtained from adjusting 1970 PRS by partial information available from 1970 Census

The Township, at only 75 percent of its residential capacity, passed through its first major wave of growth from 1950 to 1960. It continues to grow but in a somewhat more selective manner. Although the Township population increased by over 3,000 from 1960 to 1970, its average annual growth rate was only 3 percent compared to 9.3 percent in the decade 1950-1960. The problem of land availability, although not as severe as in the Borough, has now become a controlling factor in the Township's residential expansion.

A general decrease in household size has accompanied the lack of growth in the Borough and the declining growth rate in the Township. While a declining household size is more characteristic of the Township than of the Borough, it must be remembered that the single, divorced and widowed population is larger in the Borough and that its household size is affected to a lesser degree by trends which influence the "intact family" size.

Notwithstanding the trends of central stability and peripheral growth in the presence of decreasing household size, there is another more subtle change occurring within the population of the Princeton community. As the home of Princeton University, Princeton Theological Seminary and Westminster Choir College, Princeton has a large number of students living within its borders. In many respects, Princeton is an impacted area whose housing market and population growth are abnormally affected by "semi-transient" residents (Exhibit I-6).

After studying the impact of students on Princeton's housing market in the years from 1950 to 1960, Astrid Monson of Raymond and May

EXHIBIT I-6

RESIDENTIAL DISTRIBUTION OF THE MAJOR STUDENT POPULATIONS
(PRINCETON UNIVERSITY [PU], PRINCETON THEOLOGICAL
SEMINARY [PTS], WESTMINSTER CHOIR COLLEGE [WCC])

STUDENT GROUP	1960[1]	1970	PU	PTS	WCC
Single Students on Campus in Group Quarters (Borough)	3592	3950[2]	3400	200	350
Single Students on Campus in Group Quarters (Township)	0	300[3]	300	0	0
Married Students in College Housing (Borough)	44	54	0	54	0
Married Students in College Housing (Township)	245	400[3]	400	0	0
Single Students in Private Housing (Borough)	196	353[4]	350	3	0
Single Students in Private Housing (Township)	49	151[4]	150	1	0
Married Students in Private Housing (Borough)	310	180[5]	172	8	0
Married Students in Private Housing (Township)	77	79[5]	73	6	0

[1] Monson, Astrid, "Social and Economic Trends" (Borough of Princeton), Raymond and May Associates, New York, January 1966, p.6.

[2] Estimates obtained from respective realty offices

[3] New construction — Princeton University 1964-1966.

[4] PU figure — 1970 estimate — off-campus graduate and undergraduate (625) assuming 80 percent locate in Princeton community of which the Borough/Township splits 70/30. (20 percent of those who reside in both communities double-up. See Kendree and Shepherd, "Housing Need in the Princeton Community" — Background data Part 1 — 1967, p. 12.) PTS figures from realty office.

[5] PU figure — 1970 estimate — off-campus, graduate and undergraduate (350) — assuming 70 percent locate in Princeton Community of which Borough/Township splits 70/30. PTS figures from realty office.

Source: Princeton Housing Study — Summer 1970.

Associates concluded: "This would seem to indicate a decline between 400 and 500 in the number of permanent borough residents and an approximately equal increase in the number of students living off campus." Projecting these findings to 1970 and expanding their applicability at least in part to Princeton Township provides some insight into current trends.

EXHIBIT I-7

STUDENT AND RESIDENT POPULATIONS — PRINCETON — 1950-1970

	1950	Borough 1960	1970
Student Population	3,660	4,098	4,537
Other Resident Population	8,570	7,792	7,774
		Township	
Student Population	NA[1]	371	930
Other Resident Population	NA	10,040	12,721

Sources: Monson, Astrid, "Social and Economic Trends," Raymond and May Associates, 1966, p.6

McHugh, F. D., *Proposed Master Plan Revisions — Programs and Related Studies,* 1960, p.13

[1]Not available

While the figures displayed above show this to be much more a factor in the Borough, where the residential capacity has essentially been reached, student expansion is nonetheless an increasing part of the Township growth pattern. From 1960 to 1970 the Borough's student population increased by close to 4 percent. The effect of this was much more noticeable since the Borough's resident population actually experienced a slight decline. In the Township, however, while the student population rose more than 5 percent, the prime concern was anticipating future services necessary to sustain a decade of total growth exceeding 25 percent.

As shown in Exhibit I-7, when only the permanent resident populations of both communities are considered, it is evident that the approximate 60/40 population ratio evidenced in the PRS foretells a Township "drain" on mutual services that is only beginning to be compensated for. Schools, libraries, recreation facilities and other joint efforts must eventually be planned for, and subsequently be compensated, on the basis of at least 70 percent Township usage of all mutual facilities.

The impact of student growth on the Borough was initially eased and subsequently made more acute by a series of Princeton University decisions which, with great foresight, sought to expand married graduate student facilities in the Township, yet misinterpreted the effect of draft requirements and thereby caused 550 single graduate students to look to the briefly relieved Borough housing market.

The effect of students on the local housing market is a factor noted by Princeton residents and Princeton University personnel as well. It is not really apparent, however, until the Borough housing capacity is viewed as fixed and the University seen as a continually growing entity. The University-created student housing demand is increasing and — as far as the Borough is concerned — continuing to eliminate locals for every housing unit it takes for itself.*

HOUSEHOLD CHARACTERISTICS

The use of the telephone directory to determine a survey sample has its most serious weakness in terms of household characteristics. There is obviously some tendency to underestimate the number of single-person households or transient student accommodations. Subject to this weakness and realizing that the majority of questions concerning household characteristics were directed to the head of household, a summary of resident characteristics was compiled.

EDUCATION

A reprint of a magazine article distributed by the local Chamber of Commerce notes:

> "Prestigious, socially-correct Princeton is located in a small ivy-covered, tree lined valhalla. Princeton is synonymous with prestige, *brains*, success, savoir-faire." [3]

Professional and managerial occupations of the Princeton head of household reflect this somewhat florid observation. In 1960, the median level of education for males 25 years and over in both Borough and Township was greater than 16 years. [4] Ten years later, the PRS found

---

*Princeton University, frequently cast in the role as a source of increasing local housing demand, must also be looked upon as a significant housing generator. Princeton University has constructed the great majority of the 16 percent of Borough/Township housing stock which it now maintains.

the median level of education for the head of household (male or female) in these same communities to be 15.1 and 16.0 years respectively. Since the sampling procedure eliminated a considerable proportion of the graduate school population, some of whom are over 25 and therefore included in the census tabulation, it would appear that the local education skew obvious in 1960 at least has been preserved and may well be more accentuated in 1970.

In the exhibit which follows, Princeton's 1970 educational statistics are compared to those of Wellesley, Massachusetts, and Garden City, New York, in 1960. These communities were selected for comparison because each has a suburban location, is noted for its relative affluence and has an institution of higher education within its borders.

When compared with these communities, Princeton's educational achievement imbalance is apparent. In the Princeton community, 78

EXHIBIT I-8

MEDIAN YEARS OF FORMAL EDUCATION — PRINCETON AND OTHER COMMUNITIES
(PERCENT OF MALE OR HOH[1] POPULATION — 1960-1970)

	COMMUNITY		
EDUCATION	Wellesley Mass. 1960 (Males 25+)	Princeton N.J. 1970 (HOH 21+)	Garden City N.Y. 1960 (Males 25+)
Eight or less years of school completed	9.1	4.9	12.6
High school (1-4)	29.4	16.8	31.9
College (1-4 and over)	61.5	78.3	55.5
Median (Years)	15.1	15.9	13.8

Median School Years (1960):		
Trenton	10.5	
Boston	12.1	
New York	10.6	

Source: U. S. Census 1960 — PRS 1970
[1]Head of household

PRINCETON: ITS PEOPLE AND THEIR HOUSING

percent of the heads of household have at least a bachelor's degree, 30 percent have doctoral or post-doctoral training, while only 5 percent have not completed high school. In support of this local concentration, over 95 percent of Princeton's municipal employees stated that Princeton was a good place to be a teacher, policeman, engineer, etc., specifically because of the stimulation received from the educational characteristics of the residents. [5]

AGE

While comparisons between age structure of the population and age of head of household must be made with care, the 20-year comparison shown in Exhibit I-9 provides some interesting insights. A substantial proportion of the trends evident in 1960 persists in 1970.

The Borough shows a continuing decline in the proportion of its population between ages 25 and 34 and a similar increase in the proportion of its population over 50. The most important factors in the age distribution of the community are the steady increase in the number of elderly persons (+3.6 percent — 1950-1960; +2.2 percent — 1960-1970) and the stabilization of the middle-aged population.

The Township, with its increasingly expensive housing, is no longer a place of residence for the area's youngest or oldest households. The

EXHIBIT I-9

AGE DISTRIBUTION OF THE PRINCETON POPULATION — 1950-1970
(HOH[1] — 1970)

| | PRINCETON MUNICIPALITY | | | | | |
| | Princeton Borough | | | Princeton Township | | |
AGE DISTRIBUTION	Pop 1950(%)	Pop 1960(%)	HOH[1] 1970(%)	Pop 1950(%)	Pop 1960(%)	HOH 1970(%)
25-34	29.2	23.4	19.2	NA[2]	25.4	17.5
35-49	32.5	29.5	31.6	NA	40.3	42.5
50-64	23.1	27.3	28.2	NA	23.4	29.5
65 and Over	15.2	18.8	21.0	NA	10.9	10.5

Source: U. S. Censuses 1950 and 1960 — PRS 1970
[1]Head of household
[2]Not Available

Township is thus slowly developing a population structure similar to that of the Borough, but which currently has slightly more middle-aged residents.

MARITAL STATUS

Marital status differences of Township and Borough residents, as indicated by Exhibit I-10, occur in two specific areas; i.e., their widowed and single sub-populations. The Borough has almost double the single and four times the widowed population found in the Township, both concentrations occurring at the expense of its married population.

Mindful of the differences in definitions appearing at the top of the table, Township and Borough in 1970 are compared to two other communities in 1960 (Levittown, New York and Sausalito, California). The communities were selected for their individual life-styles, in an attempt to portray existing differences in suburban and non-suburban marital status. Notwithstanding incongruities in the divorced and widowed population, there exist obvious similarities between the two sets of communities and their degrees of marital homogeneity. The similarities of the two sets of communities and the differences between the two Princetons tend to support statements found in Osgood's *Modern*

EXHIBIT I-10

MARITAL STATUS — PRINCETON AND OTHER COMMUNITIES
(PERCENT OF MALE OR HOH[1] POPULATION — 1960, 1970)

MARITAL STATUS	COMMUNITY			
	Levittown N.Y. 1960 (Males) 14+	Princeton Township 1970 (HOH) 18+	Princeton Borough 1970 (HOH) 18+	Sausalito Calif. 1960 (Males) 14+
Single	16.4	9.8	16.2	31.9
Married	81.6	81.8	64.4	58.0
Divorced/ Widowed	2.0(0.4D) (1.6W)	8.4(4.2D) (4.2W)	19.4(4.2D) (15.2W)	10.1(6.1D) (4.0W)

Source: U.S. Census 1960 — PRS 1970
[1] Head of household

Princeton and Theilen's "Princeton: Enlightened Exurbia" as to a local urban-suburban bifurcation existing within Princeton itself. [6]

CHILDREN UNDER 18

The number of children residing in the Borough and Township is comparatively low, as indicated by the figures in Exhibit I-11. Almost half (48 percent) of the respondents in the PRS said they had no children under age 18. For those respondents with children, approximately 15 percent had one child, and 15 percent had two children.

The community chosen for comparison, Levittown, New York (1960), provides a rough approximation of the "upper end of the servicing level" (considering children) which a subdivision may be expected to bestow upon a local community. Given this example, and keeping in mind that a garden apartment with a majority of three-bedroom structures may be expected to contribute 1.03 school children per unit locally, [7] the Township, with its preponderance of four-bedroom, single-family homes, produces a relatively small number of children per household.

EXHIBIT I-11

PROPORTION OF JUVENILES RESIDING WITHIN PRINCETON AND LEVITTOWN
(PERCENT 1960, 1970)

	COMMUNITY		
AGE GROUP	Levittown N.Y. 1960(%)	Princeton Township 1970(%)	Princeton Borough 1970(%)
Juveniles (0-18)	48	37.5	18.7
Working Age Adults (19-64) + The Elderly (65 +)	52	62.5	81.3
Mean Number of Children Per Household	2.02	1.30	0.80

Source: Princeton: PRS 1970
   Levittown, N.Y.: Dobriner, William, *Class in Suburbia* Prentice-Hall, Englewood Cliffs, 1963, p. 140

Princeton Borough has a smaller proportion of juveniles, as well as a much lower mean number of children per household. This void in the population is taken up by the elderly, who make up a 10 to 15 percent greater share of the Borough's population than of the Township's. It should be noted that the Princeton community's combined mean of 1.11 children per household in 1970 is only 55 percent of Levittown's 2.02 in 1960.

The burden of the public school system is considerably less in Princeton than it is in Levittown. Based on a relatively low per-household child rate, and the fact that, on the average, local schools receive only 83 percent potential usage,* a public school rate of 0.89 and 0.55 children per household in the Township and Borough respectively is not too surprising.

OTHERS LIVING IN THE HOME

More than 17 percent of those interviewed in the PRS said they have others besides primary family members living in their household. [8]

EXHIBIT I-12

FAMILY INCOME — PRINCETON AND OTHER COMMUNITIES
(1960, 1970)

	COMMUNITY		
	Wellesley Mass.	Garden City N.Y.	Princeton N.J.
INCOME	1960	1960	1960 / 1970
Under $1,000	1.6[1]	1.1	1.8
$1,000-9,999	41.1	26.7	51.2	25.8
$10,000-14,999	24.5	28.5	20.3
$15,000-24,000	20.5	26.6	15.8	46.4
$25,000 +	12.3	17.1	10.9	27.8
(Median Income Families in $)	$11,478	$13,875	$9,323 $17,500

Source: U.S. Census 1960 — PRS 1970
[1] Amounts are expressed in percentages

*377 out of 456 potential school age children whose families were surveyed were utilizing the public system. The single child family is the single greatest non-user; i.e., only 52 of 91 are enrolled in public school.

/81/22

In two-thirds of the cases, this was just one additional person, with less than ten at the three or more level.

The first and largest category of nonprimary family was that of *unrelated* individuals (52 to 87). In 90 percent of these cases the unrelated individuals were students; the remaining 10 percent were almost exclusively domestic help.

The second and somewhat smaller category of non-primary family was that of *related* individuals (35 of 87). The most frequent boarder was the mother of the respondent (over 44 percent of the cases), while fathers, in-laws and children over 18 equally divided the remaining 56 percent.

The only noted difference between Borough and Township in the above comparisons was a greater proportion of unrelated individuals residing in homes of the former (mostly students), while there was an equally greater preponderance of related individuals (mostly fathers) found in homes of the latter.

INCOME

Exhibits I-12 and I-13 summarize and compare family income in Princeton and in two other communities. Other than a $2,150 disparity in median income, Princeton's income structure was similar to a "sister" academic suburb, Wellesly, Massachusetts.

In 1960, when salaries for assistant and associate professors were below the $10,000 mark[9] and the Borough with its lower incomes exerted a like influence on any overall community median, the bulk of Princeton residents fell below the $10,000 income level. Princeton, unlike Garden City, New York, in 1960 had not experienced in quantity the filtering of the upper-middle class into its peripheral, developing neighborhoods.

By 1970, Princeton's median family income had risen by over $8,000. Business executives, who have purchased the larger, more expensive homes in the Township, have raised the overall community median by close to 90 percent. (Note the Borough underwent a similar increase from 1950-1960.) [10]

The disparity between Township and Borough incomes is noteworthy.* A major contributor to the Township's high median income is its monopoly (eleven to one) on the $51,000-$76,000 per year salaried head of household (Exhibit I-13). An equally important factor is the imbalance in the distribution of the lower incomed (under $10,000 — two to

---

*Median family income in the Township in 1960 was $9,965; in 1970, $21,075. Median family income in the Borough in 1960 was $8,833; in 1970, $13,290.

EXHIBIT I-13

TOTAL HOUSEHOLD INCOME BY PRINCETON MUNICIPALITY

MUNICIPALITY	Under $10,000	10,000-15,999	16,000-20,999	21,000-30,999	31,000-50,999	51,000-75,999	76,000-124,999	125,000 and over	No Response/ Don't Know	Total
Princeton Township	45[1]	46	44	70	30	11	4	1	57	308
Princeton Borough	62	31	23	19	18	1	3	1	35	193
Total	107	77	67	89	48	12	7	2	92	501
Princeton Township	14.6[2]	14.9	14.3	22.7	9.7	3.6	1.3	0.3	18.5	100
Princeton Borough	32.1	16.1	11.9	9.8	9.3	0.5	1.6	0.5	18.1	100
Average	21.4	15.4	13.4	17.8	9.6	2.4	1.4	0.4	18.4	100

Source: PRS — Summer 1970 — n=501 (Non-responses Included)
[1] Number
[2] Percent

one in the Borough) and the upwardly mobile, middle class ($20,000-$30,000 — two to one in the Township).

Additional cross-tabulation data shows the individuals earning $51,000-$76,000 per year are generally involved in professional (67 percent) or managerial (33 percent) work. The age distribution at this income level is split 50-50 with heads of households falling into one of two classes — 36-49 or 49-64 years of age.

Lower income individuals, found mainly in the Borough, are found in all age groups and educational levels. A broad range of occupational categories is also evident, the major ones being students, retirees, technical workers, clericals, laborers and household workers.

EXHIBIT I-14

OCCUPATIONAL GROUPS OF RESIDENTS
PRINCETON AND OTHER COMMUNITIES — 1960, 1970
(PERCENT)

	MUNICIPALITY			
OCCUPATIONAL GROUP	Princeton Community (HOH[1] 1970)	Princeton Community (M—F[2] 1960)	Wellesley Mass. (M[3] 1960)	Garden City N. Y. (M[3] 1960)
Professional, Technical and Kindred	56.5	37.7	23.8	26.3
Managers, Officials and Proprietors	24.6	12.5	27.0	35.5
Clerical and Kindred (Including Sales)	5.6	17.6	21.3	20.1
Craftsmen, Firemen and Kindred	2.7	4.6	9.2	8.0
Operatives and Kindred	0.7	3.1	4.6	2.0
Service Workers	1.2	9.7	4.0	3.5
Laborers and Private Household (Including Farm)	6.3	10.3	3.7	1.3
Not Reported	2.4	4.5	6.4	3.3
Total Employed	100.0	100.0	100.0	100.0

Source: U.S. Census 1960 — PRS 1970
[1] Head of household
[2] Male—female
[3] Male

The upper-middle-class individual ($21,000-$30,000) predominantly found in the Township is characterized by similar age, education and occupational traits as the $51,000-$76,000 per year individual. He is a professional or a manager (70 percent/30 percent), more often in the 36-49 age bracket and likely to have a Ph.D. (45 percent of the cases).

In summary, the Borough provides for the single, the retired and the widowed, and has historically housed the lower-income laborer, houseworker and service employee. [11] The Township, in attracting a very select housing buyer, is contributing toward a family income of upwards of $20,000.

OCCUPATIONAL GROUP AND INDUSTRIAL CLASSIFICATION

Exhibit I-14 summarizes the occupational grouping of Princeton's residents in 1960 and 1970. Comparative information for Garden City, New York, and Wellesley, Massachusetts, is also provided.

In 1960, Princeton residents show a marked professional concentration and a somewhat greater-than-average proportion of service and domestic employees. In 1970, the skew is even more pronounced. Over 56 percent of those surveyed placed themselves in the "professional, technical and kindred" category. This is 20 percent greater than 1960.

The major difference between Borough and Township figures is the somewhat higher student and laborer concentrations in the Borough (13 percent) and the higher professional and managerial concentrations in the Township (15 percent).

The industrial classifications of Princeton residents are shown in Exhibit I-15. It is obvious that in 1960 as well as in 1970 the service trades play a major role in the local economy. The service grouping appears almost equally divided between specific *educational* services and the other service classifications. Princeton's educational concentration is evident in light of the service split and further amplified when one considers that close to 60 percent of Princeton's populace is currently engaged in one or another service-related occupation.

The only apparent difference in the industrial classifications of the two communities is the Township's heavier concentration of finance, insurance and real estate employees and the Borough's educational service bias.

PLACE OF EMPLOYMENT

The 1970 PRS and the 1960 Census have different breakdowns for the place of work of the "head of household" and "all workers." The PRS divides place of work into five categories; i.e., Princeton, three

EXHIBIT I-15

INDUSTRIAL CLASSIFICATIONS OF RESIDENTS
PRINCETON COMMUNITY — 1960, 1970
(PERCENT)

	MUNICIPALITY		
INDUSTRIAL CLASSIFICATION	Princeton Community (HOH[1] 1970)	Princeton Borough (HOH 1970)	Princeton Borough (M[2] 1960)
Manufacturing, Construction, Agriculture, Mining	15.7	15.0	12.5
Transportation, Communications and Public Utilities	3.4	3.0	2.1
Retail/Wholesale	13.3	13.8	15.8
Finance, Insurance, Real Estate	4.8	1.7	3.1
Educational Services	29.8	35.1	37.5
Services (Household, Business, Entertainment, Hospital, Research, Non-Profit, Professional)	28.4	26.7	25.3
Not Reported	4.6	4.7	3.7
Total	100.0	100.0	100.0

Source: U.S. Census 1960 — PRS 1970
[1] Head of household
[2] Male

mileage increments away from Princeton, and New York or Philadelphia. The Census segregates place of work into "county of residence" or "outside county of residence" classifications.

Assuming that the categories of Princeton and a radius of 20 miles is equal to "county of residence" and that the New York or Philadelphia category and 20 miles or more is equal to "outside county of residence," then place of work distributions have not changed substantially since 1960. In 1960, 75 to 85 percent of Princeton residents worked in the county of their residence, while 5 to 15 percent worked outside. More conclusive data will be forthcoming in the 1970 Census. However, on the basis of this information it appears that new entrants to the Princeton job and housing markets are continuing the work patterns which have characterized the previous ten years.

EXHIBIT I-16

PLACE OF EMPLOYMENT OF PRINCETON RESIDENTS — 1960, 1970
(PERCENT)

PLACE OF EMPLOYMENT	PRINCETON MUNICIPALITY	
	Borough (1960 All Workers)	Township (1960 All Workers)
County of Residence	81.8	79.1
Outside County of Residence	13.4	15.9
Not Reported	4.8	5.0
Total	100.0	100.0
	1970 HOH[1]	*1970 HOH*
Princeton (Township or Borough	57.4	47.2
5 Mile Radius	10.1	15.8
6-20 Mile Radius	13.5	16.8
New York or Philadelphia	8.8	11.1
Over 20 Miles and Not New York or Philadelphia	0.6	0.0
Not Reported	9.6	9.1
Total	100.0	100.0

Source: U.S. Census 1960 — PRS 1970
[1] Head of household

HOUSING

HOME OWNERSHIP

"The median value (as reported by the owner) of owner occupied single family units rose from $19,057 to $26,600 — an increase of almost 40 percent." [12] Such was the conclusion of an earlier study comparing the increase in housing value between 1950 and 1960 in Princeton Borough. An extension of this analysis is undertaken in the present study.

PRINCETON: ITS PEOPLE AND THEIR HOUSING

EXHIBIT I-17

LOCATION OF RESIDENTS' EMPLOYMENT BY
PRINCETON MUNICIPALITY

| MUNICIPALITY | Princeton | LOCATION OF EMPLOYMENT | | | | |
		5 Mile Radius	6-20 Mile Radius	New York Philadelphia	Over 20 Mile Radius	Total
Princeton Township	126[1]	42	45	30	0	243
Princeton Borough	85	15	20	13	1	134
Total	211	57	65	43	1	377
Princeton Township	51.9[2]	17.3	18.5	12.3	0.0	100
Princeton Borough	63.4	11.2	14.9	9.7	0.7	100
Average	56.0	15.1	17.2	11.4	0.3	100

Source: PRS — Summer 1970 — n=501 (Non-responses Excluded)
[1] Number
[2] Percent

The median 1970 home value in the Borough is $47,670, while the median for the Township is $52,410 (Exhibit I-18). Our estimates for 1970 suggest that cost trends of the 1950-1960 decade have been sharply accelerated by the start of the 1970s.

There is little variation between Township and Borough distributions. In the combined totals (Exhibit I-19) only 15 percent of the single-family residences in the survey area are valued under $31,000, while 17.4 percent are valued in excess of $76,000. With respect to monthly mortgage payments, 40.5 percent fall within the $200 to $400 range.

RENTAL STRUCTURE

Substantial variation exists between rental structures of the Township and Borough. Over three-quarters of all Borough units presently rent for under $200 per month, while less than 60 percent of the Township rentals are found below this figure (Exhibit I-20).

Whether the Township and Borough are considered together or separately, the largest single proportion of rental units falls into the $150 to $199 per month range. The modes of the rental distributions are therefore somewhat similar. While the greatest proportion of Borough units falls below the modal range, the greatest proportion of the

EXHIBIT I-18

HOME VALUE CHARACTERISTICS OF
DWELLING UNITS BY PRINCETON MUNICIPALITY

PRINCETON BOROUGH

Value	1960[B] (%)	1970[C] (%)
Owner Occupied		
Under $15,000	18.1	1.2
$15,000-25,000	28.9	10.1[1]
Over $25,000	53.0	88.7[1]
Median $	$26,600	$47,670
Gross Rent		
Under $100	44.5	18.6
$100 or More	45.5	81.4
Median $	$103	$159

PRINCETON TOWNSHIP

Value	1960[A] (%)	1970[C] (%)
Owner Occupied		
Under $15,000	7.9	1.3
$15,000-25,000	26.4	9.5[1]
Over $25,000	65.7	89.2[1]
Median $	$29,400[3]	$52,410
Gross Rent		
Under $100	53.3	15.6
$100 or More	46.7	84.4
Median $	$ 70[3]	$183[2]

[1] Figures adjusted to comply with Census breakdowns
[2] Includes Princeton University graduate-student housing
[3] Estimate — unable to obtain figure

Source: (A) Kendree and Shepherd; *Housing Need in the Princeton Community.*
(Part 1: Background Data), Feb. 1967, p. 2.
(B) Raymond and May; *Social and Economic Trends* (Borough of Princeton),
Jan. 1966, Table XIII.
(C) PRS — Summer 1970.

EXHIBIT I-19

CURRENT SELLING PRICE OF HOME BY PRINCETON MUNICIPALITY

MUNICIPALITY	SELLING PRICE							
	Under $15,000	15,000-30,999	31,000-50,999	51,000-75,999	76,000-100,000	Above 100,000	No Response/Don't Know	Total
Princeton Township	3[1]	31	62	62	31	10	31	230
Princeton Borough	1	12	27	17	10	4	14	85
Total	4	43	89	79	41	14	45	315
Princeton Township	1.3[2]	13.5	27.0	27.0	13.5	4.3	13.5	100
Princeton Borough	1.2	14.1	31.8	20.0	11.8	4.7	16.5	100
Average	1.3	13.7	28.3	25.1	13.0	4.4	14.3	100

Source: PRS — Summer 1970 — n=315 (Non-responses Included)
[1] Number
[2] Percent

EXHIBIT I-20

MONTHLY RENT (WITHOUT UTILITIES) BY PRINCETON MUNICIPALITY

MUNICIPALITY	$10-99	$100-149	$150-199	$200-269	$270-349	$350-449	$450-999	Total
Princeton Township	10[1]	10	18	17	6	1	2	64
Princeton Borough	18	25	31	16	3	3	1	97
Total	28	35	49	33	9	4	3	161
Princeton Township	15.6[2]	15.6	28.1	20.6	9.4	1.6	3.1	100
Princeton Borough	18.6	25.8	32.0	16.5	3.1	3.1	1.0	100
Average	17.4	21.7	30.4	20.5	5.6	2.5	1.9	100

Source: PRS — Summer 1970 — n=186 (Non-responses Excluded)
[1] Number
[2] Percent

Township units lies above it. This produces median differences of approximately $25 per month. The higher monthly rental structure in the Township is a function of the greater number of single-family homes available there for rent. In the Borough, conversions and multifamily development have generated the classic multiple-dwelling-unit rental pattern.[13]

PREVIOUS RESIDENCY COMPARISONS

A comparison between housing costs in a previous residence and costs presently incurred. Exhibit I-21 shows that residents pay more to live in Princeton.

Changes in the purchasing power of the dollar create distortion when applied to the commodity of housing. According to the PRS sample, however, almost 60 percent of the respondents have experienced *significant* increases in housing costs specifically as a result of their entry into the Princeton housing market. The ability to absorb this cost increase would indicate that the present accommodations of Princeton residents are the result of an upgrading of status, at least as measured by housing expenditures.

TYPE OF RESIDENCE

Exhibit I-22 shows the proportion and type of residence in the Township and Borough. However, since the residential composition is more

EXHIBIT I-21

HOUSING COSTS NOW AS COMPARED TO PREVIOUS ADDRESS BY PRINCETON MUNICIPALITY

MUNICIPALITY	Comparing What You Spend on Housing Now With What You Were Spending on Housing at Your Previous Residence Would You Say You Were Spending:				
	Much More?	Little More?	Little Less?	Lot Less?	Total
Princeton Township	169[1]	64	19	9	261
Princeton Borough	83	53	15	5	156
Total	252	117	34	14	417
Princeton Township	64.8[2]	24.5	7.3	3.4	100.0
Princeton Borough	53.2	34.0	9.6	3.2	100.0
Average	60.4	28.1	8.2	3.4	100.0

Source: PRS — Summer 1970 — n=501 (Non-responses Included)
[1] Number
[2] Percent

accurately examined in Chapter II, this topic is only reviewed here. Both communities are predominantly composed of single family homes; i.e., 78 percent and 72 percent respectively. The Township's larger share of single-family homes is compensated for by a similar greater proportion of Borough two-family dwellings. The balance, 16 to 18 percent in both communities, is made up of larger multifamily units. It will subsequently be pointed out that differences in existing zoning policies of both municipalities are causing a convergence in their residential fabrics. Both Township and Borough are approaching community means of the following magnitudes:

Single family	75.0 percent
Two family	8.5 percent
Multifamily	16.5 percent

TENURE

Of comparable importance is the form of housing tenure of the Princeton municipalities (Exhibit I-23). Slightly more than three out of five (62.7 percent) of the area's residents presently own their home. Some 27.5 percent classify themselves as renters, while 9.8 percent (a

EXHIBIT I-22

TYPE OF RESIDENCE BY PRINCETON MUNICIPALITY

	TYPE OF RESIDENCE							
	Single-Family House		2-3-4 Family House		Apartment House		Total	
MUNICIPALITY	Number	Percent	Number	Percent	Number	Percent	Number	Percent
Township	247	81.0	19	6.2	39	12.8	305	100
Borough	96	51.9	37	20.0	52	28.1	185	100
Total Number Average Percent	343	70	56	11.4	91	18.6	490	100

Source: PRS — Summer 1970 — n=501 (Non-responses Excluded)

EXHIBIT I-23

FORM OF HOUSING TENURE BY PRINCETON MUNICIPALITY

	FORM OF TENURE							
	Own		Rent		Princeton Contract		Total	
MUNICIPALITY	Number	Percent	Number	Percent	Number	Percent	Number	Percent
Township	226	73.9	53	17.3	27	8.8	306	100
Borough	86	44.8	84	43.8	22	11.5	192	100
Total Number Average Percent	312	62.7	137	27.5	49	9.8	498	100

Source: PRS — Summer 1970 — n=501 (Non-responses Excluded)

possible understatement) are involved in some way or another in contractual arrangements with Princeton University.* The Township has a greater proportion of homeowners, approximately 75 percent, while the Borough is almost equally split between owners and the other two categories of housing tenure.

Local housing tenure is shown on the map in Exhibit I-24. Clusters of renters are found predominantly in the Borough, usually within walking distance of the institutions of higher education. Renters are also found to a lesser extent in the Township. Representative of this category are the Princeton University housing projects for graduate students and faculty on South Harrison Street, Hartley Avenue, Faculty Road, Western Way and so on. Non-university rentals and "Princeton contract" arrangements also dot the Township.

Ownership tenure, Princeton's mainstay, is common, particularly in the Township. Many of the Township areas immediately adjacent to the Borough are populated almost exclusively by ownership tenure. In the Borough and in newly developing Township areas, both ownership and rental tenure exist. Princeton has a high demand for *single-family* rentals in part created by the needs of those in the service industry and enhanced by the exclusionary multifamily zoning of Princeton Township. [14]

In 95 percent of the sample, owners occupy single-family homes, whereas renters are divided between apartments (47.7 percent) and either single- (27.7 percent) or two- to four-family homes (24.6 percent). Those who classified themselves as Princeton contract people were either apartment dwellers (59.6 percent) or shared two- to four-family homes (25.5 percent); 14.9 percent live in single-family units.

BEDROOMS VERSUS NEED

Owner-renter cost distinctions and tenure analysis do not show the interrelationship between unit size and the position of the individual in the life cycle. Within the United States it is common for families in the child-rearing life-stage to be most in need of space, and least able to afford it. [15] Conversely, families whose children have formed their own households can afford more and usually occupy larger residences.

This pattern is characteristic of the Princeton housing market. A large percentage of three- and four-bedroom homes are occupied by

---

*"Princeton contract" is a term coined by this study to include rental, ownership or mortgage arrangements between Princeton University and its locally residing personnel. The understatement referred to is the possibility that those Princeton University personnel who responded failed to recognize the classification and categorized themselves merely as owners or renters.

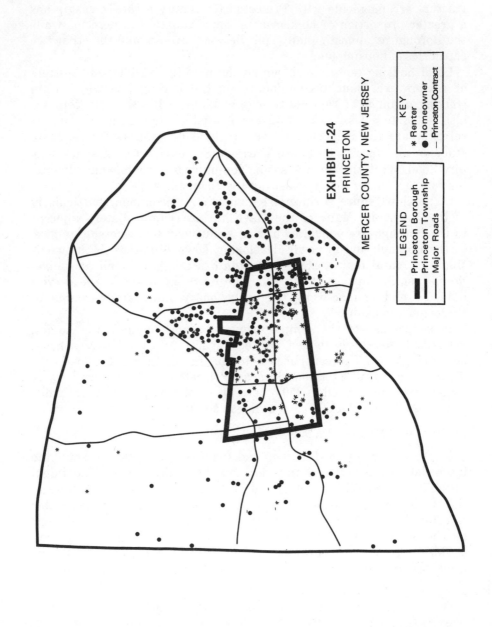

EXHIBIT I-24
PRINCETON

MERCER COUNTY, NEW JERSEY

LEGEND

█ Princeton Borough
─ Princeton Township
─ Major Roads

KEY

✳ Renter
● Homeowner
─ Princeton Contract

EXHIBIT I-25

SIZE OF HOUSEHOLD BY TOTAL NUMBER OF BEDROOMS

	SIZE OF HOUSEHOLD								
NUMBER OF BEDROOMS	One	Two	Three	Four	Five	Six	Seven and Eight	Nine to Twenty	Total
Zero	2^1	0	0	0	0	0	0	0	2
One	27	17	3	0	0	1	0	0	48
Two	11	34	28	15	7	0	3	0	98
Three	20	54	37	27	17	4	2	0	161
Four or More	8	39	45	38	34	17	8	3	192
Total	68	144	113	80	58	22	13	3	501
Zero	100.0^2	0.0	0.0	0.0	0.0	0.0	0.0	0.0	100.0
One	56.3	35.4	6.2	0.0	0.0	2.1	0.0	0.0	100.0
Two	11.2	34.7	28.6	15.3	7.1	0.0	3.1	0.0	100.0
Three	12.4	33.5	23.0	16.8	10.6	2.5	1.2	0.0	100.0
Four or More	4.2	20.3	23.4	19.8	17.7	8.9	4.2	1.6	100.0
Average	13.6	28.7	22.6	16.0	11.6	4.4	2.6	0.6	100.0

Source: PRS — Summer 1970 — n=501 (Non-responses Included
[1] Number
[2] Percent

households comprised of two or fewer individuals. The number of a-vailable bedrooms for underhoused, large, young families is not great, although there is evidence that such families exist in the Greater Princeton Area. More importantly, Exhibit I-25 shows that there is a strong local tendency for mature families to remain in larger housing units.

AGE STRUCTURE

The above exhibit summarizes the age of Princeton's housing stock. Over 40 percent of the Township's current stock is under ten years of age; this reflects the degree to which new construction has concentrated in this municipality. The Borough, however, over two decades has maintained an age imbalance in its standing housing stock. Current annual production, in many cases assisted by the demolition of retired structures, barely exceeds the aging process, which results in a more

EXHIBIT I-26

DWELLING UNITS BY AGE OF STRUCTURE
PRINCETON BOROUGH AND TOWNSHIP 1950-1970
(PERCENT)

| | MUNICIPALITY | | | | | |
| | Princeton Borough | | | Princeton Township | | |
AGE OF STRUCTURE	1950	1960	1970	1950	1960	1970
Under 5 Years	14.9	4.4	3.1	NA[1]	NA	12.7
5 to 10 Years		8.5	10.4	NA	NA	28.0
11 to 20 Years	5.0	12.4	15.5	NA	NA	30.5
20 Years and Over	80.1	74.7	71.0	NA	NA	28.8
Total	100.0	100.0	100.0			100.0

Source: U. S. Census of Housing 1950-1960
      PRS 1970
[1] Not available

aged housing stock. In this type of situation, the Borough must be a-ware of increasing pressure on maintenance quality and the potential necessity for widespread structural rehabilitation.

HOUSING DEFICIENCIES

In the PRS, 501 residents were asked if there were any community housing deficiencies which would inhibit future household plans (Exhibit I-27). Forty percent replied affirmatively. If the same proportion is applied to the entire Princeton population, 2,700 out of a total of 6,600 households feel local housing deficiencies. Borough residents were more negative in their feelings about housing deficiencies than were Township residents; 46 percent of the former and 36.6 percent of the latter felt that there were sufficient local housing deficiencies to limit future moves.

While overall, 40 percent of the residents interviewed said they were limited due to local housing deficiencies, the percentage dissatisfied rose to 60 percent when only renters of apartments were considered. Further, when all renters were considered, including those in apartments and single-family homes, 70 percent felt that they were limited

EXHIBIT I-27

HOUSING DEFICIENCIES INHIBITING FUTURE PLANS BY PRINCETON MUNICIPALITY

| | *Are There Specific Housing Deficiencies in Princeton Which Would Inhibit Any Future Plans?* | | | | | |
| | YES | | NO | | TOTAL | |
MUNICIPALITY	Number	Percent	Number	Percent	Number	Percent
Princeton Township	106	36.3	184	63.4	290	100
Princeton Borough	80	46.0	94	54.0	174	100
Total Number	186		278		464	
Average Percent		40.1		59.0		100

Source: PRS — Summer 1970 — n=501 (Non-responses Excluded)

by inadequacies in the local market. Thus, apartment dwellers and renters in general felt the most immobile, while those who owned their home were relatively free to contemplate future moves.

The group most severely depressed due to the non-availability of local housing appeared to be lower-middle-income families earning from $10,000 to $16,000 per year. In six out of ten cases, respondents in this income bracket said that future plans were limited because of a lack of moderately priced owner or rental units in the Princeton community.

A total of 188 respondents cited specific inadequacies in the overall housing supply; half of the sample said that garden apartments with monthly rents of $100 to $135 or $135 to $174 were unavailable. Almost 40 percent of the respondents said single-family homes in the $17,500 to $25,000 range were not on the market. Proponents of increased garden apartment construction typically included families now living in apartments, those earning less than $10,000 a year and households with three or less members. Greater single-family construction was advocated by families currently living in two- to four-family homes, by those earning from $10,000 to $16,000 a year and by households with four or five members (Exhibit I-28). In a related observation, almost 70 percent of all survey respondents cited a lack of rental units as the major local housing deficiency. There is, therefore, a definite community acknowledgement of local rental deficiencies.

EXHIBIT I-28

MOST SERIOUS HOUSING DEFICIENCY CONSIDERING MONTHLY COST OR TOTAL SELLING PRICE BY PRINCETON MUNICIPALITY

MONTHLY COST OR TOTAL SELLING PRICE

MUNICIPALITY	Under $100 or Under $12,000	$100-135 or $12-14,999	$136-174 or $15-24,999	$175-249 or $25-39,999	$250-399 or $40-59,999	$400-600 or $60-80,000	Total
Princeton Township	12[1]	21	42	13	5	1	94
Princeton Borough	11	23	28	9	5	0	76
Total	23	44	70	22	10	1	176
Princeton Township	12.8[2]	22.3	44.7	13.8	5.3	1.1	100
Princeton Borough	14.5	30.3	36.8	11.8	6.6	0.0	100
Average	13.8	25.9	41.2	12.9	5.9	0.6	100

Source: PRS — Summer 1970 — n=186 (Non-responses Excluded)
[1] Number
[2] Percent

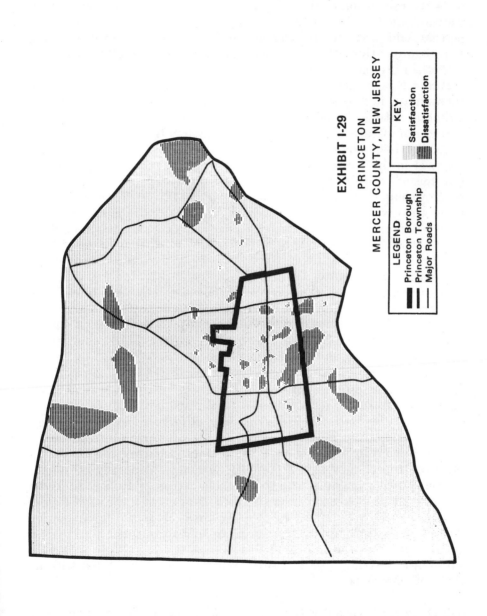

EXHIBIT I-29

PRINCETON

MERCER COUNTY, NEW JERSEY

LEGEND

Princeton Borough
Princeton Township
Major Roads

KEY

Satisfaction
Dissatisfaction

DISSATISFACTION WITH HOUSING

At the conclusion of the PRS respondents were asked whether they were satisfied or dissatisfied with their current housing. Although 40 percent said that the offerings on the local market were inadequate, less than one-third (12.4 percent) said they were actually dissatisfied with their present housing.

If 87.6 percent housing satisfaction is taken as representative of the community, it is possible through the SYMAP presentation (Exhibit I-29) and voting district analysis (Exhibit I-30*) to isolate graphically patterns of dissatisfaction within both municipalities.

Exhibit I-30 shows that 16 out of 20 voting districts (9 in the Borough, 11 in the Township) do not differ from the "community satisfaction mean" by more than 10 percent. Of those that do, one district in the Township shows no housing dissatisfaction (Riverside Drive — Lake Drive area), while two of three others, both of which are in the Borough, show extreme discontent. The Witherspoon area, Palmer Square, Shirley Court, Lytle and McLean Street and Hulfish and Bank Streets are the worst. Housing dissatisfaction here is three times the community "norm." These areas are more fully studied in the Underhoused portion of this report (Chapter VI). If, however, one were to compare roughly the Borough and the Township based on the community mean (Exhibit I-31) the Township would be approximately two to three points above this artificial satisfaction level, while the Borough would fall a corresponding number of points below it.

Lack of space (39 percent) and structural deficiencies (10 percent) were cited most often as reasons for dissatisfaction with present housing. Only two respondents, out of a total of 60 noting dissatisfaction, said local taxes were too high. The only difference between Borough and Township dissatisfaction is that Borough residents tend to have a higher proportion of structural complaints, whereas the Township residents report they have "too much housing." Generally there is a high level of housing satisfaction within most areas of Princeton. Those few who speak of housing dissatisfaction want more of the same type of housing in terms of increased physical space or household amenities. terms of increased physical space or household amenities.

But what does the future hold? The past ten years have witnessed substantial housing price increases. Will they continue? What will the shape of housing be?

If one were to capsulize the import of this chapter, it would be to say that the social and economic dimensions of the Princeton community initially appearing in 1960 are well established in 1970. Princeton is an

EXHIBIT I-30

PATTERNS OF HOUSING DISSATISFACTION SHOWN AS DEVIATING NEGATIVELY FROM A COMMUNITY SATISFACTION MEAN — 1970

PRINCETON BOROUGH

Community Mean — 87.6

Voting District	Deviation From Community Mean	Location of Dissatisfaction
1	+ 1.0	—
2	−10.3	Prospect and Olden Sts.
3	+ 5.5	—
4	+ 0.6	—
5	− 2.1	Vandeventer and Nassau Sts.
6	−27.6	Palmer Sq., Bank St. Hulfish St.
7	−26.7	Witherspoon Lane Shirley Ct. Lytle & McLean Sts.
8	+ 8.1	—
9	+ 1.9	—

PRINCETON TOWNSHIP

Voting District	Deviation From Community Mean	Location of Dissatisfaction
1	+ 6.8	—
2	+ 8.1	—
3	− 2.2	Broadmead and S. Harrison Sts.
4	+ 4.3	—
5	+ 2.4	—
6	− 4.3	N. Harrison St. Below Terhune Rd.
7	+ 1.3	—
8	+ 4.1	—
9	+12.4	—
10	− 8.4	Herrontown Circle & Rd.
11	+ 6.2	—

Source: PRS — Summer 1970

affluent, highly educated suburban community, the bulk of whose residents demonstrate strong community allegiance and minimal housing dissatisfaction. There appears to be a local acknowledgement of Princeton's environmental uniqueness in the regional area, and a realistic appraisal of the increased economic costs (in many cases expressed in housing value) to those who choose to live there.

EXHIBIT I-31

SATISFACTION WITH PRESENT ACCOMMODATIONS BY PRINCETON MUNICIPALITY

	Are You Satisfied With Your Present Accommodations?		
MUNICIPALITY	Yes	No	Total
Princeton Township	274[1]	34	308
Princeton Borough	165	28	193
Total	439	62	501
Princeton Township	89.0[2]	11.0	100
Princeton Borough	85.5	14.5	100
Average	87.6	12.4	100

Source: PRS — Summer 1970 — n=501
[1] Number
[2] Percent

NOTES

1. *U.S. Census of Population-1970-Advance Report* (U.S. Bureau of the Census, U.S. Government Printing Office, Washington, D.C.), General Social and Economic Characteristics, PC (Vol. 1)-32, p. 5.

2. Harvard University, Department of City and Regional Planning, Graduate School of Design, *SYMAP* (Harvard University, Laboratory of Computer Graphics, Cambridge, Massachusetts, 1963).

3. "An Introduction to the Community of Princeton, New Jersey," reprinted from *Philadelphia Magazine* (Greater Princeton Chamber of Commerce, 1967), p. 1.

PRINCETON: ITS PEOPLE AND THEIR HOUSING

4. *U.S. Census of Population-1960* (U.S. Bureau of the Census, U.S. Government Printing Office, Washington, D. C.), General Social and Economic Characteristics, Vol. 32, p. 215.

5. See Chapter VII, The Municipal Employees — "The Attitude of the Municipal Employee."

6. Osgood, Charles G.: *The Modern Princeton* (Princeton University Press, Princeton, New Jersey, 1947); Theilen, Benedict: "Princeton: The Enlightened Exurbia" (*Holiday Magazine*, November, 1965.)

7. Sternlieb, George: *The Garden Apartment Development: A Municipal Cost-Revenue Analysis* (Bureau of Economic Research, Rutgers — The State University, New Brunswick, New Jersey, 1964) p. 6.

8. Present Residents Survey — Question #20.

9. Interviews with realty personnel. Princeton University, Princeton Theological Seminary, Westminster Choir College.

10. Monson, Astrid: *Social and Economic Trends: Borough of Princeton, New Jersey* (Raymond and May Associates, White Plains, New York, 1966), p. 10.

11. Collins, Varnum Lansing: *Princeton Past and Present* (Princeton University Press, 1931), pp. 10-11.

12. Monson, op. cit., p. 16.

13. See Smith, Wallace T.: *Housing: Social and Economic Elements* (University of California Press, Berkeley, California, 1970), Chapter 2.

14. *1968 Master Plan for Princeton Township* (Kendree and Shepherd Planning Consultants, Philadelphia, Pennsylvania, 1968), p. 2.

15. Lansing, John B.; Charles Wade Clifton, and James N. Morgan: *New Homes and Poor People* (Institute for Social Research, The University of Michigan, Ann Arbor, Michigan, 1960), p. 10.

II

LAND AVAILABILITY
AND THE DEMAND FOR HOUSING

Of the many factors which influence the local housing market, two of the most important are the availability of land and the demand for new housing. Although national monetary policy and regional demographic trends largely determine the rate at which future growth takes place, it is local factors — particularly those discussed here — that determine the direction and character of growth.

The Housing and Land Inventory presented in Chapter II reviews Princeton's residential development from 1960 to 1970, and, on the basis of growth during this period, projects the character of housing development over the next decade. This chapter is followed by an analysis of the demands for new housing which major employers in the Princeton area are likely to make.

Through a review of these factors, this section outlines the potentialities for residential growth which now exist in Princeton Township and Borough. If no changes are made in public policy, this is a probable look at Princeton's housing market in the year 1980.

Chapter II

HOUSING AND LAND INVENTORY

HOUSING GROWTH AND RESULTANT
LAND AVAILABILITY

PRINCETON BOROUGH

Princeton Borough has an estimated total of 3,125 residential units in 1970, an increase of 186 units or 6.3 percent more than the 1960 total (2,939). Over the past decade there has been an average net gain of only 18.6 units per year.

Changes in the housing stock are due to: 1) an increase of 213 newly constructed units; 2) an increase of 27 units from conversion of larger residential and non-residential buildings; and, finally, 3) a decrease of 54 units through local demolition. The majority of these changes occurred before 1967; in the last four years there has been a net gain of only eight residential units.

Of the 213 new units added to the housing stock, 37 percent (78 units) were single family structures, six percent (12 units) were two-family, while 57 percent (123 units) were larger multifamily buildings, including those of public housing. The 27 conversions in most cases occurred in single-family homes which were subdivided into two-family structures, and additionally, in the conversion of a hotel's dormitory spaces into multifamily residential housekeeping units. Thus, of the gross additions to the housing supply since 1960 (240 units), 162 units or 68 percent were multifamily structures.

Detailed examination of Exhibit II-1 shows that no new multifamily dwellings, excluding public housing, have been built since 1963, with only one conversion since that date. The only new additions to the total housing stock since 1963 have been 29 single-family homes. At the beginning of 1970, Princeton Borough has approximately the same housing supply that it had at the beginning of the 1960s. The various

EXHIBIT II-1

HOUSING STARTS, CONVERSIONS AND DEMOLITIONS
PRINCETON BOROUGH 1960-1970
(IN RESIDENTIAL HOUSEKEEPING UNITS)

	HOUSING ADDITIONS							
YEAR	Single Family	Two Family	Multi- Family	Public Housing	Total	Conver- sions (+)	Demoli- tions (−)	Net Gain
Existing 1960	2170	338	431	70[1]	2939	—	—	—
1960	27	8	0	0	35	0	2	33
1961	10	2	59[2]	0	71	4	16	59
1962	5	0	0	0	5	2	2	5
1963	7	2	14	0	23	18	12	29
1964	6	0	0	0	6	0	5	1
1965	8	0	0	0	8	2	5	5
1966	2	0	50	50[1]	52	1	6	47
1967	6	0	0	0	6	0	2	4
1968	2	0	0	0	2	0	3	−1
1969	2	0	0	0	2	0	1	1
1970 (June)	3	0	0	0	3	0	0	3
Increases 1960-70	78	12	123	50	213	27	54	186
Total 1970	2248	350	554	120	3152	+27	−54	3125

Source: *Report of Building Permits Issued and Local Public Construction.*
(New Jersey Department of Labor and Industry — Form C-404 — N. J. Monthly Tabulations 1960-1970.)

[1] Included in Multifamily count
[2] Completed 1963 (figure verified by Borough Building Inspector)

housing types have maintained a relatively constant percentage of the overall housing stock.

The only significant change was in the multifamily category, which was, however, somewhat inflated by the inclusion of public housing. Since most of this multifamily construction was undertaken prior to 1966, the major deviations from the 1960 pattern occurred at that time.

The net result of the decade's building activity, then, has been to reduce the land available for residential construction to that presented in Exhibit II-2, "Buildable Land Inventory." Only 31.54 acres of total usable land is available for residential development in all Borough zoning density categories.

EXHIBIT II-2

BUILDABLE LAND INVENTORY BY RESIDENTIAL ZONING DISTRICTS — PRINCETON BOROUGH — 1970 (IN ACRES)

| | LAND INVENTORY | | | | |
ZONE	Gross Available Land[1]	Usable Land 1970[2]	Vacant Land McHugh 1960[3]	Vacant Land Re-Survey 1962[4]	Known Acreage Built 1962-1970[5]
R-1	9.75	9.59	—	37.28	2.99
R-2	3.20	3.14	—	24.08	9.11
R-3	13.27	13.87	—	13.86	4.63
R-4	1.57	1.17	—	1.08	0.76
RO-1	2.60	2.30	—	—	—
RO-2	2.30	2.07	—	—	—
Total	32.69	31.54	92	76.30[6]	17.49

[1] Tabulated from tax records after public open space had been deducted

[2] Usable Land — Gross Available Land minus lots too small to be feasibly improved
  Borough cut off point — plots which lack necessary frontage and whose total acreage is less than 0.08

[3] McHugh, F. D. Proposed Master Plan Revisions — Programs and Related Studies — (For the Borough of Princeton, N. J.) October 1960, p. 23.

[4] See Williams, Norman, "Summary of McHugh Statistical Material." no date, p. 8

[5] Survey of Borough building permits and tax records

[6] There has been a redefinition of residential districts between 1962 and 1970. In addition, park land was included in original surveys (1960, 1962) as vacant land, in 1970 it was not.

Source: Housing and Land Inventory — Summer 1970

Additional interpretation can be made by converting from land units to those of population. This is accomplished in Exhibit II-3, "Zonal Holding Capacity." In Princeton Borough, the acreage in each residential zoning category has been converted into building lots and considered potentially developable to the limit of existing neighborhood dwelling unit capacities. By employing a population per household total unique to each density zone, the "full development population" is established.

EXHIBIT II-3

RESIDENTIAL ZONING HOLDING CAPACITY — PRINCETON BOROUGH — 1970

ADDITIONAL POPULATION AS A FUNCTION OF AVAILABLE LAND

ZONING	No. of Building Lots/Sites[2]	Highest Residential Land Use Permitted	No. of Dwelling Units[3]	House-hold Size[1]	Additional Population
R-1	16	Single Family	16	3.1	49
R-2	11	Single Family	11	2.81	31
R-3	13	Two Family	115	2.81	322
R-4	8	Multifamily	12	2.5	30
RO-1	1[4]	Multifamily	78	2.2	172
RO-2	2[4]	Multifamily	122	2.2	268
Total	51		354	—	872

[1] Middle cases' household size obtained from Present Residents Survey — Others adjusted + or — by a factor of 0.3

[2] A better estimate than acreage due to scarcity of land

[3] Windshield survey determined most appropriate intensity of development for each land parcel

[4] Specific development proposals have been included in these totals

Source: Housing and Land Inventory — Summer 1970

According to this analysis, if all available vacant residential land were used to the same capacity as the land which surrounds it, approximately 872 new residents would be absorbed into the community.

PRINCETON TOWNSHIP

While Princeton Borough's housing supply remained relatively constant from 1960 to 1970, Princeton Township, which was comparatively underdeveloped, experienced significant changes. Its housing supply increased by 39.4 percent, a rate more than six times that of the Borough. This Borough-Township disparity is not unique to Princeton, but is typical of urban-suburban growth rates. However, the Princeton environs present a unique context for this phenomenon as most negative effects of such a pattern of growth have not yet affected the older, more urbanized Borough.

The Township has an estimated 1970 total of 4,273 residential housekeeping units, a gain of 1,187 units over the 3,086 which existed in 1960.

EXHIBIT II-4

HOUSING STARTS, CONVERSIONS AND DEMOLITIONS
PRINCETON TOWNSHIP 1960-1970
(IN RESIDENTIAL HOUSEKEEPING UNITS)

YEAR	HOUSING ADDITIONS					Conversions (+)	Demolitions (−)	Net Gain
	Single Family	Two Family	Multi-family	Public Housing	Total			
Existing 1960	2543	269	274	0	3086	—	—	—
1960	105	0	96	0	201	0	1	200
1961	97	0	0	0	97	0	2	95
1962	114	0	0	0	114	0	0	114
1963	77	0	0	0	77	0	1	76
1964	68	0	96	0	164	0	1	163
1965	93	0	150	0	243	0	1	242
1966	57	0	0	0	57	0	0	57
1967	55	0	27	0	82	0	1	81
1968	68	0	32	0	100	0	5	95
1969	47	0	0	0	47	0	1	46
1970 (June)	18	0	0	0	18	0	0	18
Increases 1960-70	799	0	401	0	1200	0	13	1187
Total 1970	3342	269	675	0	4286	+0	−13	4273

Source: *Report of Building Permits Issued and Local Public Construction.* (New Jersey Department of Labor and Industry — Form C-404 — N. J. Monthly Tabulations 1960-1970.)

This represents a net average gain of 118.7 residential units per year for the ten-year period. This included a gross increase of 1,200 newly constructed units along with the loss through demolition of 13 units. In contrast to the Borough, whose growth was concentrated in the early 1960s, the Township's growth has continued steadily since 1960.

The total increase in new units (1,200) consisted of two residential types: 799 (66 percent) single-family units and 401 (34 percent) multi-family units. This pattern is somewhat different from what occurred in the Borough over the same time period. In the Borough, the increase was 37 percent in single-family units and 57 percent for multifamily units, with the remainder in two-family units.

The Township had a much higher rate of increase in the single-family category, and a much lower rate in multiple dwellings. This situation is again frequently found in urban-suburban growth patterns. However, the significance of the Borough-Township relationship is diminished if absolute increases in housing units are considered. Although the Borough had a higher *rate* of multifamily increase, the Township had an *absolute* gain almost four times as great.

Because of its growth rate from 1960 to 1970, Princeton Township had a somewhat different housing structure at the end of the decade than it did at the beginning. With the high rate of university apartment construction, multifamily units represented 15.8 percent of the total number of housing units; this was almost twice the proportion accounted for by this housing type in 1960.

Thus in 1970, a comparison of the two municipalities (Exhibit II-5)

EXHIBIT II-5

RESIDENTIAL TYPES BY PERCENT OF TOTAL UNITS
PRINCETON — 1960, 1970

| RESIDENTIAL CATEGORY | TOTAL EXISTING HOUSING | | | |
| | 1960 | | 1970 | |
	Borough	Township	Borough	Township
Single Family	73.8	82.4	71.6	77.9
Two Family	11.5	8.7	11.0	6.3
Multifamily	14.7	8.9	17.4	15.8

Source: Percentages calculated from Exhibits II-1 and II-4

shows that the residential patterns of the Township and Borough are both tending toward a similar structure. In each case single-family homes represent approximately 75 percent of the local housing stock, with multifamily and two-family homes filling out the remaining 25 percent in a ratio of two to one.

Since 1960, the supply of vacant or usable land in the Borough has been all but exhausted. In 1970, only 32 acres of land remained available for further residential development. The Township, however, currently has 2,289 acres of undeveloped land within its borders which may be used for construction of new housing units.

EXHIBIT II-6

BUILDABLE LAND INVENTORY BY RESIDENTIAL ZONING DISTRICTS — PRINCETON TOWNSHIP — 1970
(IN ACRES)

ZONE	Gross Available Land[1]	Road Wastage (12%)[2]	Platting Wastage (4%)[3]	Flood-way[4]	Usable Land 1970	Kendree and Shepherd 1967[5]	Known Acreage Built 1967-70[6]
R-1	2300	276	92	260	1672	2021	163
R-2	604	80	—	12	512	823	63
R-3	22.5	2.7	—	19	0	0	3
R-4	66	7.9	—	0	58.1	92.5	17.5
R-5	34	4.0	—	0	30.0	0	23.2
R-6	19.5	2.3	—	0	17.2	9	4.4
Total	3046.0	372.9	92	291	2289.3	2945.5	274.1

Source: Housing and Land Inventory — Summer 1970

[1] Tabulated from tax records after public open space had been deducted.
[2] Figure contained in local ordinance obtained from Mr. S. Robson, Tax Assessor, Princeton Township, N. J
[3] Pertains only to Zone R-1
[4] Floodway deductions obtained via planimeter and large acetate maps of Stony Brook (Princeton, N. J.) produced as a by-product of N. J. Department of Conservation and Economic Development Flood Plain Study
[5] "Princeton's Population," Shepherd and Kendree/Planning Consultants, October 1967, p. 1
[6] Survey of Township building permits and tax records. Building lots upon which no improvement has been made are not included in total

As is the case of the Borough, conversion from land units (usuable acreage) to units of potential population dramatizes the extent to which the Township can increase its growth (Exhibit II-7). The Borough can theoretically add 354 new housing units; the Township with present zoning can accommodate 1,382 units. Translated into people, this would mean 5,111 additional residents for the Township.

With these elements in mind, it becomes important to examine housing quality over the past ten years to gauge the cost structures within which future housing supply will fall.

EXHIBIT II-7

RESIDENTIAL ZONAL HOLDING CAPACITY
PRINCETON TOWNSHIP — 1970

ADDITIONAL POPULATION AS A FUNCTION OF AVAILABLE LAND

ZONING	Usable Acreage[2]	Highest Residential Land Use Permitted	No. of Dwelling Units	Household Size[1]	Additional Population
R-1	1672	Single Family (2 acres)	836	3.9	3260
R-2	512	Single Family (1½ acres)	341	3.6	1230
R-3	0	Single Family (1 acre)	0	3.34)	0
R-4	58.1	Single Family (¾ acre)	77	3.34)	257
R-5	30.0	Single Family (½ acre)	60	3.0	180
R-6	17.2	Single Family (¼ acre)	68	2.7	184
Totals	2289.3		1382	—	5111

Source: Housing and Land Inventory — Summer 1970

[1] Middle cases' household size obtained from Present Residents Survey — others adjusted + or — by a factor of 0.3

[2] Gross available land minus road and platting wastages and floodway acreage equals usable acreage

EXHIBIT II-8

ADDITIONS TO THE SINGLE FAMILY HOUSING STOCK
BY CONSTRUCTION COST[1]
PRINCETON BOROUGH, 1960-1970

COST RANGE	HOUSING ADDITIONS BASED ON BUILDING PERMIT APPLICATIONS						
	1960-1961	1962-1963	1964-1965	1966-1967	1968-1969	June 1970	Total
Under $10,000	0	0	0	0	0	0	0
$10,000-12,999	0	0	0	1	0	0	1
$13,000-15,999	1	1	1	0	0	0	3
$16,000-20,999	27	8	5	3	0	0	43
$21,000-25,999	5	3	4	2	0	0	14
$26,000-29,999	2	0	1	0	1	0	4
$30,000-39,999	1	0	0	0	2	3	6
$40,000-59,999	1	0	1	2	0	0	4
$60,000+	0	0	2	0	1	0	3
Total	37	12	14	8	4	3	78

[1] Over the period 1960-1970 building permit construction cost estimate x 1.04 = occupancy permit construction cost estimate (100% sample — n = 78)

Source: Building Permits — Princeton Borough 1960-1970

PAST AND FUTURE HOUSING COSTS: CURRENT HOLDERS OF VACANT RESIDENTIAL LAND

THE BOROUGH AND THE TOWNSHIP: PAST COSTS

The number and price of single-family units constructed in Princeton Borough from 1960-1970 are listed in Exhibit II-8. In the last three years, almost all new housing has been in the more expensive price categories. This is illustrated in Exhibit II-9. Since 1960 the price of the median unit has steadily increased. In fact, construction costs of the median units have nearly doubled over the ten-year period. Although housing costs are demonstrably increased, this does not necessarily mean that more luxurious housing has been put in place locally; inflation has pushed the price of land and housing to a point where changes in value over time are not calculable. If, for example, the 27 units of housing constructed in 1960-1961 were built today, a marked shift to a higher cost cohort would probably be evident. In terms of possible future building activity, it is likely that the "builder" cost of a single-family home will be $30,000 or more. Examination of Borough assessment records over the past three years provides a conversion multiplier of 2.4 which can be used to change "builder cost" into "purchaser cost." Based on its utilization, it is not realistic to expect any additions to the Borough's single-family housing stock at a purchaser cost of less than $60,000. Increased housing costs, coupled with limited land availability under present zoning, forecasts the limited future growth of the Borough's housing supply.

Extensive housing activity in the Township provides a greater opportunity to establish valid trends for future development than was possible in analysis of the Borough. Exhibits II-10 and II-11 list the cost of the Township's median housing unit from 1960 to 1970. As was found in the Borough, the building cost of the median housing unit shows a steady increase over the ten-year period.

By the middle of 1970, the median had shifted to a cost cohort approximately three times greater than that found in 1960. This rate of change is even greater than the increase noted in the Borough, as shown in Exhibit II-9.

The increase in construction costs may be the result of the decreasing availability of the smaller acreage zones throughout the Township. The basic fact remains, however, that open market forces have generated much higher construction costs in the Township during the last decade. Again, conversion of construction costs to consumer cost is necessary to

---

*Refers in this instance to a simple taxonomic grouping category.

appreciate this trend. Township assessment records for 1968 and 1969 show a conversion multiplier of 2.4 which, if applied to the builder cost, approximates the potential purchaser cost. Using this as a base, initial housing costs to the Township buyer must be viewed as increasingly falling in the $60,000-$70,000 range.

EXHIBIT II-9

MEDIAN CONSTRUCTION COST COHORTS[1]
PRINCETON BOROUGH, 1960-1970

| | MEDIAN AND COHORT OF INDIVIDUAL UNITS | |
DEVELOPMENTAL PERIOD	Median Unit	Cohort of Median Housing Units
1960-1961	19	$16,000-20,999
1962-1963	6-7	$16,000-20,999
1964-1965	7-8	$21,000-25,999
1966-1967	4-5	$21,000-25,999
1968-1969	2-3	$30,000-39,999
1970-June	2	$30,000-39,999

[1] Refers in this instance to a simple taxonomic grouping category.

Source: Cohorts calculated from Exhibit II-8

THE BOROUGH AND THE TOWNSHIP:
FUTURE COSTS

The basic market processes seem to guarantee a high standard of development, in both the Borough and Township which is exclusively limited to upper-middle-income families. A straight line projection of building costs from the 1960s into the 1970s suggests that a $60,000 cost may, in fact, be conservative. Cost increases over the period 1960-1961 to 1968-1969 were used to establish cost magnitudes likely to be found in Princeton over the next decade. Assuming that previous rates of increase will continue throughout the coming decade, median builder costs by 1980 may rise to the $60,000-$79,999 level. This would result in minimum purchaser costs of $100,000 or more. Such a high figure is at first difficult to accept; however, there are no valid reasons why cost increases

EXHIBIT II-10

ADDITIONS TO THE SINGLE FAMILY HOUSING STOCK
BY CONSTRUCTION COST[1]
PRINCETON TOWNSHIP, 1960-1970

COST RANGE	*HOUSING ADDITIONS BASED ON BUILDING PERMIT APPLICATIONS*						
	1960-1961[2]	1962-1963[2]	1964-1965[2]	1966-1967	1968-1969	June 1970	Total
Under $10,000	0	0	0	0	0	0	0
$10,000-12,999	1	2	1	0	2	0	6
$13,000-15,999	11	7	4	1	1	0	24
$16,000-20,999	113	83	57	34	19	2	308
$21,000-25,999	21	29	29	14	11	3	107
$26,000-29,999	18	15	24	8	18	1	84
$30,000-39,999	24	42	32	35	32	0	165
$40,000-59,999	13	9	10	17	20	9	78
$60,000+	1	4	4	3	12	3	27
Total	202	191	161	112	115	18	799

Source: Building Permits — Princeton Township 1960-1970

[1] Over the period 1960-1970 building permit construction cost estimate x 1.04 = occupancy permit construction cost estimate (100% sample — n = 799)

[2] Kendree and Shepherd. *Housing Need in Princeton Community—Part 1 Background Data,* p. 3

EXHIBIT II-11

MEDIAN CONSTRUCTION COST COHORTS
PRINCETON TOWNSHIP, 1960-1970

| | MEDIAN AND COHORT OF INDIVIDUAL UNITS | |
DEVELOPMENTAL PERIOD	Median Unit	Cohort of Median Housing Units
1960-1961	101-102	$16,000-20,999
1962-1963	96	$21,000-25,999
1964-1965	81	$21,000-25,999
1966-1967	56-57	$26,000-29,999
1968-1969	58	$30,000-39,999
1970-June	9-10	$40,000-59,999

Source: Cohorts calculated from Exhibit II-10

EXHIBIT II-12

BUILDING COST PROJECTION
PRINCETON COMMUNITY — 1960-1980

| | BUILDING COST AND PERCENT INCREASE | |
DEVELOPMENTAL PERIOD	Cohort of Median Housing Units	Percent Increase
1960-1961	$16,000-20,999	—
1968-1969	$30,000-39,999	100%
1976-1977	$60,000-79,999	100%

Source: Comparison drawn from Exhibits II-9 and II-11

in the 1970s should be less than those of the 1960s. Certainly the rates in the late 1960s are much higher than those found in earlier parts of the decade.

Thus, in the early 1970s, the most significant amount of housing built on the private market will be in the Township, with purchaser costs gradually increasing from $60,000 to $100,000 through the decade. This will most certainly occur if the current technology of housing construction and local governmental restraints remain unchanged.

EXHIBIT II-13

VACANT RESIDENTIAL ACREAGE BY
RECEIVERSHIP CLASSIFICATION
PRINCETON BOROUGH-TOWNSHIP — 1970

	NUMBER OF ACRES	
CLASSIFICATION	Borough	Township
Individual Holdings (Two building lots or less)	14.20	703.60
Individual Holdings (Three building lots or more)	0.00	323.40
Developer/Realty Agency Holdings	11.86	244.75
Corporate Holdings	2.43	58.20
Developable Institutional Holdings	4.20	528.60[1]
Specifically Designated Farmland	0.00	1188.05[2]
Total (Based on gross available land totals previously calculated in the Land Inventory)	32.69	3046.00

Source: Inventory of Borough and Township Tax Records — Summer 1970

[1] There are approximately 750 acres of additional vacant Township land held by institutions considered for the most part not residentially developable due to educational zoning, planned institutional growth, restrictive land covenants, etc. These were *not* included in the gross available land total. (Specific building lots and acreage estimates were obtained from Mr. S. Robson, Township Tax Assessor.)

[2] Farmland is divided in the Township as follows: individual holdings 2 or less (13.5%), individual holdings 3 or more (84.4%), corporate holdings (2.1%). (107 acres of institutional farmland not included in gross available totals.)

CURRENT HOLDERS OF VACANT RESIDENTIAL LAND

Vacant residential acreage in the Borough and Township is broken down by ownership classifications in Exhibit II-13. In the Borough 87 percent (14 acres) of the buildable residential land is in the possession of individual holders who own less than two building lots. The way this land is developed will be a function of a variety of private and public decisions. Land holdings by developers are relatively and absolutely secondary, thus precluding any single or uniform development mode within the Borough's future housing additions.

In contrast, the Township has 568.15 acres, or 18 percent, of its developable land held by private developers, realty agencies or by individuals who own more than three building lots. It is the land owned by the group, supplemented by similar holdings in what is now designated as farmland, that is the most susceptible to the increasing pressures of rapid development. Individual holders of two building lots or less (703.6 acres — 23 percent of total) and other institutional holdings (528.6 acres — 17

EXHIBIT II-14

FUTURE HOUSING BOUNDARIES

	MUNICIPALITY	
CONSIDERATION	Princeton Borough	Princeton Township
A. Available Land	31.54 Acres	2,289.3 Acres
B. Potential Dwelling Capacity Units and Population	354 Units/ 872 Residents	1,382 Units/ 5,111 Residents
C. Development Options Due to Ownership Categories (Open Market)	Fairly Limited	Extensive Alternatives
D. Potential Unit and Population Increase to 1980 at 1960-70 Rate	186 Units/ 494 Residents	1,187 Units/ 4,392 Residents
E. Potential Unit Cost 1970/1980	$60,000/$80,000	$60,000/$120,000

Source: Housing and Land Inventory — Summer 1970

percent) are also sufficiently extensive, and parcels so large, that the possibilities for development are no less real, although one would expect these developments to be more varied and to take a longer period of time to reach completion.

In summation, one may view the development potential of the limited and individually owned vacant land in the Borough as supplementing over time the character of this municipality's existing housing supply. In the Township, however, there are many large parcels of land owned by developers, individuals in multiple assemblages and institutions, each of which may choose a variety of development patterns.

Exhibit II-14 summarizes future growth possibilities. Township and Borough differences as well as their extent, are clearly portrayed.

The Borough shows little building activity, reflecting its limited growth potential. In the Township, building is going on at six to seven times the Borough's rate. The building realizable potential, however, is considerably more extensive.

Since the Borough's stock is essentially filled (90 percent), contemplated additions will do little to alter its existing residential pattern.* The Township, at only 75 percent of its housing capacity, can expect housing additions different from the existing mode to affect its residential pattern to a slightly greater degree.

---

*1970 census definitions equating condominiums to single-family homes and contemplated Borough growth in this area further reenforce existing residential type ratios.

Chapter III
LOCAL EMPLOYMENT GROWTH

This chapter describes the extent to which local employment in the Princeton area creates demands for housing in the Township and the Borough.

While this research in part supplements similar efforts by the Township Advisory Committee (1959-1960)[1] and the Middlesex-Somerset-Mercer Regional Study Council is 1970,[2] it is somewhat different in its approach. Housing demand is predicted in relation to job growth. In other words, the demand for future housing is derived in this study by an analysis of the kinds of employers now located in the Princeton area and the extent to which their employees use, or want to use, local housing.

Firms located in Princeton (those utilizing/not utilizing a Princeton mailing address yet found in the immediate Princeton vicinity and of sufficient size to influence its housing market) were categorized into employer groups in accordance with the Standard Industrial Classifications (SIC) established by the U. S. Bureau of the Census.

The employer groups analyzed in the study were those of significance locally; i.e., SIC categories of: 1) Manufacturing; 2) Transportation, Communications and Public Utilities; 3) Finance, Insurance and Real Estate; 4) Wholesale and Retail; and 5) the Service Industry.

Agriculture, Mining and Construction firms were eliminated because they either did not constitute a sufficient local employment concentration or because future growth or competition expectations were nil.

Once categorized, a random sample of the estimated population of each group was taken, in which from 16 to 50 percent of the firms were sampled.

An effort was made to sample heavily both the manufacturing and service industries in accordance with their weight locally. As will be indicated in the section devoted to the service group (module), even though the largest segment of interviews was conducted in this industrial grouping, the number and variety of these firms in the Princeton area make conclusions based on this study tentative rather than definitive.

Personnel directors or ranking officials from each firm were interviewed in depth to determine occupational profiles and existing Princeton housing usage. Current usage was compared with other usage indices, and future need based upon existing use was projected to 1975.

Manufacturing firms were separated into large and small employers. This was necessary due to significant differences in the wage and occupational structures occasioned by substantial numbers of operatives in the former category. The division was fixed at 35 employees or under for the small firms and 100 employees or over for those of the larger variety. Middle-sized manufacturing firms (36-99 employees) were not significant in either structure or quantity, and thus were eliminated from the analysis.

In no other modular grouping was this refinement of large from small necessary. The characteristics which profile a small real estate or transportation firm generally hold true for their larger equivalents. These and other similarities, specifically within the transportation, communications and public utility; finance, insurance and real estate; and the wholesale and retail modules, were so intense that further sampling after five to six interviews proved redundant.

This was not the case, however, in the service module, where internal differences were so extensive that the sample mean underwent adjustment with almost every interview.

Exhibits III-1 and III-2 detail both the individual types and specific firms surveyed in each module. The 50 firms were surveyed in an attempt to document the occupational and housing needs of Princeton's employer concentrations. The lists, while not exhaustive, hopefully are representative. In some cases numbers are much too low for extensive generalizations. The basic goal of this limited rather than definitive conclusion is to provide insight into the dynamic linkage between job development and housing demand.

EXHIBIT III-1

CONSTITUENTS OF THE LOCAL EMPLOYER MODULE

PRINCETON-ORIENTED EMPLOYER MODULES (BY TYPE)

Manufacturing (Large and Small)

    Food and Kindred Products
    Textile Mill Products
    Printing and Publishing Products
    Chemicals and Allied Products
    Electrical Machinery Products
    Instruments and Related Products
    Miscellaneous Manufacturing Products

Transportation, Communications and Public Utilities

    Transportation
        Surface Passenger Transportation
        Trucking and Local Warehousing

    Communications
        Direct Voice Communication
        Airwave Broadcasting

    Public Utilities
        Electric and Gas Services
        Sanitary Services

Wholesale and Retail Trade

    Apparel and Accessory Goods
    Grocery and Specialty Goods
    Hardware and Mechanical Goods
    Other General Merchandise

Finance, Insurance and Real Estate

    Banking
    Insurance Carriers
    Real Estate Agents
    Stockbrokers and Investment Organizations

The Service Industry

    Business Services
    Educational Services
    Hotels and Travelling Accommodations
    Medical and Health Services

Source: Local Employers Survey — Summer 1970

EXHIBIT III-2

CONSTITUENTS OF THE LOCAL EMPLOYER MODULE

PRINCETON-ORIENTED EMPLOYER MODULES (BY FIRM)

Manufacturing Firms — Small

Gardner Cyrogenics Corp.
Haskins Press
Intertech Corp.
Keene Interiors
Kent Corp.
Princeton Biomedix Laboratories
Princeton Packet
Princeton Photo Process Co.

Manufacturing Firms — Large

Coca-Cola Bottling Co.
Cointreau, Ltd.
Creative Playthings, Inc.
Data-Ram
Fifth Dimension, Inc.
I.B.M. Corp.
Princeton Applied Research Corp.
Princeton University Press
Shell Chemical Company

Transportation, Communication & Public

Utilities
American Telephone & Telegraph Co.
Irish's Express & Storage
Nassau Broadcasting Co.
Princeton Disposal Service
Princeton Water Co.
Public Service Electric & Gas Co.
Tiger Bus Company
Tiger Cab Company

Finance, Insurance & Real Estate

Jenny E. Cortese, Real Estate
Dun & Bradstreet, Inc.
First National Bank of Princeton
The Gulick Agency
Hilton Realty
Princeton Bank & Trust Co.

Wholesalers & Retailers

Bamberger's Inc.
Langrock — Princeton
Mettler Instruments, Inc.
Thrift-Way of Princeton
Tia Electric Co.
Tiger Auto Stores, Inc.

The Service Industry

American Cyanamid Co.
Applied Data Research, Inc.
Benson and Benson, Inc.
FMC Corporation
The Gallup Organization, Inc.
Institute for Advanced Study
Mobil Oil Corporation
The Nassau Inn
Opinion Research Corporation
Princeton Hospital
Princeton Theological Seminary
RCA (Astro-Electronics Division)
RCA (David Sarnoff Research Center)

Source: Local Employers Survey — Summer 1970

SMALL MANUFACTURING FIRMS

The small manufacturing firm which generally caters to the immediate needs of the Mercer County area is a relative newcomer to the Princeton area. A majority of the firms selected for analysis have been in the immediate area* for a period of less than ten years. There are, however, noted exceptions, such as a small weekly newspaper whose history and local presence date back to the Revolutionary War period.

Three distinct reasons for selecting Princeton as a business environment were given by representatives of small manufacturing firms. The most common rationale is the prestige of the local community; i.e., the association with a community long renowned for its intellectual air and for its affluence.

The regional location of the community and its concomitant accessibility to neighboring municipalities was the second most frequent reply. For example, a small, high-priced furniture manufacturer and a liquid helium producer located in Princeton primarily because of the unencumbered access to the major urban centers of the East Coast which the community offers.

The third most frequent explanation for selecting Princeton was its nearness to competition. Few single, small manufacturing types dominate the Princeton economy. In most cases there are several firms engaged in similar, if not duplicate, endeavors, all with an eye frequently cast on the activities of their competition.

OCCUPATIONS

White-collar employees comprise the majority of the small manufacturing firm's staff. In the modular case, professionals and technicians, managers and officials, and white-collar clericals make up more than 75 percent of the payrolled force. In the most diminutive of firms analyzed, i.e., a small pharmaceutical producer, the entire staff is professionally classified.

There are, however, notable exceptions. A photo-process company has 65 percent of its staff classified as operatives or service workers. Other small firms engaged principally in publishing activities may retain as much as one-third of their staff in the form of craftsmen.

In these small firms (the mean size within the sample is 14 full-time employees) management personnel comprise an unusually high percentage of the work force (17 percent). It is not uncommon for managers to equal half the total of the combined clerical craftsman and operative labor forces.

*Princeton's zoning ordinances which limit heavy industry cause most manufacturing firms to locate adjacent to rather than within the confines of the community itself.

EXHIBIT III-3

OCCUPATIONAL/INCOME PROFILE — SMALL MANUFACTURING FIRMS

SUMMARY TABLE:

Mean Size	14 Full Time Employees
Male/Female Distribution	82/18%

Labor Force Composition (Total-14)

Classification	Percent of Modular Employee Mean	Number of Modular Employees So Classified
Professional, Technical & Kindred Workers	35%	5
Managers, Officials & Proprietors	17	2
Clerical & Kindred Workers	22	3
Craftsmen, Foremen & Kindred Workers	8	1
Operatives & Kindred Workers	13	2
Service Workers	1 }	1
Laborers & Private Household Workers	4 }	

Income Scale of All Employees (Total-14)

Classification	Percent of Modular Employee Mean	Number of Modular Employees So Classified
Under $ 4,000	0%	0
4,000- 6,999	32	4
7,000- 9,999	16	2
10,000-15,999	28	4
16,000-20,999	20	3
21,000-30,999	4	1
31,000-50,999	0	0
Over $51,000	0	0

Income Scale of Princeton Residing Employees (Total-1)

Classification	Percent of Princeton Modular Employee Mean	Number of Modular Employees So Classified
Under $10,000	100%	1
10,000-15,999	0	0
16,000-20,999	0	0
21,000-30,999	0	0
31,000-50,999	0	0
51,000-75,999	0	0

Sample Data

        Number of Such Firms in the Princeton Area: 26
        Number Sampled: 8

Source: Local Employees Survey — Summer 1970

INCOMES

More than half of the employees in Princeton's small manufacturing firms earn above $10,000. No firm acknowledged salaries higher than $21,000 or lower than $4,000. Two distinct wage-scales exist within these firms; i.e., in the $4,000-$7,000 and the $10,000-$16,000 salary brackets.

Thus, if one were to capsulize both the employment and income profiles of these small firms, they would be considered as top-heavy with management and professional personnel, who earn middle-level salaries. Few extremes exist in either occupational classifications or income ranges.

PRESENT USE OF PRINCETON'S HOUSING

The small manufacturers in the sample rely on Princeton to provide less than 1 percent of the housing accommodations for their employed personnel. Twenty-five percent of those surveyed could name no one from their roster who resided in either Princeton jurisdiction. A small laboratory instrument company, whose receptionist lives in town, is typical of the firms with only one employee housed within the community. A current exception is the weekly newspaper, which attracts 20 percent of its employees (mostly operatives) from the Princeton community.

All of the employees of small manufacturing firms who currently reside in Princeton earn less than $10,000. They are either long-term residents of Princeton or wives of graduate students attending one of the local institutions of higher learning. The long-term residents (not necessarily heads of households) are predominantly homeowners, while the students' wives and a small proportion of single girls contribute to a limited rental market.

The major portion of the labor supply for Princeton's small manufacturing firms is provided by Trenton, an old industrial city 12 miles away, or communities within Trenton's "inner ring." Included in this category are Lawrenceville, Ewing, Hamilton Township, Montgomery Township, and the Pennsylvania communities of Yardley and Levittown. Commuters from either New York or Philadelphia are a rare phenomenon.

Although most of the employees have established residence outside the community, a significant proportion want to relocate in the immediate Princeton area. Representative firms acknowledge a desire on the part of one-quarter (a mean of four) of their current staff to become Princeton residents. At the laboratory instrument company, the personnel director stated that a large portion of those with this desire were senior management personnel.

Two types of housing accommodations were seen as deficient by the small manufacturers; i.e., single-family homes and garden apartments.

Apartment-style living in Princeton is considered by those surveyed as practically non-existent. Single-family units at prices within reach of the "workingman" are also considered to be in short supply.

EXHIBIT III-4

CURRENT AND DESIRED PRINCETON HOUSING USAGE: GROWTH AND COMPETITION EXPECTATIONS — SMALL MANUFACTURING FIRMS

SUMMARY TABLE:

	Percent of Modular Employee Mean*	Number of Modular Employees Affected
Current Princeton Housing Usage:	6.5	1
As Owners	4.0	1
As Renters	2.5	0
	Percent of Modular Employee Mean	**Number of Modular Employees Affected**
Desired Additional Princeton Housing Usage:	25.0	4
As Owners in the $17,500-$40,000 Range	18.0	3
As Renters at the $136-$175 Level	7.0	1
Housing Maintained in the Community:	None	
Anticipated Growth by 1975 (Mean):	200%	
Expectation of Competition:	4 - 5 additional non- publishing firms	
Princeton Housing Market as a Barrier to Growth or Recruitment:	No (100%)	

*Modular Employee Mean — 14 Full Time Employees

Source: Local Employers Survey — Summer 1970

Employers consider the availability of single-family homes with a purchase price of $17,500-$20,000 the most severely deficient and list rentals in the range of $136 to $175 in a similar category.

FUTURE COMPETITION AND/OR EXPECTED GROWTH

There is no consensus among small manufacturers concerning anticipated competition within the next five years. None is envisioned by the small publishing firm, although there is an expectation among computer service firms of an influx of competition in the not-too-distant future.

Internal growth is expected by all the firms in the small manufacturing category. Increases of 100, 250 and 500 percent are not uncommon predictions for 1975. The mean employment growth expectation is almost 200 percent above current size.

The apparent housing shortage is not expected to affect any of the expansion plans of the small manufacturers. Only one firm, a small furniture production operation, contended that the lack of apartment facilities in the municipality would adversely affect its operations.

The other firms held that the housing supply in the immediate vicinity was of sufficient quantity to offset any shortages currently existing in Princeton.

LARGE MANUFACTURING FIRMS

Large manufacturing institutions are not a new phenomenon in the Princeton area, although very few are actually located in the community itself. Three of the nine representative firms contacted have been on its fringe for more than 80 years. It should not, however, be considered a closed market, as several of the firms in this modular type also have been residents of the area for less than 10 years. Of this latter group, an information systems corporation is representative. The older residents are typified by a local publishing company bearing the university's name.

The large manufacturers also considered the "prestige of Princeton" as one of the three major factors which attracted them to the area, although to considerably less extent than the smaller producers. The availability of land on which to build and expand physical facilities was first given priority.

Unlike their smaller counterparts, the large producers export heavily to the major markets of the East Coast. Accessibility to the regional road network was the third factor listed by this type of firm.

OCCUPATIONS

The typical large manufacturer's labor force within the sample is comprised largely of blue-collar workers. Craftsmen, foremen and operatives represent 45 percent of the working force.

Professionals and technicians account for the majority of the white-collar employees. At the information systems corporation they account for over 31 percent of this group. For the module as a whole the professional category comprises 24 percent of the labor force.

Within all of the large manufacturing installations, males outnumber females by two to one. This is a more equitable distribution than the one found in the smaller firms where, as shown in Exhibit III-3, males represent 82 percent of the labor force.

INCOMES

Except at the highest levels, wages and salaries in large-scale manufacturing are well below those of their smaller counterparts. Seventy percent of the employees in the modular case earn below $10,000 annually. The majority, 41 percent, earn under $7,000. At the other end of the income scale, only four percent earn above $21,000.

PRESENT USE OF PRINCETON'S HOUSING

As with the previous modular group, less than 10 percent of the employees who work in the Princeton area also reside within the Princeton community. The companies polled ranged from a low of two employees out of 275 at a major oil company to a high of 38 out of 158 at the local publisher.

Long-time Princetonians form the major block of employed residents. Blue-collar workers earning less than $10,000 a year represent 55 percent of this total. These workmen, who have been with their companies for a considerable period, generally are homeowners. Among the representative firms only 13 percent of the employees who live in Princeton participate in the local rental market.

Employees who have the desire to be renters and, additionally, to live close to their place of work, have frequently selected either the Hightstown or Cranbury areas. Both of these sections offer a large selection of garden apartment rentals at relatively moderate prices within a 10-mile drive.

Though the Trenton area provides residence for the majority of the lower-level labor force, the commuting radius of specific employees may exceed 50 miles in any direction. Lawrenceville was referred to as the community most often chosen by professionals and executives who either did not have the desire or the capital to reside in Princeton.

The desire among large-manufacturing employees to relocate to Princeton is almost negligible. Eight of nine employers contacted could not recall the Princeton housing situation as a subject of discussion at either official or unofficial group sessions. Reasons given for this lack of interest were the comparatively high tax structure and the overall high cost

EXHIBIT III-5

OCCUPATIONAL/INCOME PROFILE — LARGE MANUFACTURING FIRMS

SUMMARY TABLE:

Mean Size	172 Full time employees
Male/Female Distribution	66/34%

Labor Force Composition (Total-172)

Classification	Percent of Modular Employee Mean	Number of Modular Employees So Classified
Professional, Technical & Kindred Workers	24	41
Managers, Officials & Proprietors	13	22
Clerical & Kindred Workers	16	28
Craftsmen, Foremen & Kindred Workers	13	22
Operatives & Kindred Workers	32	55
Service Workers	1	2
Laborers & Private Household Workers	1	2

Income Scale of All Employees (Total-172)

Classification	Percent of Modular Employee Mean	Number of Modular Employees So Classified
Under $ 4,000	0	0
4,000- 6,999	41	70
7,000- 9,999	29	50
10,000-15,999	16	28
16,000-20,999	10	17
21,000-30,999	3	5
31,000-50,999	1	2
Over $51,000	0	0

Income Scale of Princeton Residing Employees (Total-14)

Classification	Percent of Princeton Modular Employee Mean	Number of Modular Employees So Classified
Under $10,000	55	8
10,000-15,999	10	1
16,000-20,999	22	3
21,000-30,999	7	1
31,000-50,999	6	1
51,000-75,999	0	0

Sample Data

Number of Such Firms in the Princeton Area: 18
Number Sampled: 9

Source: Local Employers Survey — Summer 1970

EXHIBIT III-6

CURRENT AND DESIRED PRINCETON HOUSING USAGE: GROWTH AND COMPETITION EXPECTATIONS — LARGE MANUFACTURING FIRMS

SUMMARY TABLE:

	Percent of Modular Employee Mean*	Number of Modular Employees Affected
Current Princeton Housing Usage:	8	14
As Owners	7	12
As Renters	1	2

	Percent of Modular Employee Mean	Number of Modular Employees Affected
Desired Additional Princeton Housing Usage:	20	34
As Owners in the $25,000-$40,000 Range	14	24
As Renters at the $136-$175 Level	6	10

Housing Maintained in the Community:	None
Anticipated Growth by 1975 (Mean):	40%
Expectation of Competition:	Limited - Computer Related Firms Only
Princeton Housing Market as a Barrier to Growth or Recruitment:	No (100%)

*Modular Employee Mean — 172 Full Time Employees

Source: Local Employers Survey — Summer 1970

of living associated with the Princeton area.

There is, however, a relatively strong desire to live in Princeton on the part of the members of newer firms in the area. A branch of a major bottling company, located in Princeton for only five years, notes that nearly one-quarter of its 200 employees expressed a desire to become residents of the Princeton community. Another large manufacturing firm, the information systems corporation, also acknowledged a similar desire by 10 percent of its staff. Both of these firm's employees, exceptions to the modular case, would generally prefer to be owners. Renting appeals to only 20 percent of those desirous of a Princeton address.

The housing shortage was seen as acute, though not limiting, by eight of nine large-manufacturing employers. Single-family homes in the $25,000-$40,000 price range which would attract the younger, upwardly mobile professional, were most often regarded as deficient. The $40,000-$60,000 home appealing to those in upper management levels also was mentioned as lacking in several instances. Few employers, however, mentioned the needs of the lower echelon "working man," assuming possibly that "if one does not have money, he *does not* live in Princeton."

Rentals, particularly for secretaries and younger professionals, were also noted as lacking by four of the nine firms. The rental level most often mentioned as missing was at the $136-$175 per month range for a one-bedroom unit.

FUTURE COMPETITION

As with the small manufacturer, the computer-oriented producer envisions that competition will locate in the immediate Princeton area within the next five years. Two large business/computer corporations also contemplate this happening.

Most other large manufacturing firms either do not acknowledge the existence of competition or do not envision a shift in location by any of their major adversaries.

Internal growth is not expected by all the firms representing the large manufacturing group. One-half of them anticipate their payroll size to remain the same for the next several years; decreases are expected by one firm because of rearrangement of its priorities, while only four out of nine expect organizational increases and then only of a magnitude of 35 percent by 1975.

Housing market deficiencies in Princeton are not expected to hamper any of the expansion plans held by these employers. Manufacturers feel that there is sufficient housing supply in the surrounding municipalities to accommodate the majority of new employees. Companies also contend that shelter for employees is not one of their direct responsibilities. (The lack of attention here would seem to bolster the argument of an adequate *regional* housing supply.)

TRANSPORTATION, COMMUNICATION AND PUBLIC UTILITY FIRMS

Firms which comprise the transportation, communication and public utility (TCU) module are not subject to competition in the immediate market. Most of these firms have been granted licenses through state, local or federal agencies, and several also serve as the local business offices for statewide agencies.

The unique nature of the TCU module permits few new enterprises to enter the market. The latest arrival, a regional broadcasting company, has been in operation since 1962. All of the other firms representing the group have maintained a Princeton address for a minimum of 30 years. Representatives unaffected by the licensing procedure settled within the community primarily because of the availability of land.

OCCUPATIONS

Like the small and large manufacturing firms, the transportation, communication and utility companies are staffed primarily with male employees. Of the eight companies which represent the modular category, not one had staffs with more than 20 percent female members.

Operatives comprise the largest single segment of the labor force. These, together with repairmen, installation men, drivers and other types of blue-collar workers, account for almost 60 percent of the average TCU firm's payroll. Professionals are not considered essential to most company operations, and with the exception of the local radio station, professionals and technicians are rare in this group's labor force.

INCOMES

The high proportion of non-professional and non-managerial labor force helps to explain why 70 percent of those employed earn less than $10,000 annually. In a typical TCU firm, such as a local carting company, 35 percent of its payrolled force receive between $7,000 and $9,999 a year. Another 16 percent earn between $10,000 and $16,000. Wages are lower in this group than in any other; several individuals within each organization receive less than $4,000 in annual salaries.

PRESENT USE OF PRINCETON'S HOUSING

Transportation, communication and utility firms have been located in Princeton for several years. As a result, employees were able to purchase homes before the current housing shortage became acute. Fifteen percent of the TCU employees live in Princeton. No one with a Princeton address in the sample, however, earns above $21,000. Most of the employed Princeton residents earn between $10,000 and $16,000. For

EXHIBIT III-7

OCCUPATIONAL/INCOME PROFILE –
TRANSPORTATION, COMMUNICATIONS AND PUBLIC UTILITIES

SUMMARY TABLE:

Mean Size	27 Full Time Employees
Male/Female Distribution	82/18%

Labor Force Composition (Total-27)

Classification	Percent of Modular Employee Mean	Number of Modular Employees So Classified
Professional, Technical & Kindred Workers	17%	5
Managers, Officials & Proprietors	9	2
Clerical & Kindred Workers	11	3
Craftsmen, Foremen & Kindred Workers	2	1
Operatives & Kindred Workers	58	15
Service Workers	3	1
Laborers & Private Household Workers	0	0

Income Scale of All Employees (Total-27)

Classification	Percent of Modular Employee Mean	Number of Modular Employees So Classified
Under $ 4,000	2%	1
4,000- 6,999	33	9
7,000- 9,999	35	9
10,000- 15,999		
16,000- 20,999	22	5
21,000- 30,999	6	2
31,000- 50,999	2	1
Over $51,000	0	0

Income Scale of Princeton Residing Employees (Total-4)

Classification	Percent of Princeton Modular Employee Mean	Number of Modular Employees So Classified
Under $10,000	38%	2
10,000-15,999	57	2
16,000-20,999	4	0
21,000-30,999	1	0
31,000-50,999	0	0
51,000-75,999	0	0

Sample Data

Number of Such Firms in the Princeton Area: 24
Number Sampled: 8

Source: Local Employers Survey – Summer 1970

example, employees of a small bus company who live in Princeton are in the $10,000-$16,000 bracket. All but one of these residents live in single-family homes.

As in the preceeding modular groups, the largest share of the labor force emanates from Trenton and its surrounding communities. The high percentage of low-skilled operatives employed by TCU firms comes from the city of Trenton itself. More highly paid employees have a wider range of housing options and are thus likely to choose one of the less affluent suburban communities such as Levittown, Pennsylvania, as their place of residence.

There is a lack of consensus on the part of employers regarding their employees' desire to live in Princeton. Half of the firms contacted could not envision serious relocation plans. The other half, however, disclosed strong desires of perhaps a quarter of their employees to move to the Princeton area.

The transportation and communication employers polled believed that their people would readily relocate if housing were to become available at "realistic" prices. The manager of a taxi company said that his men drive an exhausting amount during their working day and thus want to live closer to the job. Employees in the market to relocate are generally interested in becoming homeowners, and less than 20 percent indicate a preference in becoming renters.

All but one of the TCU employers interviewed believed Princeton was suffering from an acute housing shortage, particularly in the $15,000-$25,000 single-family home category. The one dissenting opinion held that Princeton is already *overhoused* and thus must not be considered as a catch-all for all levels of employment.

There were also several employers who believed that housing of all types was a necessity for the community. This included not only the single-family variety, but also garden apartments renting for less than $175 monthly. This was the first group of employers to mention a need for studio apartments which would rent for an average of $100 monthly and cater to the bachelor blue-collar worker.

FUTURE COMPETITION AND/OR EXPECTED GROWTH

Due to the extra-market nature of this module, competition is not envisioned by most of the transportation, communication and utility employers. Furniture-moving companies, however, do expect competitors to be drawn by the availability of vacant land in surrounding areas.

As the Princeton region continues to grow, the companies which serve this area also expect employment growth. Internal increases are expected to average 70 percent over the next five years for the bulk of the TCU firms.

All but one of the firms contacted do not consider the housing shortage severe enough to deter future plans for expansion. Concomitantly, these employers are reluctant to consider employee shelter as one of their responsibilities. The only company feeling that housing deficiencies would cause hiring problems was one of the local taxi firms.

EXHIBIT III-8

CURRENT AND DESIRED PRINCETON HOUSING USAGE: GROWTH AND COMPETITION EXPECTATIONS— TRANSPORTATION, COMMUNICATIONS AND PUBLIC UTILITIES

SUMMARY TABLE:

	Percent of Modular Employee Mean*	Number of Modular Employees Affected
Current Princeton Housing Usage:	13	4
As Owners	11	3
As Renters	2	1
	Percent of Modular Employee Mean	Number of Modular Employees Affected
Desired Additional Princeton Housing Usage:	25	7
As Owners in the $17,500-$25,000 Range	22	6
As Renters at the $100-$175 Range	3	1
Housing Maintained in the Community:	None	
Anticipated Growth by 1975 (Mean):	70%	
Expectation of Competition:	None	
Princeton Housing Market as a Barrier to Growth or Recruitment:	No (75%)	

* Modular Employee Mean — 27 Full Time Employees

Source: Local Employers Survey — Summer 1970

FINANCE, INSURANCE AND REAL ESTATE FIRMS

The fourth modular type is comprised of firms engaged in finance, insurance and real estate (FIRE) activities. These employers are predominantly small, white-collar organizations which have been located in Princeton's core for more than 20 years. A typical case is a local bank, bearing the community's name, which has been providing services to residents since before the turn of the century.

OCCUPATIONS

The typical FIRE office (excluding the banks) maintains a full-time staff of 13 employees. It is not uncommon to find a small office, for example, a Nassau Street realtor, which is staffed by only three people, catering to a select housing shopper. The two major local banks, however, each maintain more than 100 full-time employees on their payrolls.

White-collar employees comprise fully 90 percent of the labor force within the FIRE category. Due to the nature of the activity, clerical, sales and servicing personnel account for more than half of these employees.

INCOMES

Salary levels are slightly higher than those recorded by the three previous modular employers. The highest wage in the group, $21,000-$31,000 is received by 10 percent of the representative firms' employees. Forty-five percent of the labor force receives more than $10,000. Less than one-fourth of the labor force earns under $7,000 per year.

PRESENT USE OF PRINCETON'S HOUSING

The outstanding characteristic of the FIRE module is the high percentage of employees who both work and live in the community. Thirty-seven percent of its employees live in Princeton Township or Borough. Of these, all but a few currently are homeowners.

Residents' incomes are higher than in any of the preceding modular groups. Two-thirds of the resident employees earn more than $10,000 a year. One Nassau Street realtor has no employee living in Princeton earning less than $10,000.

Communities in the immediate vicinity of Princeton provide the major portion of the labor force to FIRE employers. The apartment developments in East Windsor, Plainsboro and Cranbury are attractive to banking's young assistant cashiers and the female clericals of the insurance industry. The Trenton area also provides similar accommodations, although to a considerably lesser degree. Not all employees reside in

EXHIBIT III-9

OCCUPATIONAL/INCOME PROFILE –
FINANCE, INSURANCE AND REAL ESTATE FIRMS (FIRE)

SUMMARY TABLE:

Mean Size	Banks — 120 Full Time Employees
	Other FIRE — 13 Full Time Employees (Range)
Male/Female Distribution	60/40%

Labor Force Composition (Totals-120/13)

	Percent of Modular	Number of Modular Employees So Classified	
Classification	*Employee Mean*	*(Banks)*	*(Other FIRE)*
Professional, Technical & Kindred Workers	16%	19	2
Managers, Officials & Proprietors	19	23	3
Clerical & Kindred Workers	53	64	7
Craftsmen, Foremen & Kindred Workers	0	0	0
Operatives & Kindred Workers	0	0	0
Service Workers	3	4	0
Laborers & Private Household Workers	9	10	1

Income Scale of All Employees (Totals-120/13)

	Percent of Modular	Number of Modular Employees So Classified	
Classification	*Employee Mean*	*(Banks)*	*(Other FIRE)*
Under $ 4,000	0%	0	0
4,000- 6,999	24	29	3
7,000- 9,999	31	37	4
10,000-15,999	20	24	3
16,000-20,999	15	18	2
21,000-30,999	10	12	1
31,000-50,999	0	0	0
Over $51,000	0	0	0

Income Scale of Princeton Residing Employees (Totals-45/5)

	Percent of Princeton Modular	Number of Modular Employees So Classified	
Classification	*Employee Mean*	*(Banks)*	*(Other FIRE)*
Under $10,000	36%	16	2
10,000-15,999	20	9 ⎫	
16,000-20,999	18	8 ⎬	2
21,000-30,999	26	12	1
31,000-50,999	0	0	0
51,000-75,999	0	0	0

Sample Data

Number of Such Firms in the Princeton Area: 2/36
Number Sampled: 2/4

Source: Local Employers Survey — Summer 1970

Mercer or even Middlesex Counties. Employers referred to a 60-mile commuting distance as a not-uncommon journey to work.

Because of the large number of employees already living in the community, the desire to relocate in Princeton is minimal. FIRE organizations were unable to recall a single case where a member of their staff wanted to move to the Princeton community.

Reasons for this lack of desire include: the economic commitment one must make when acquiring a Princeton address; the established relationships which must be broken when leaving present neighborhoods; and, finally, the feeling that there are alternatives to Princeton which offer comparable accommodations at greatly reduced rates. If, however, housing were to become available at prices employees considered within their reach, most employers stated that this general lack of interest would quickly dissipate.

No other employer group is as involved with the Princeton housing situation as is the FIRE module. The daily activities of finance, insurance and real estate firms directly affect supply and demand in the local market. All of the firms representing this category indicated their belief that Princeton is currently plagued by a serious housing shortage.

The single most obvious deficiency referred to by FIRE employers is the lack of garden apartments. Spokesmen for these firms indicated a desire to have a wide range of rentals available for those who want to rent in the Borough. The $136-$174 monthly rent is considered most necessary to accommodate students and secretaries. Both higher and lower price accommodations are also viewed as necessary, but far less urgent than those falling in the range in which students offer severe competition.

FUTURE COMPETITION AND/OR EXPECTED GROWTH

No significant number of newcomers is envisioned by FIRE organizations. Spokesmen contend that there are sufficient firms already in business in Princeton to meet various demands of current and future residents.

Internal growth is expected to average 40 percent over the next five years. As in the previous modular group, FIRE employers expect to increase their staff in accordance with the demands of a growing populace.

Employers representing the FIRE category are confident they can obtain qualified competent personnel regardless of the local housing situation. Expansion plans appear to be unaffected by any deficiencies which currently exist in the housing supply. The ease of commuting to Princeton and the prestige associated with Princeton firms are expected to offset any inconveniences caused by the local housing situation.

EXHIBIT III-10

CURRENT AND DESIRED PRINCETON HOUSING USAGE:
GROWTH AND COMPETITION EXPECTATIONS –
FINANCE, INSURANCE AND REAL ESTATE FIRMS (FIRE)

SUMMARY TABLE:

	Percent of Modular Employee Mean*	Number of Modular Employees Affected	
		Banks	Other FIRE
Current Princeton Housing Usage:	37	45	5
As Owners	35	43	5
As Renters	2	2	0

	Percent of Modular Employee Mean	Number of Modular Employees Affected	
		Banks	Other FIRE
Desired Additional Princeton Housing Usage:	0	0	0
As owners	0	0	0
As renters	0	0	0

Housing Maintained in the Community:	None
Anticipated Growth by 1975 (Mean):	40%
Expectation of Competition:	None
Princeton Housing Market as a Barrier to Growth or Recruitment:	No (100%)

*Modular Employee Mean - Banks - 120 Full Time Employees
Other FIRE - 13 Full Time Employees

Source: Local Employers Survey — Summer 1970

WHOLESALE AND RETAIL FIRMS

The retail core of Princeton's central business district has undergone few noticeable changes over the past decade; the majority of the establishments have been located in the community for protracted periods of time.

Retail expansion, a common occurence in the surrounding municipalities, has been relatively small in the Princeton community itself. The heaviest concentration of employers in this modular group are the gourmet/delicacy grocery, "specialty" hard and soft goods, and purveyors of higher grade food service.

Wholesaling, locally present in only limited fashion, is restricted primarily to the electronics and precision instrument categories. These firms, which are somewhat new to the Princeton area, (15-20 year vintage) are nevertheless firmly entrenched.

Wholesalers and retailers originally selected Princeton as their business address because of the presence of a very select market. Representative merchants indicated a desire to provide "specialty" merchandise to a unique community, as the basis of their locational strategy. Wholesalers pointed to the availability of land as well as the accessibility to neighboring market areas as their motive for locating locally.

OCCUPATIONS

Excluding the minute "Mama and Papa" store, a typical retail establishment in Princeton maintains a staff of approximately 20 full-time employees. The largest establishment in the community, a major department store branch, retains more than 120. Firms representing wholesale enterprises employ staffs averaging 60 or more employees on a full-time basis.

The characteristic activities engaged in by retail establishments necessitate a large proportion of sales and clerical employees. In the firms questioned of the wholesale-retail modular type, 60 percent were so categorized. Craftsmen, including butchers, tailors, bakers and skilled electricians, are also found in abundance within this modular group. They comprise an additional 22 percent of the combined labor force.

INCOMES

Retail wages rank as the lowest of any of the modular types of employers. In a typical retail outlet, more than 50 percent of the full-time employees earn less than $7,000 a year. Less than 30 percent of the personnel earn over $10,000. (The latter low figure is equalled only in the TCU module.)

PRESENT USE OF PRINCETON'S HOUSING

The typical wholesale or retail firm has close to 25 percent of its staff living in Princeton. As with several of the other types of employers, single-family homeowners outnumber renters by a factor of almost ten to one. Two-thirds of the employees living in Princeton earn less than $10,000 annually. Several of these are students' wives or women who are not the primary head-of-household.

The Princeton retailer and wholesaler depend upon the Trenton suburban communities at the southern end of Mercer County to house their homeowning labor force. Renters generally live within five miles of Princeton, though rarely within one of its municipalities.

Neither retail nor wholesale employers described employees at any job level as wanting to relocate in Princeton. The high cost of living associated with the community was the reason given most often as deterring additional interest.

Each of the polled retailers and wholesalers acknowledge that a housing shortage currently exists in the Princeton community. There is, however, no consensus as to the type or price of dwelling unit considered most lacking. Single-family homes at moderate prices, as well as apartments at any cost, are considered non-existent on the local market.

A local precision instruments distributor contends that single-family homes in the $17,500-$25,000 price range are necessary to accommodate its "underhoused" personnel. A spokesman at a fashionable men's store mentioned one-bedroom garden apartments, particularly those in the $136-$175 price range, as necessary to house the bulk of his current staff.

Merchants generally would like to see more local housing, as this, of course, adds to the existing volume of current business.

FUTURE COMPETITION AND/OR EXPECTED GROWTH

Several of the retail merchants feel they offer a unique service and are well established, and are therefore largely unconcerned with the threat of future competition. The only types of employers who envision additional competition in the immediate future are the non-specialty food stores and local food chains. Gourmet and butcher/vegetable establishments in the "core" area no longer seem to be meeting the volume or price needs of the community's more peripheral residents.

In like manner, there is a growing need for additional convention and "think tank" facilities which is now going unmet. Respondents said the intellectual setting of Princeton was ideal for such meetings, although they are currently unable to accept the service aspect of all requests. Existing facilities may experience rising competition from new entrants in this field.

Internal expansion is expected to be slight in the overall wholesale-retail module. In large part this is due to lack of interest by wholesalers who claim land costs severely limit expansion.

EXHIBIT III-11

OCCUPATIONAL/INCOME PROFILE—
WHOLESALE AND RETAIL FIRMS

SUMMARY TABLE:

| Mean Size | Wholesalers — 60 Full Time Employees |
| | Retailers — 24 Full Time Employees |

Male/Female Distribution — 64/36%

Labor Force Composition (Totals-60/24)

	Percent of Modular	*Number of Modular Employees So Classified*	
Classification	*Employee Mean*	*(Wholesale)*	*(Retail)*
Professional, Technical & Kindred Workers	2%	1	1
Managers, Officials & Proprietors	8	5	2
Clerical & Kindred Workers	60	36	14
Craftsmen, Foremen & Kindred Workers	22	13	5
Operatives & Kindred Workers	7	4	2
Service Workers	1	1	0
Laborers & Private Household Workers	0	0	0

Income Scale of All Employees (Totals-60/24)

	Percent of Modular	*Number of Modular Employees So Classified*	
Classification	*Employee Mean*	*(Wholesale)*	*(Retail)*
Under $ 4,000	0%	0	0
4,000- 6,999	49	30	12
7,000- 9,999	22	13	5
10,000-15,999	8	5	2
16,000-20,999	17	10	4
21,000-30,999	4	2	1
31,000-50,999	0	0	0
Over $51,000	0	0	0

Income Scale of Princeton Residing Employees (Totals 13/5)

	Percent of Princeton Modular	*Number of Modular Employees So Classified*	
Classification	*Employee Mean*	*(Wholesale)*	*(Retail)*
Under $10,000	66%	9	3
10,000-15,999	16	2	1
16,000-20,999	7	1	0
21,000-30,999	11	1	1
31,000-50,999	0	0	0
51,000-75,999	0	0	0

Sample Data

Number of Such Firms in the Princeton Area: 8/16
Number Sampled: 2/4

Source: Local Employers Survey — Summer 1970

Retailers, even in the categories previously mentioned, do not anticipate substantial growth. A local following has been established and a labor force necessary to serve this following has been recruited. With few applicants interested in an admittedly low wage scale, local retailers do not want to overextend themselves and do not feel that they have the ability to serve an enlarged clientele. The group's mean anticipated growth is a scant 10 percent.

The housing assets that would be most instrumental in establishing an adequate labor reserve are identical to the deficiencies which are characteristic of the Princeton housing market; single-family homes selling for below $25,000 and apartments renting for less than $175.

Limited expansion is anticipated, even if there is no easing of the tight local housing market.

THE SERVICE INDUSTRY

The research element of the service modular group has increased steadily over the past 15 years to a level which now makes Princeton a research, as well as an educational center. The typical research firm has been in Princeton for the past 12 years. These firms were attracted to the area by the propinquity of Princeton University, and by the intellectual prestige which the name "Princeton" brings to a firm's mailing address.

A significant amount of choice land in neighboring communities is zoned specifically for research firms and this also has helped accent the locational attractiveness of the "Greater Princeton Area."

Finally, Princeton's central location and the accessibility to the major eastern cities have reinforced almost all decisions to locate in this area.

OCCUPATIONS

The number of employees varies so much within the service employers group that it is difficult to describe the typical size of a service firm. Staff size ranges from 18 people at an advertising and market research firm to 3,800 full-time employees at Princeton University, the community's largest employer. The average payroll size, *excluding* these two organizations, however, is approximately 240 full-time employees.

The service organization is more dependent upon the professional worker than any other type of employer. Approximately 50 percent of the labor force is comprised of professional or technical personnel; only 20 percent fall into the blue-collar categories of craftsmen, operatives, service workers and laborers.

The largest deviation from this norm can be found at the community's

EXHIBIT III-12

CURRENT AND DESIRED PRINCETON HOUSING USAGE: GROWTH AND COMPETITION EXPECTATIONS — WHOLESALE AND RETAIL FIRMS

SUMMARY TABLE:

	Percent of Modular Employee Mean*	Number of Modular Employees Affected	
		(Wholesale)	(Retail)
Current Princeton Housing Usage:	22	13	5
As Owners	20	12	5
As Renters	2	1	0

	Percent of Modular Employee Mean	Number of Modular Employees Affected	
		(Wholesale)	(Retail)
Desired Additional Princeton Housing Usage:	0	0	0
As Owners	0	0	0
As Renters	0	0	0

Housing Maintained in the Community:	None
Anticipated Growth by 1975 (Mean):	10%
Expectation of Competition:	1 or 2 Chain Groceries
	2 or 3 New Dining Establishments
	1 Small Wholesaler
Princeton Housing Market as a Barrier to Growth or Recruitment:	No (75%)

*Modular Employee Mean — Wholesalers - 60 Full Time Employees
                                           Retailers - 24 Full Time Employees

Source: Local Employers Survey — Summer 1970

oldest and most historic hotel. Professionals there are almost non-existent, while service workers represent 81 percent of the total labor force.

INCOMES

A sizeable proportion, 24 percent, of the service labor force earns above $16,000 annually. Several employers readily acknowledge other managerial salaries above the $31,000 level. However, the largest segment of the service industry (55 percent) earns well below $10,000.

A renowned post-doctoral research institute pays 63 percent of its personnel less than $10,000 annually. At the other end of the wage scale, however, 24 percent of its senior staff members receive between $31,000 and $50,000.

PRESENT USE OF PRINCETON'S HOUSING

Slightly more than 20 percent of the employees of the representative service firms live in the Princeton community. This total, conservative in its estimate, is not inflated by inclusion of faculty members or graduate students who currently live in housing maintained by any of the locally based educational institutions.

Renting is a more accepted form of housing tenure among service-related employees than in any other category of worker. Approximately 40 percent of the employees in the service group who live in Princeton reside in rented facilities.

The wage profile for service workers living in Princeton is similar to that of other groups. Almost 50 percent of the group earns under $10,000. The remaining portions are found in lesser quantities at the other wage levels.

As is the case in other modular groups, the majority of the labor force commutes daily from Trenton or non-Princeton suburban communities. The larger firms, such as a major electronic research center, claim to attract a substantial portion of their labor force from as far as 75 miles away.

Executives who receive high salaries are not adverse to living away from Princeton and form the bulk of those who commute long distances. To a lesser extent, lower-level managers are also commuters. These people originate, however, not from New York or Philadelphia, but rather from Levittown, Pennsylvania, and other Lower Bucks County communities.

Service employees showed the greatest desire of all employees in any group to live in the Princeton community. Several older firms have had employees forced out of the community because of local economic constraints. These employees are now a small but vocal segment of the ser-

EXHIBIT III-13

OCCUPATIONAL/INCOME PROFILE –
THE SERVICE INDUSTRY

SUMMARY TABLE:

Mean Size	240 Full Time Employees
Male/Female Distribution	59/41%

Labor Force Composition (Total-240)

Classification	Percent of Modular Employee Mean	Number of Modular Employees So Classified
Professional, Technical & Kindred Workers	47%	113
Managers, Officials & Proprietors	8	19
Clerical & Kindred Workers	24	58
Craftsmen, Foremen & Kindred Workers	6	14
Operatives & Kindred Workers	4	10
Service Workers	10	24
Laborers & Private Household Workers	1	2

Income Scale of All Employees (Total-240)

Classification	Percent of Modular Employee Mean	Number of Modular Employees So Classified
Under $ 4,000	0	0
4,000- 6,999	30	72
7,000- 9,999	24	58
10,000- 15,999	23	55
16,000- 20,999	11	26
21,000- 30,999	7	17
31,000- 50,999	5	12
Over $51,000	0	0

Income Scale of Princeton Residing Employees (Total-50)

Classification	Percent of Princeton Modular Employee Mean	Number of Modular Employees So Classified
Under $10,000	47	23
10,000-15,999	21	11
16,000-20,999	14	7
21,000-30,999	12	6
31,000-50,999	6	3
51,000-75,999	0	0

Sample Data	Number of Such Firms in the Princeton Area: 80
	Number Sampled: 13

Source: Local Employers Survey — Summer 1970

vice personnel who are currently seeking or "re-seeking" housing in the Princeton area.

Employers contend that an additional 20 percent of their personnel are seriously contemplating a move to Princeton. Researchers and professionals with a family want to purchase single-family homes locally. There is also a significant number of secretaries and young unmarried employees who would contribute strongly to any newly formed rental market. The lack of housing availability and cost constraints deters participation of these groups in the local market.

INSTITUTIONALLY PROVIDED HOUSING

The service classification has several employers who provide housing for their personnel. Research firms which are branches of larger corporations generally have policies which insure the sale of a transferred employee's home. These firms do not, however, maintain their own stock of homes.

Housing provided directly by the employer to its staff is limited to institutions which are physically located in Princeton. These primarily include Princeton University, the Institute for Advanced Study and Princeton Hospital. To a lesser extent this category includes Westminster Choir College and Princeton Theological Seminary.

Princeton University currently maintains 1,038 rental dwelling units within the community which are divided between the Township and the Borough. Rents range from $60 to $400 a month. These apartments accommodate 400 married graduate students and 638 junior faculty members.

The University also has a mortgage program for its more senior faculty members. The only limitation is that homes must be within an eight-mile radius of the University. This program currently involves 328 homes, all but eight of which are in the Township. The Institute for Advanced Study maintains 130 rental units for members and four single-family ownership units for its permanent staff.

Princeton Hospital provides dormitory-type accommodations to its young technicians at an average weekly rent of $10. Sixty units of this type are maintained, of which one-half are used intermittently by student nurses during their training periods. The hospital also owns eight single-family homes which provide residences for its senior, on-call staff members.

Finally, both the Choir College and the Seminary maintain a limited amount of housing for a few senior personnel. However, this number is relatively small.

All but one of the organizations representing the service category indicated that Princeton has an insufficient housing supply. In contrast to others in the labor force (who for the most part desire ownership housing), service employers feel that the more immediate local shortage is among rental units.

Price ranges which are deficient follow the precedent set by the other employment groups. Single-family homes below $40,000, as well as rentals under $250 monthly, are believed to be in short supply.

EXHIBIT III-14
CURRENT AND DESIRED PRINCETON HOUSING USAGE:
GROWTH AND COMPETITION EXPECTATIONS—
THE SERVICE INDUSTRY

SUMMARY TABLE:

	Percent of Modular Employee Mean*	Number of Modular Employees Affected
Current Princeton Housing Usage:	21	50
As Owners	14	33
As Renters	7	17
	Percent of Modular Employee Mean	Number of Modular Employees Affected
Desired Additional Princeton Housing Usage:	20	48
As Owners	12	29
As Renters	8	19
Housing Maintained in the Community:	(See Exhibit III-15)	
Anticipated Growth by 1975 (Mean):	75%	
Expectation of Competition:	3 – 4 Additional Research Firms	
Princeton Housing Market as a Barrier to Growth or Recruitment	None (100%)	

*Modular Employee Mean — 240 Full Time Employees

Source: Local Employers Survey — Summer 1970

FUTURE COMPETITION AND/OR EXPECTED GROWTH

Growth is expected to continue within the service module both internally and externally. Only the educational institutions do not envision competition locating in Princeton. The other firms in the category expect new companies to come to the area for reasons similar to those given in the wholesale/retail module; i.e., insufficient supply to meet demonstrated demand.

Internal growth is anticipated to average 75 percent by 1975 and several (three to four) major researchers are expected to locate in the area during this five-year period.

Housing deficiencies, while considered severe, are not enough to inhibit future plans for internal expansion. A large spacecraft firm grew from a staff of 60 to 1,600 and was never directly affected by any demonstrable Princeton housing shortage.

A representative of an opinion-polling firm succinctly described the situation: "As long as there is a Trenton and a Lawrenceville existing regionally, and commuting poses no problem, the housing supply of Princeton will not be a factor influencing the expansion plans of any local employer."

Princeton's locally employed housing users are largely white-collar workers in the banking, manufacturing and service industries. In the

EXHIBIT III-15

NON-DORMITORY HOUSING MAINTAINED BY INSTITUTIONAL EMPLOYERS

INSTITUTION	TYPE OF HOUSING		
	Single Family	Multifamily	Total
Princeton University	55	983	1,038
Princeton Theological Seminary	24	6	30
Westminster Choir College	2	0	2
Institute for Advanced Study	4	130	134
Princeton Hospital	8	0	8
Total	93	1,119	1,212

Source: Local Employers Survey — Summer 1970

first case, this support is only minimal as most of these Princeton residents are women drawn to the area by the employment of their husbands. In the latter cases, these industries offer executives and other personnel salaries which bring the offerings of the local market within financial reach.

To a limited degree, service industry firms maintain local housing to offset economic strain in the Princeton area. With this exception, however, the bulk of the housing demand is centered in the region surrounding Princeton. To date the extensive availability of housing in peripheral areas has created a sense of security within the minds of local employers. Whether this is realistic in the face of future demand is open to question. Housing assistance is not provided as a service, nor is the housing situation deemed limiting. This may prove to be a costly oversight in light of anticipated shortages.

"Our region is highly overzoned for industry and research and is failing to provide housing suited to the needs of the people it is attracting. There is little time in which to alter our course. Our residential lands will approach saturation under present zoning by 1985 as the population of the region nears one-half million persons." [3]

This statement, a conclusion of the report "Housing and the Quality of Our Environment" by the Middlesex-Somerset-Mercer Regional Study Council, foreshadows the findings of this study.

As demonstrated in Exhibit III-16, workers located within the Greater Princeton area currently utilize two-thirds of Princeton's existing housing stock. Maintaining present usage ratios and applying internal growth and additional competition estimates, these firms will require 3,862 additional units by 1975.* Based on current Township production rates (120 units/year) and assuming that the Borough will be 92 percent developed by 1975 (with the addition of approximately 100 units), a five-year building period would net only 700 additional housing units, or 18 percent of the projected ratios of demand.

If Princeton's housing market today is viewed as select, it will be even more so in 1975. At this particular juncture no relief is foreseen; a continued inflation of local housing prices and a concomitant rise in the average income levels of the community are seen as inevitable.

---

*It should be noted that employer growth within the physical limits of the Princeton community will contribute to only 47 percent of this total projected housing demand (1805 units — see "A Note on the Housing Demand of Princeton Based Employers," *supra* pp. 267-268).

EXHIBIT III-16

HOUSING DEMAND OF THE LOCAL EMPLOYERS
(PYRAMIDED TOTALS)

METHODOLOGY LEADING TO DEMAND CALCULATION

EMPLOYER MODULE	Current Modular Housing Usage		Number of Firms in the Area	Current Housing Demand 1970		Modular Internal Growth by 1975	Modular Housing Usage 1975		Additional Firms 1970-1975	Total Firms in Area 1975	Total Housing Demand in 1975	
	Owner	Renter		Owner	Renter		Owner	Renter			Owner	Renter
Manufacturing (Small)	1	0	26	26	0	200%	2	0	5	31	62	0
Manufacturing (Large)	12	2	18	216	36	40%	17	3	3	21	357	63
Transportation, Communication and Public Utilities	3	1	24	72	24	70%	5	2	0	24	120	48
Finance, Insurance and Real Estate												
Banks	43	2	2	86	4	} 40%	60	3	0	2	120	6
Other F.I.R.E.	5	0	36	180	0	}	7	0	0	36	252	0
Wholesale and Retail												
Wholesale	12	1	8	96	8	} 10%	13	1	1	9	117	9
Retail	5	0	16	80	0	}	6	0	4	20	120	0
The Service Industry	33	17	80	2,640	1,360	75%	58	30	4	84	4,860	2,520
Total Usage				4,792							8,654	

Total Housing Stock = Local Employers + Commuters + Students + Retirees, Unemployed
(1970)   Those Not Included In Survey
7,300   4,800   825   800   875

Source: Local Employers Survey — Summer 1970

NOTES

1. "Employee Survey — Princeton Area" (12 Organizations — 1377 Responses) (Township Advisory Committee on Multi-Family Housing 1960), Summary Sheets.

2. *Housing and the Quality of Our Environment* (Middlesex-Somerset-Mercer Regional Study Council, Princeton, New Jersey, January 1970), pp. 1-14.

3. *Ibid.*, p. 1.

A CLOSER LOOK AT HOUSING DEMAND
AND THE IMPACT OF HOUSING NEED

The preceding chapters have established the limits of housing demand and supply in the Township and the Borough, and, with the results of the Present Residents Survey, have outlined the socioeconomic characteristics of the Princeton population. This section reviews the impact of special demand created by four segments of the population.

The population sectors analyzed in this section were selected for a variety of reasons. First, to understand and predict changes in the socioeconomic character of the Princeton community, it was necessary to know what groups are now moving into the community and the reasons why they chose to move to Princeton. These issures are considered in Chapter IV, "The Newcomers," in which recent home buyers and renters are compared with established Princeton residents. Second, to predict and categorize the factors which may cause present residents to move out of Princeton (or possibly to seek a new residence within the community), a study of the reshaped household was undertaken. This analysis is presented in Chapter V.

Comparisons between those who have recently moved into Princeton, and those who, because of a change in family size, may soon seek a new residence, provide detailed information on two groups which influence the demand for local housing. On one level, what is really being asked is: Who can afford to move into Princeton, who can afford to stay, and who is forced to leave? On another level, this kind of analysis examines the effects of housing demand on the overall supply of residential stock.

Chapter VI, "The Underhoused," considers the special demands for housing generated by those who are poorly housed, those who live in overcrowded conditions, or those who are forced to remain in "inadequate" units because of economic or racial pressure. These residents cannot, in many cases, compete for housing on the open market.

In Chapter VII the study considers the local demand engendered by the municipal labor force. Is there a desire by this sub-population to live within the local community? Does this residence decision in some way affect work performance? Finally, is the goal of closing the gap between what municipal workers can afford to pay and current housing prices on the local Princeton market realizable in terms of evidenced need? This chapter attempts to answer these questions.

Chapter IV

THE NEWCOMERS

An analysis of new entrants into the Princeton housing market yields insight into the supply of housing that is potentially available to newcomers to the area.

The housing accommodations of the non-moving population generally reflect previous needs and circumstances. In contrast, a description of the newcomer's characteristics represents a current adjustment of their housing to changed circumstances. [1] These new entrants can be classified as a marginal group:

> The dynamic market in any period is determined by the marginal group who are in the process of making such adjustments. The remaining households do exert influence on current market behavior because they might move and might react to major shifts in the market. Their influence, however, is muffled because it is felt in the market only through a cloak of inertia and lack of immediate interest. [2]

Within this framework the chapter includes a socioeconomic portrait of the new entrants, a description of their origin, present accommodations and reasons for moving. Comparative references will be made with the PRS to emphasize the distinctive character of the newcomer households.

The information in this chapter was drawn from a sample of 50 new homeowners and 50 new renters. To secure the names of all new home buyers for the 1969-1970 year, a list of all property transactions in

Princeton Borough and Township was obtained from the Mercer County clerk. From this list of transactions, all purchases of commerical facilities and land, all transfers of property from one family member to another, and all sales of homes to persons with unlisted telephone numbers were eliminated. The transactions which remained to be surveyed numbered 235. The 235 homes were divided into six groups according to the purchase price of the home. Personal interviews were conducted with a specified number of households within each category. The 50 interviews represent a stratified sample; the number of interviews conducted within each price category is based on the proportion of the total number of homes purchased within that category.

The choice of the new renters sample was less clear-cut due to difficulties encountered in securing the data. Originally the study group sought to secure names of new renters by obtaining lists of new subscribers from the New Jersey Bell Telephone Company or Public Service Gas and Electric Company. These lists were not made available, however, and new lists had to be compiled from a cross-tabulated combination of renters residing in Princeton under a year, and additional lists obtained from local realty agencies. From these lists 50 new renters who moved between January, 1969, and July, 1970, were interviewed. It is possible that the renters of private homes are under-represented.

To highlight the differences in social profiles, reasons for moving and type of accommodations chosen between new renters and new owners,

EXHIBIT IV-1

SAMPLE SELECTION: NEW HOMEOWNERS

PURCHASE PRICE	Total Number New Homeowners	Sample Number
Under $15,000	0	0
$15-30,999	24	5
$31-50,999	84	18
$51-75,999	66	14
$76-100,000	47	10
$100,000 +	14	3
Total	235	50

Source: Newcomers Survey — Summer 1970 — sub n=50

A CLOSER LOOK AT HOUSING DEMAND

and, secondly, between Princeton area local movers as opposed to more distant movers, cross-tabulations were run for all variables by these two factors. For convenience the Princeton area and other local movers will be referred to as intracity movers, the balance as intercity movers. Both sets of data reveal distinctive patterns of socioeconomic characteristics within each group, accounting for their housing accommodations differential. As mentioned previously, the questionnaire contained questions similar to those administered to the present residents, municipal employees and underhoused segments of the study to facilitate additional comparison if so desired.

SOCIOECONOMIC PORTRAIT

ORIGIN

The newcomers to Princeton represent a diverse pattern of previous locations. As shown below in Exhibit IV-2, 50 percent came from a distant New Jersey area or another state, 7 percent moved from areas outside the continental United States, and 43 percent came from local areas, either Princeton or a surrounding area.

Tenurial differences vary with the origin of the mover. The new owners predominately represent the intracity Princeton movers, the new renters (including Princeton contract), the intercity movers. The high

EXHIBIT IV-2

ORIGIN OF NEW HOMEOWNERS AND RENTERS

			FORM OF TENURE					
	Owner		Renter		Princeton* Contract		Total	
ORIGIN	Num- ber	Per- cent	Num- ber	Per- cent	Num- ber	Per- cent	Num- ber	Per- cent
Princeton	21	42.9	7	21.2	3	16.7	31	31.0
Local Areas	9	18.4	1	3.0	2	11.1	12	12.0
Distant N. J. Other States	18	36.7	22	66.7	10	55.6	50	50.0
Outside U. S.	1	2.0	3	9.1	3	16.7	7	7.0
Total	49	100.0	33	100.0	18	100.0	100	100.0

Source: Newcomers Survey — Summer 1970 — n=100

*All but one are renters

local mobility of intracity Princeton movers suggests a possbile second move among renting intercity movers. This second move would represent an adjustment of housing needs within the community.

AGE COMPOSITION

The age characteristics of the new movers also differ between origin group and tenurial type. The former Princeton resident and foreign entrant are older than the local and outside area mover; the respective median ages are 37 and 33. Similarly, the new homeowner is older than the renter or Princeton-contract respondent, 39 years as opposed to 31 and 28 respectively. The elderly represent a small but significant proportion (6 percent) of the new homeowners and renters.

HOUSEHOLD COMPOSITION AND SIZE

As expected, the most common marital status among movers is the married couple; there is little variation among intra- and inter-Princeton movers, except that all divorced movers (6 and 2 percent respectively) originated in Princeton. Similar to the findings in other sectors, the bulk of single persons live in rental units, while those who are married, divorced or widowed are homeowners. From the exhibit below one notices a higher proportion of incoming singles in the Borough than in the Township and relative to the present residents. Furthermore, for the latter case the widowed proportion is lower and the divorced higher.

Similar to the findings for both the present residents and the underhoused, the newcomers do not have large families; 41 percent have no

EXHIBIT IV-3

MARITAL STATUS: NEWCOMERS AND PRESENT RESIDENTS (PERCENT)

	1970 New Residents		1970 Present Residents	
MARITAL STATUS	*Township*	*Borough*	*Township*	*Borough*
Single	4.8	22.2	9.8	16.2
Married	88.9	66.7	81.8	64.4
Divorced/ Widowed	6.4 (4.8D) (1.6W)	11.1 (8.3D) (2.8W)	8.4 (4.2D) (4.2W)	19.4 (4.2D) (15.2W)

Source: Present Residents Survey — Summer 1970
Newcomers Survey — Summer 1970

A CLOSER LOOK AT HOUSING DEMAND

children under 18 at home. The median family size for owners is 3.6 compared to 3 for renters and 2 for Princeton-contract respondents. The typical case for those reporting children was one or two dependents, 27.1 and 40.7 percent respectively. As anticipated, the larger proportion (78 percent) of children reside in the Township.

The newcomers appear to be utilizing the public schools slightly more than the present residents — 88 percent usage compared to 83 percent. Those attending private school are concentrated among the ranks of homeowners, regardless of origin.

Almost one-fifth of the new movers have other persons besides a spouse and children under 18 living in their households. In 90 percent of the cases this was just one additional person. A child over 18 represented one-fifth of the responses. The largest category of non-primary family was a roomer or companion (8 out of 19). The second largest category was that of related individuals. Domestic help accounted for only 3 out of 19 cases.

EDUCATION

The educational level of the newcomers is similar to that of the present residents — a median of 16.5 years compared to 15.9 years. The difference can be attributed to the higher proportion of persons with a Ph.D. entering than presently reside in Princeton. Forty percent of the newcomers possess Ph.D. degrees; only 10 percent did not receive a college (B.S./B.A.) degree.

OCCUPATIONAL GROUP, INDUSTRIAL CLASSIFICATIONS,
PLACE OF EMPLOYMENT

A characterizing feature of the Princeton community is the high degree of professional occupations among the residents. This is a constant for the new homeowners as well as the renters. Over three out of five household heads work in a professional or technical capacity. An additional 14 percent work as managers or officials, and 11 percent are students. There is a noticeable absence of blue-collar and service workers among the newcomers; this reflects the lack of available homes for households with modest incomes.

Further analysis reveals a higher proportion of professionals among intra-Princeton movers and foreign movers than inter-Princeton movers; the latter group contains the highest percentage of managers and officials. Here renters rather than owners exhibit a higher incidence of professional occupations. This can be attributed to the drawing power of Princeton University.

Aside from looking at the occupational characteristics of the households, it is also important to review the employment distribution of these newcomers. The major employers of the newcomers are the educational institutions; second are the service industries (including research). These two categories account for almost three out of every four of the newcomers' jobs. Manufacturing and construction are the next most important employers, representing 13 percent. Although there is little variation between intra- and inter-Princeton movers, there is a significant difference between homeowners and renters. Eighty-six percent of the latter are employed by service and educational institutions, compared to 60 percent of the former. The homeowners represent a more diversified industrial classification with a significant proportion (20.5 percent) of manufacturing and construction executives. The small incidence of self-employment is concentrated among previous Princeton movers and homeowners.

Similar to the distribution in the entire community, the job location of the newcomers is predominately local, or at least within the county.[3] This short journey to work is most prevalent among renters, Princeton-contract holders and previous Princeton movers. The New York or Philadelphia commuter represents less than one-fifth of the respondents; they are concentrated among homeowners and inter-Princeton movers.

Due to the discrepancies in annual incomes among the tenurial groups and intra- and inter-Princeton movers, a three-way cross-tabulation was run for these variables. For ease and comprehensiveness of presentation, only the median incomes are presented visually (Exhibit IV-4).

EXHIBIT IV-4

MEDIAN INCOMES BY TENURE AND ORIGIN

ORIGIN	FORM OF TENURE							
	Owner	Sub n	Renter	Sub n	Princeton Contract	Sub n	Total	Sub n
Princeton	$23,141	17	$ 5,831	7	$ 7,500	3	$16,624	27
Local areas	18,499	8	*	1	*	2	15,000	11
Distant N. J./ Other U. S. States	35,443	18	15,142	20	7,140	10	19,331	48
Outside U. S.	*	1	22,499	3	13,000	3	19,749	7
Total	$26,711	44	$14,125	31	$ 7,497	17	—	—

*Sample size too small for generalization
Source: Newcomers Survey — Summer 1970 — n=100 (Non-responses Excluded)

A CLOSER LOOK AT HOUSING DEMAND

It is clear that homeowners, particularly the inter-Princeton movers, earn the highest annual incomes. Among renters the intra-Princeton movers have the lowest incomes. The lower incomes of the local area movers, renters and Princeton-contract respondents can be attributed to the younger ages of these groups. As shown in Exhibit IV-5, income is directly related to age up to the $50,999 level and age 65 and over. More than 70 percent of those 50-64 earn $31,000-$50,999.

Further analysis of Exhibit IV-5 reveals:

1. There is a greater concentration of higher incomes in the Township than in the Borough, which is reminiscent of the differences found in the PRS; the median incomes of movers are $20,665 and $15,250 respectively.
2. Income is directly related to educational achievement; three out of the seven respondents with only a high school education earn under $10,000. In contrast, 46 percent of those respondents with Ph.D.s earn over $21,000.
3. A higher proportion of managerial personnel earn $31,000 or more than do professionals. As anticipated, 70 percent of all those who are retired or are students earn under $10,000.

SUMMARY PROFILES

Exhibit IV-6, which compares the basic social data of the newcomers and the entire Princeton community, is self-explanatory. The following is simply a brief recapitulation.

INTRA-PRINCETON MOVERS

Homeowners

The intra-Princeton movers who recently purchased a home represent 62 percent of all new home-buyers in the sample, and 72 percent of all intra-Princeton movers. This person is typically married, middle-aged and a professional employed for the most part by the local and surrounding educational institutions and service industries. Over 50 percent of these individuals earn between $21,000 and $50,999 annually. These homeowners are from either Princeton or the surrounding localities.

Renters

The counterpart of the home-owning intra-Princeton mover is the renter, including a smaller proportion of the total sample, 24 percent of new renters, 28 percent of intra-Princeton movers. The new renter is younger than the homeowner and works in the same professional capacity; however, the total family income is lower. The median income for

EXHIBIT IV-5

INCOME DISTRIBUTION BY SELECTED SOCIAL CHARACTERISTICS

	Under $10,000		$10,000-15,999		$16,000-20,999		$21,000-30,999		$31,000-50,999		$51,000-75,999		$76,000-124,000		Total	
	Number	Per cent	Number	Per cent	Number	Per cent	Number	Per cent	Number	Per cent	Number	Per cent	Number	Per cent	Number	Per cent
RESIDENCE																
Township	13	22.4	9	15.5	6	10.3	15	25.9	13	22.4	1	1.7	1	1.2	58	100.0
Borough	10	29.5	8	23.5	8	23.5	3	8.8	5	14.7	0	0.0	0	0.0	34	100.0
Total	23	25.0	17	18.4	14	15.2	18	19.6	18	19.6	1	1.1	1	1.1	92	100.0
AGE																
21-25	11	84.6	1	7.7	0	0.0	0	0.0	1	7.7	0	0.0	0	0.0	13	100.0
26-35	10	27.8	10	27.8	3	8.3	9	25.0	3	8.3	1	2.8	0	0.0	36	100.0
36-49	1	2.9	5	14.3	8	22.8	9	25.7	11	31.4	0	0.0	1	2.9	35	100.0
50-64	0	0.0	1	25.0	0	0.0	0	0.0	3	75.0	0	0.0	0	0.0	4	100.0
65+	1	25.0	0	0.0	3	75.0	0	0.0	0	0.0	0	0.0	0	0.0	4	100.0
EDUCATION																
Less Than High School	0	0.0	1	100.0	0	0.0	0	0.0	0	0.0	0	0.0	0	0.0	1	100.0
High School	3	42.8	2	28.6	1	14.3	1	14.3	0	0.0	0	0.0	0	0.0	7	100.0
2 Yr. College	1	50.0	0	0.0	1	50.0	0	0.0	0	0.0	0	0.0	0	0.0	2	100.0
College (BS/BA)	9	39.2	2	8.7	1	4.3	6	26.1	4	17.4	0	0.0	1	4.3	23	100.0
Masters Degree	4	19.0	6	28.6	3	14.3	3	14.3	5	23.8	0	0.0	0	0.0	21	100.0
Ph.D	6	15.8	6	15.8	8	21.1	8	21.1	9	23.7	1	2.5	0	0.0	38	100.0

EXHIBIT IV-5 (Cont'd.)

INCOME DISTRIBUTION BY SELECTED SOCIAL CHARACTERISTICS

	Under $10,000		$10,000-15,999		$16,000-20,999		$21,000-30,999		$31,000-50,999		$51,000-75,999		$76,000-124,000		Total	
	Number	Per cent	Number	Per cent	Number	Per cent	Number	Per cent	Number	Per cent	Number	Per cent	Number	Per cent	Number	Per cent
OCCUPATION																
Professional	9	15.3	13	22.0	11	18.7	13	22.0	12	20.3	1	1.7	0	0.0	59	100.0
Managerial	0	0.0	0	0.0	0	0.0	4	36.4	6	54.5	0	0.0	1	9.1	11	100.0
Clerical, Sales	3	60.0	1	20.0	0	0.0	1	20.0	0	0.0	0	0.0	0	0.0	5	100.0
Laborer	0	0.0	2	100.0	0	0.0	0	0.0	0	0.0	0	0.0	0	0.0	2	100.0
Retired, Students	12	75.0	1	6.3	3	18.7	0	0.0	0	0.0	0	0.0	0	0.0	16	100.0

Source: Newcomers Survey — Summer 1970 — n=100 (Non-responses Excluded)

EXHIBIT IV-6

SUMMARY PROFILE: INTRA VS. INTER MOVER BY TENURE

SOCIAL CHARACTERISTICS	Intra-Princeton Mover		Inter-Princeton Mover		Princeton Community	
	Owner	*Renter**	*Owner*	*Renter**	*Owner*	*Renter**
RESIDENCE						
Township	71.0	41.7	29.0	60.5	72.4	43.0
Borough	29.0	58.3	21.0	39.5	27.6	57.0
Total	100.0	100.0	100.0	100.0	100.0	100.0
AGE						
21-35	29.0	91.7	31.5	67.6	7.1	48.4
36-49	48.4	0.0	57.9	29.7	41.6	27.5
50-64	9.7	8.3	5.3	0.0	35.2	14.3
65+	12.9	0.0	5.3	2.7	16.1	9.8
Median	41.5 yrs.	29.2 yrs.	39.5 yrs.	32.1 yrs.	49.5 yrs.	35.8 yrs.
EDUCATION						
Less than H.S.	0.0	0.0	0.0	2.7	4.6	5.5
High School	6.5	25.0	5.3	2.7	14.4	19.2
2 Yrs. College	3.2	8.3	0.0	0.0	—	—
College (BS/BA)	22.6	16.7	42.1	24.3	35.0	25.8
Masters Degree	25.8	25.0	21.1	21.6	17.3	13.7
Ph.D.	41.9	25.0	31.5	48.7	28.8	35.8
Median	16.7 yrs.	16 yrs.	16.1 yrs.	17 yrs.	15.9 yrs.	16.5 yrs.
INCOME						
Under $10,000	4.0	84.6	0.0	33.3	13.9	43.9
$10,000-15,999	24.0	7.7	5.3	25.0	13.4	25.4
$16,000-20,999	20.0	7.7	5.3	19.5	19.3	12.4
$21,000-30,999	36.0	0.0	26.3	11.1	28.7	12.4
$31,000-50,999	16.0	0.0	52.5	11.1	16.0	5.9
$51,000-75,999	0.0	0.0	5.3	0.0	5.0	0.0
$76,000-124,999	0.0	0.0	5.3	0.0	2.9	0.0
$125,000 & Over	0.0	0.0	0.0	0.0	0.8	0.0
Median	$21,554	$10,000	$35,999	$13,000	$22,175	$11,465

*Princeton Contracts Included.

Source: Newcomers Survey, PRS — Summer 1970

renters and Princeton-contract holders is under $10,000 as compared to $21,554 for the intra-Princeton-moving homeowners. This group is also characterized by a larger proportion of single individuals than the homeowners.

INTER-PRINCETON MOVERS

Homeowners

In contrast to the intra-Princeton-moving homeowners, homeowners are the minority in the group of inter-Princeton movers, representing only one-third of the group sample. Typically the new homeowning entrant is a middle-aged executive. He is employed for the most part by the research and light industrial firms surrounding Princeton and to a smaller degree by firms in the immediate environs of either New York or Philadelphia. Over three out of five of these persons earn more than $30,000 a year. The inter-Princeton movers are characteristically from Northern New Jersey, other states or outside the continental United States.

Renters

Inter-Princeton-moving renters are younger and work in professional capacities in the service industries or local educational institutions. Typically they have a higher educational level than the inter-Princeton-moving homeowner, yet they have a lower family income.

MOBILITY STIMULUS

The decision to move involves the consideration of present and future needs, desires and aspirations. Mobility is closely associated with household composition and its subsequent changes; new moves should reflect some shifts in size, tenure and type of residence for the reshaped households. Frequency of job shifts among the nation's employed, especially professionals, is another factor which influences mobility. Here we will review the reasons for moving given by the new homeowners and renters in Princeton. It is important to note that there may be more than a single reason for mobility; i.e., a change in family size and a simultaneous job change. In the following cases, the reason cited is the one which movers said was most important or influential in making the decision to move.

REASONS FOR MOVING

The most frequent cause of mobility is a job change; second is a desire to change housing. Although the incidence of changes in family size appears to be small, persons who may possibly be moving for this reason may simply specify a desire for larger housing units and, thus, appear in the housing desires category (Exhibit IV-7).

It is also evident that there are distinctive differences among the various originating groups. The intra-Princeton movers exhibit the widest variation of responses, emphasizing housing desires; the inter-Princeton movers cite job changes almost exclusively. A small group of intra-Princeton movers are also moving specifically to change social environments. One-third of "other" responses are students who moved for educational advantages.

There are also distinctions between the new homeowners and renters. Over one out of three homeowners moved because of job changes, compared to almost three out of four renters (including Princeton contracts). Homeowners moved more frequently for reasons pertaining to housing need, including favorable environment and changes in family size. There is little differentiation between Township and Borough residents.

Income is related to the various mobility reasons. The income distribution is wide with regard to job changes, but concentrated in the lower and upper brackets for family size changes and housing and favorable environments desires respectively. Two out of three persons moving because of family size changes earn under $16,999 a year; 50 percent of those moving for housing desires and over 60 percent of those moving for a favorable environment earn $21,000-$50,999 a year. As mentioned before, the "other" category includes moves made by students and retired persons; 77.8 percent in this category earn under $10,000 annually.

Deeper analysis of mobility reasons reveals differences within the individual categories. Among those who shifted because of job changes, 70.5 percent of the moves involved changes in employer as opposed to locational assignment shifts. The former reason is concentrated among renters, the latter among homeowners. The bulk of family size changes are related to changes in marital status — a new household formation, divorce or death. The need for larger homes was cited by 48 percent of those moving because of housing desires; more land and a change of tenure were cited by 19 percent. A shift for environmental reasons most commonly meant good schools for the children or the physical appearance of the neighborhood, the latter being the most important of the two reasons.

HOUSING ACCOMMODATIONS: DIMENSIONS OF COST, TYPE, SIZE AND AGE

COSTS OF HOMEOWNERSHIP

The sample of new homeowners provides a profile of the successful home buyer and reflects the availability of homes within the current

EXHIBIT IV-7

REASONS FOR MOBILITY BY INCOME

REASONS FOR MOBILITY	INCOME							
	Under $10,000	10,000-15,999	16,000-20,999	21,000-30,999	31,000-50,999	51,000-75,999	76,000-124,999	Total
Job Changes	12[1]	12	7	8	11	1	1	52
Family Size Changes	2	2	1	1	0	0	0	6
Housing Desires	2	1	4	6	5	0	0	18
Favorable Environment	1	2	1	3	1	0	0	8
Other	7	0	1	0	1	0	0	9
Total	24	17	14	18	18	1	1	93
Job Changes	23.1[2]	23.1	13.4	15.4	21.2	1.9	1.9	100.0
Family Size Changes	33.3	33.3	16.7	16.7	0.0	0.0	0.0	100.0
Housing Desires	11.1	5.6	22.2	33.3	27.8	0.0	0.0	100.0
Favorable Environment	12.5	25.0	12.5	37.5	12.5	0.0	0.0	100.0
Other	77.8	0.0	11.1	0.0	11.1	0.0	0.0	100.0
Total	25.8	18.3	15.1	19.4	19.4	1.0	1.0	100.0

[1] Number
[2] Percent

Source: Newcomers Survey — Summer 1970 — n=100 (Non-responses Excluded)

local market. The unsuccessful buyers should be partially represented by the missing or scanty price category(ies). As shown in Exhibit IV-8 no homes were purchased for less than $15,000; a small proportion (10 percent) were secured for $15,000-$30,999; this latter figure is two-thirds that of the entire community figure. [4] In contrast, an extraordinary 24 percent of the homes purchased are valued in excess of $76,000, although homes of this value account for only 17.4 percent of the housing stock in the entire community. These figures reinforce previous indices which emphasize the unavailability of homes in the local market for all but higher income groups.

This conclusion is also evident in the level of monthly mortgage payments; the median payment is $374. It is important to note that over one out of five (21.7 percent) of all new home-buyers have no mortgage; this is concentrated among previous Princeton movers.

Further analysis of the data in Exhibit IV-8 reveals differences among the groups of movers. The inter-Princeton mover is the most frequent buyer of the most expensive homes. In turn the local area mover, typically from a community such as Rocky Hill or Lawrence Township, is purchasing the least expensive homes, a reflection of his younger age and lower family income. Although the local area mover has paid a lower purchase price, the lower median monthly mortgage costs are held by previous Princeton movers, a finding which reflects the high incidence of mortgage-free holders in that group.

COSTS OF RENTAL UNITS

The range of rental prices is extremely broad, from less than $99 to almost $600 a month. The extreme cases represent a minority; the median monthly rent paid by new renters is $152. As shown in Exhibit IV-9 there is a wide disparity between renters in the normal open market and those holding Princeton contracts. The rents paid by university affiliates living in the institution's facilities are significantly lower than those paid in the competitive market; the monthly median rents are $146 and $176 respectively.

Aside from this disparity, the data emphasizes what we have already found in the case of ownership potential: namely, that the opportunity for new residence within Princeton is limited to those in the higher-income groups. Only 8.2 percent of the new renters are paying less than $100 per month; the equivalent figure for the entire community is 17.4 percent. A larger proportion of new renters (14.3 percent) are paying high rents than are present residents (10 percent). Thus, successful newcomers within the rental and homeowner markets are more affluent than those who presently live in the community.

A CLOSER LOOK AT HOUSING DEMAND

EXHIBIT IV-8

CURRENT PURCHASE PRICE OF HOME BY ORIGIN OF HOMEOWNER

ORIGIN OF HOMEOWNER	PURCHASE PRICE (1969-1970)							
	Under $15,000	$15,000-30,999	$31,000-50,999	$51,000-75,999	$76,000-100,000	$100,000 +	Total	Median
Princeton	0[1]	3	6	7	4	1	21	
Local Areas	0	2	5	1	1	0	9	
Distant N. J./ Other States	0	0	6	6	5	1	18	
Outside U. S.	0	0	1	0	0	0	1	
Total	0	5	18	14	10	2	49	
Princeton	0.0[2]	14.3	28.6	33.3	19.0	4.8	100.0	$56,355
Local Areas	0.0	22.2	55.6	11.1	11.1	0.0	100.0	$40,999
Distant N. J./ Other States	0.0	0.0	33.3	33.3	27.8	5.6	100.0	$63,497
Outside U. S.	0.0	0.0	100.0	0.0	0.0	0.0	100.0	*
Total	0.0	10.0	36.0	28.0	20.0	4.0	100.0	$53,676

Source: Newcomers Survey – Summer 1970 – sub n=50 (Non-responses Excluded)
*Sample Size Too Small For Generalization
[1] Number
[2] Percent

EXHIBIT IV-9

MONTHLY RENT (WITHOUT UTILITIES) BY TYPE OF RENTER

TYPE OF RENTER	$59-99	$100-149	$150-199	$200-249	$250-299	$300-599	Total	Median
Regular Market	3[1]	7	11	4	3	4	32	
Princeton Contract	1	8	7	1	0	0	17	
Total	4	15	18	5	3	4	49	
Regular Market	9.4[2]	21.9	34.4	12.5	9.4	12.4	100.0	$160.00
Princeton Contract	5.9	47.1	41.2	5.9	0.0	0.0	100.0	$137.00
Total	8.2	30.6	36.7	10.2	6.1	8.2	100.0	$152.00

Source: Newcomers Survey — Summer 1970 — sub n=50 (Non-responses Excluded)
[1] Number
[2] Percent

PREVIOUS RESIDENCY COST COMPARISONS

A comparison of the housing costs of a previous residence and costs presently incurred by new homeowners and renters gives additional meaning to the above observation. Although data regarding the cost of housing is distorted by changes in the purchasing power of the dollar, it is clear that those who move into Princeton pay more for housing than they did before. Over 54 percent of all respondents have experienced significantly higher increases in the costs of housing. This figure is slightly higher for owners than for renters or Princeton-contract holders; 58.3 percent, 50 percent and 50 percent respectively. Furthermore, another 14.4 percent are experiencing slightly higher payments than before. Thus, the accommodations of the newcomers reflect an upgrading of status as measured by housing expenditure. This is characteristic of both the intra- and inter-Princeton mover.

TYPE OF RESIDENCE

As shown in Exhibit IV-10 the single-family unit is the most common type for both homeowner and renter in the Township and Borough. It is important to note the high incidence of single-family home rentals. Although rental of single-family homes is a common phenomenon within Princeton, this tendency is more pronounced among the new renters. The proportion for the present resident renters is 27.7 percent as compared to 33.3 percent for the new renters. The greater proportion of both two- to four-family units and apartments within the Borough, evident from this data, has also been documented in the housing inventory chapter.

EXHIBIT IV-10

TYPE OF RESIDENCE BY TENURE AND LOCATION

	Single Family		2-3-4 Family		Apartment		Other		Total	
	Num-ber	Per-cent	Num-ber	Per-cent	Num-ber	Per-cent	Num-ber	Per-cent	Num-ber	Per-cent
Owner	49	100.0	0	0.0	0	0.0	0	0.0	49	100.0
Renter	11	33.3	9	27.3	11	33.3	2	6.1	33	100.0
Princeton Contract	1	5.6	1	3.6	15	83.3	1	5.6	18	100.0
Total	61	61.0	10	10.0	26	26.0	3	3.0	100	100.0
Township	43	67.2	5	7.8	16	25.0	0	0.0	64	100.0
Borough	18	50.0	5	13.9	10	27.8	3	8.3	36	100.0

Source: Newcomers Survey — Summer 1970 — n=100

Comparing present and past residences of the newcomers one finds the most diverse pattern among previous apartment dwellers (Exhibit IV-11). Over two out of five (44.2 percent) of these persons moved into single-family homes, 14 percent moved into two- to four-family units, while 39.5 percent again chose apartments. In contrast, the previous home dwellers overwhelmingly chose single-family units. Those previously living with their parents or relatives, the majority of whom are newly formed households, chose apartment units.

TENURE

It is important to recall the differing origins of both new homeowners and renters. Over three out of five (62 percent) of all new homeowners are intra-Princeton movers; in contrast, 76 percent of all new renters (including Princeton contracts) are inter-Princeton movers. These distinctions reflect the possibility of second moves among the intra-Princeton movers, once they become familiar with the area, and the influence

EXHIBIT IV-11

PREVIOUS TYPE OF RESIDENCE BY PRESENT TYPE OF RESIDENCE

	Single Family		2-3-4 Family		Apartment		Other		Total	
PRESENT TYPE OF RESIDENCE										
PREVIOUS TYPE OF RESIDENCE	Number	Percent	Number	Percent	Number	Percent	Number	Percent	Number	Percent
House	39	84.8	2	4.3	4	8.7	1	2.2	46	100.0
Apartment	19	44.2	6	14.0	17	39.5	1	2.3	43	100.0
Parents/Relatives	1	14.3	0	0.0	5	71.4	1	14.3	7	100.0
Other	1	50.0	1	50.0	0	0.0	0	0.0	2	100.0
Total	60	61.2	9	9.2	26	26.5	3	3.1	98	100.0

Source: Newcomers Survey — Summer 1970 — n=100 (Non-responses Excluded)

EXHIBIT IV-12

FORM OF TENURE BY MUNICIPALITY

	Owner		Renter		Princeton Contract		Total	
	Number	Percent	Number	Percent	Number	Percent	Number	Percent
Township	36	56.2	12	18.8	16	25.0	64	100.0
Borough	13	36.1	21	58.3	2	5.6	36	100.0

Source: Newcomers Survey — Summer 1970 — n=100 (Non-responses Excluded)

of the university, which attracts graduate students and faculty who are unsure of permanent plans and therefore prefer to rent.

The characteristic division between Township and Borough is again evident, as the former has a greater proportion of owners, approximately 56.2 percent, while the latter has a similar proportion of renters (Exhibit IV-12). (These figures are not comparable to those for the entire community because of the structured proportions of renters and owners.)

A CLOSER LOOK AT HOUSING DEMAND

Reviewing present tenurial relationships in light of previous forms of tenure and place of origin, one finds the greatest changes among renters from Princeton and the local areas. Fifty percent and 71.4 percent of these households respectively shifted from renter to homeowner as compared to 16.0 percent and 14.3 percent for Northern New Jersey/Other United States movers and foreign movers respectively (Exhibit IV-13). As anticipated, the inclination of previous homeowners to purchase another home is very strong (91 percent).

EXHIBIT IV-13

PRESENT TENURE BY PREVIOUS TENURE AND ORIGIN OF MOVER

	PRESENT TENURE*							
	Own		Rent		Princeton Contract		Total	
PREVIOUS RESIDENCE AND TENURE	Num-ber	Per-cent	Num-ber	Per-cent	Num-ber	Per-cent	Num-ber	Per-cent
Previous Princeton Residents								
Own	12	100.0	0	0.0	0	0.0	12	100.0
Rent	9	50.0	6	33.3	3	16.7	18	100.0
Total	21	70.0	6	20.0	3	10.0	30	100.0
Previous Local Area Residents								
Own	4	100.0	0	0.0	0	0.0	4	100.0
Rent	5	71.4	0	0.0	2	28.6	7	100.0
Total	9	81.8	0	0.0	2	18.2	11	100.0
Previous Northern N. J. and Outstate Residents								
Own	14	82.4	2	11.8	1	5.8	17	100.0
Rent	4	16.0	14	56.0	7	28.0	25	100.0
Total	18	42.9	16	38.1	8	19.0	42	100.0
Previous Outside U. S. A. Residents								
Own	0	0.0	0	0.0	0	0.0	0	0.0
Rent	1	14.3	3	42.9	3	42.9	7	100.0
Total	1	14.3	3	42.9	3	42.9	7	100.0

Source: Newcomers Survey — Summer 1970 — sub n=90 (Non-responses Excluded)
*Excludes Those Previously Living with Parents or Relatives.

NUMBER OF BEDROOMS

More than any of the sub-study groups, the recent movers' accommodations should closely match the stage in the life cycle need. [5] Those who have just moved have overcome the residential inertia which causes many households to remain in a dwelling unit after it is no longer appropriate for their needs. The new movers are closer to an equilibrium adjustment than the remaining population. They have adjusted their housing to their financial position, needs and preferences, and the conditions of the existing market. [6]

As shown in Exhibit IV-14, housing of new movers matches their needs. Compared to the present residents, where it was found that a large proportion of small households occupy large units, a small proportion of small households in the newcomer population occupy large units with three, four or more bedrooms, 14 percent as opposed to 24.2 percent. The number of bedrooms is directly related to total household size. Therefore, there are enough available bedrooms for the larger households with the exception of a couple of cases.

Further analysis of the size of dwelling units reveals differences among units occupied by owners, renters and holders of Princeton contracts and between those available in the Township and Borough. As anticipated, owners are living in the largest units, Princeton-contract households in the smallest. The mean bedroom sizes are as follows:

Homeowners	3.7
Renters	2.2
Princeton Contract	1.8

There is a difference between mean values for the Township and Borough — 3.1 bedrooms and 2.5 bedrooms respectively. This can be attributed to the differing housing stock characteristics within each area.

AGE STRUCTURE

The age of the dwelling units occupied by homeowners and renters varies significantly. As anticipated by the split of owners and renters between Township and Borough and the latter's older housing stock, the dwelling units of owners are younger than those of renters. Princeton-contract holders reside in the newest units; the mean ages of the housing units are 11.8 years, 17.2 years and 8 years old respectively.

This sub-study clearly indicates that among new homeowners within Princeton there is an absence of lower and moderate income families, bringing about an increasingly homogeneous wealthy community. The characteristics of new renters, however, reflect the influence of the major educational institutions, and as such their socioeconomic profile is similar to that of the main body of renters within the entire community.

More specifically, the sample of newcomers shows the influential force of the local employers. A significant proportion of newcomers is generated by the upper positional levels of the major local employers. This is clearly evident in the high purchasing power among the new homeowners.

Although the reshaped household represents a small proportion of the new movers within Princeton, these households do constitute a sector of demand. As previously mentioned, a portion of the reshaped households may have unintentionally disguised what might be called a "change in family size" move as a desire for different housing.

The absence of low and moderate income families and municipal employees in the population of new movers confirms the survey's hypothesis that these sectors represented areas of local need rather than demand. The high purchase price of homes and lack of sufficient rental units is an

EXHIBIT IV-14

SIZE OF HOUSEHOLD BY TOTAL NUMBER OF BEDROOMS

NUMBER OF BEDROOMS	SIZE OF HOUSEHOLD							
	One	Two	Three	Four	Five	Six	Seven	Total
One	6[1]	12	0	0	0	0	0	18
Two	3	5	5	5	0	0	1	19
Three	0	10	6	4	2	1	0	23
Four or More	0	4	5	11	14	5	1	40
Total	9	31	16	20	16	6	2	100
One	66.7[2]	38.7	0.0	0.0	0.0	0.0	0.0	18.0
Two	33.3	16.1	31.3	25.0	0.0	0.0	50.0	19.0
Three	0.0	32.3	37.5	20.0	12.5	16.7	0.0	23.0
Four or More	0.0	12.9	31.3	55.0	87.5	83.3	50.0	40.0
Total	100.0	100.0	100.0	100.0	100.0	100.0	100.0	100.0

Source: Newcomers Survey — Summer 1970 — n=100
[1] Number
[2] Percent

inhibiting factor for these potential residents. As documented in the Housing Inventory chapter, the cost of new homes is increasing within both the Borough and the Township, and is, thus, available only to higher income groups. Unless the present moderately priced housing and rental units experience a greater turnover of residents, we can expect the present pattern of in-migration to continue with resulting changes in the community mix leading to an increasingly wealthy homogeneous population.

NOTES

1. Maisel, Sherman J.: "Rates of Ownership, Mobility, and Purchase" in *Essays in Urban Land Economics* ed. Grebler (University of California, 1966), p. 76.

2. *Ibid.*, p. 76.

3. *Supra*, p. 22.

4. *Supra*, p. 22.

5. *Supra*, p. 117.

6. Lansing, John B., Clifton, Charles Wade, and Morgan, James N.: *New Homes and Poor People: A Study of Chains of Moves* (Survey Research Center, Institute for Social Research, University of Michigan, Ann Arbor, Michigan, 1969), p. 25.

Chapter V

THE RESHAPED HOUSEHOLD

The demand created by the changing needs of resident households varies with the individual stages in the family life cycle. The process of adjustment between family size and housing accommodations is succinctly summarized in the paragraph below which provides the theoretical framework for this chapter:

> One of the basic processes of adjustment in the housing market is the process by which the number of people in a family is adjusted to the number of rooms in a dwelling unit. If this adjustment were the only consideration in the matching of people to housing, there would be systematic changes in the number of rooms occupied by a family as the family passed through each stage in the family life cycle. The number of rooms would increase with the transition from single to married and increase further with the birth of children. The number of rooms occupied would decrease as the children left home one by one, and decrease further with the death of one of the partners, until finally the family ceased to exist. In fact, people do seem to increase the number of rooms they occupy more or less as their families grow, but they often keep rooms needed only for occasional visits after the children have grown up and left home. [1]

The term "reshaped household" refers to either the augmented or reduced size household of families who wish to remain in the community after the size of their family has changed. The information presented in this chapter is based on a study of "reshaped households" in Princeton. The future demand generated by this sector of the Princeton housing market over the next ten years is analyzed along with social profiles, housing requirements and dissatisfaction with present accommodations. The effect of housing deficiencies within Princeton as perceived inhibitors of these households' future plans is also investigated.

The sample of reshaped households was drawn from a probability sample based on the 501 telephone interviews of the present resident population. The sample was composed of singly-listed, noncommerical, non-governmental Princeton numbers (exchanges 921 and 924) chosen at random from the February 1970, New Jersey Bell Telephone Directory for the Suburban Trenton Area. Residents of undergraduate and graduate dormitories of Princeton University, Princeton Theological Seminary and Westminster Choir College were excluded from the sample. However, non-dormitory students, both married and single, were included in the sampling population.

The households who said they expected a change in family size within the next five to ten years were separated from other resident households and were then classified as either a "reduced" or an "augmented" size household, depending upon the expected change. The total number of households in the "reshaped sample" was 182, or 38.4 percent of the total households in the PRS. The reduced size households represent 58.7 percent of the total, while the augmented households account for 41.3 percent.

To emphasize differences between the social profiles and housing requirements of the two types of potential reshaped households, the data was examined and compared to the larger resident population. Specific areas of potential transiency (i.e., the geographical location of the reshaped household) were mapped and analyzed utilizing the SYMAP computer technique.

Initially each of the 501 successful interviews of the PRS was given a set of rectangular coordinates and was plotted on the official map of Princeton Borough and Township. The reshaped households were isolated and their coordinates utilized by the SYMAP computer program, which graphically displays specific variables by their geographical location. Although this map has certain limitations, it provides a readily available visual reference for the subject under discussion.

The type of map used in this study is a conformant map, which is based on *conformance* to the boundaries of a data zone.

> The conformant map is best suited for data, either qualitative or quantitative, whose areal limits are of significance, and whose representation as a continuous surface is inappropriate. Each

A CLOSER LOOK AT HOUSING DEMAND

data zone is enclosed by a boundary "conformant" to some pre-defined spatial unit. The entire spatial unit is given the same value, and symbolism is assigned according to its numerical class. (The reduced size and augmented household would each be given such a numerical class.) Local variation of the data within the boundary will not be apparent, but on the average will be correct. [2]

THE INCREASING VERSUS THE DECREASING
HOUSEHOLD: SOCIAL PROFILE

The future plans of present Princeton residents in terms of size of household are crucial in providing the basic building blocks for a Princeton housing program. What is the projected future size of the household of present Princetonians? The proportion indicating that the size of household will remain the same is 61.6 percent; 22.6 percent believe that their household size will decrease (a tribute to the relative maturity of Princeton households). Only 15.8 percent, less than one out of six, indicate a potential increase. Therefore, if the Princeton housing market were a closed system in which household size and size of accommodation were perfectly matched, then families awaiting less space would more than balance out those who will require more space.

As expected, the reason most often cited for changes in household size is either the addition or departure of children. The first reason was given by nearly three out of five of the respondents who anticipated a reshaped household, while one out of three expected additional children. Retirement was listed by less than 1 percent of the respondents, with a small group giving a variety of other reasons.

When analysis of the potential household reshaping is undertaken by Township and Borough, it is clear that a higher proportion of those anticipating increases live in the Borough. Conversely, the Township contains a higher proportion of decreasing households. This can be seen in Exhibit V-1 on the SYMAP presentation of reshaped households.

Concentrations of increasing households are especially strong around Faculty Road in the Township, and clusters are also found in the center of the Borough bounded by Bayard Lane and Harrison Street. Generally there is a dispersed pattern of stable-sized households. More specifically, areas of family size change can be referenced by use of the Voting Districts Map, Exhibit VI-17, page 159. The areas containing the highest proportions of decreasing households are Voting Districts 3 and 9 in the Borough and 4, 5, 9 and 10 in the Township. The increasing households are concentrated in Districts 4 and 6 in the Borough and 3 in the Township. Since new and larger housing accommodations are in relatively short supply in the Borough, the Township may possibly bear the strain of accommodating increasing households, assuming that the individuals in question change the size of their housing accommodation and wish to stay in Princeton. The bulk of reshaped households anticipate a family size change within the next six to ten years. Again, Borough residents indicated much more currency of change than did Township residents.

LENGTH OF RESIDENCY AND AGE COMPOSITION

There is a significant difference in the residence patterns of the decreasing and increasing households. Members of more than three out of four increasing households have lived in Princeton for less than five years, while decreasing and stable-sized households have a more evenly distributed set of residency figures. In each of these latter two groups almost one out of every three households are comprised of long-time Princeton residents who have lived in the community for 21 years or more.

The age distribution reinforces the above trends. The increasing households are predominately young, the decreasing and stable-sized, predominately middle-aged. The median ages for these sets are 30, 47 and 49 respectively.

HOUSEHOLD COMPOSITION AND SIZE

The most prevalent household form for all groups is the married couple, although 13 percent of the increasing households are single. The household size varies with the type of potential reshaped family; the median size for the increasing household is 2.3, the stable-sized household, 2, and 3.2 for the decreasing household.

Families whose size is not expected to change within the next ten years contain a large proportion of childless households, 55.8 percent. These are families who have already passed the initial reshaping process. However, this sector also contains 8 out of the 11 large families, those with five or more children under 18 years of age living at home.

EDUCATION

The educational level of Princetonians is exceptionally high. The median level for the decreasing household is a college degree (B.A./B.S.), while the increasing household has a slightly higher level of education, 16.7 years. The larger stable-sized household population has a lower educational level, 15 years. These differences are partially a function of varying age compositions and the number of married graduate students who classify themselves as potential increasing households.

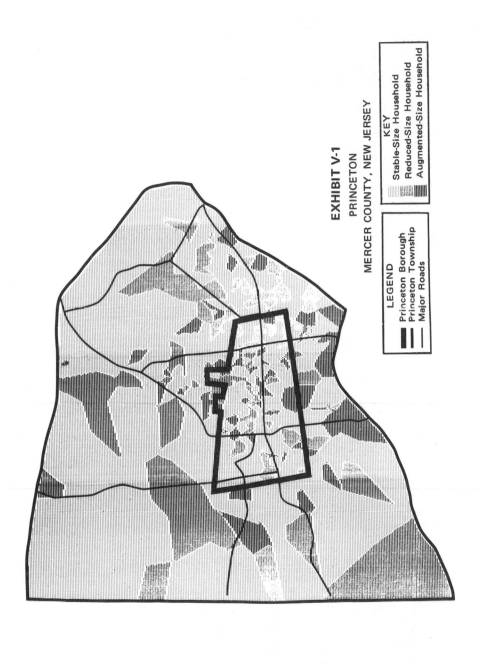

EXHIBIT V-1

PRINCETON

MERCER COUNTY, NEW JERSEY

LEGEND

Princeton Borough
Princeton Township
Major Roads

KEY

Stable-Size Household
Reduced-Size Household
Augmented-Size Household

EXHIBIT V-2

POTENTIAL RESHAPED HOUSEHOLDS BY INCOME LEVEL

	Under $10,000	$10,000-15,999	$16,000-20,999	$21,000-30,999	$31,000-50,999	$51,000-75,999	$76,000-124,000	$125,000 And Over	No Response/Don't Know	Total
				CHANGES IN FAMILY SIZE						
Remain the same	64[1]	40	39	51	24	9	5	1	59	292
Decrease	8	12	14	25	21	2	1	0	24	107
Increase	24	23	11	7	3	0	1	1	5	75
Total	96	75	64	83	48	11	7	2	88	474
Remain the same	21.9[2]	13.7	13.4	17.5	8.2	3.1	1.7	0.3	20.2	100.0
Decrease	7.5	11.2	13.1	23.4	19.6	1.9	0.9	0.0	22.4	100.0
Increase	32.0	30.7	14.7	9.3	4.0	0.0	1.3	1.3	6.7	100.0
Total	20.3	15.8	13.5	17.5	10.1	2.3	1.5	0.4	18.6	100.0

Source: PRS — Summer 1970 — n=501 (Non-responses to Reshaped Households Excluded)
[1] Number
[2] Percent

OCCUPATION

Both forms of the reshaped household are characterized by a large proportion of professional and technical workers, 48.6 percent for the reduced size and 56 percent for augmented households. Second to that, the decreasing household respondents work as managers, officials or proprietors, while over one-fifth of the increasing households are graduate students. The high educational level and occupational status of the reshaped households make such families considerably more mobile than most other families, and allow for greater choice in housing type.

INCOME

As shown in Exhibit V-2, the proportion of reduced-sized households varies directly with income levels up to $30,999. The proportion of augmented households is inversely related to income. In the latter group there are three times as many households earning less than $10,000 a year than there are in the reduced-sized sector. This emphasizes the interrelationship between age and income; younger families with increasing households have a lower earning capacity than do middle-aged, decreasing households, which are at the peak earning stage. This is evident from a comparison of the mean and median incomes of these groups.

The gaps between the mean and median figures reflect the effects of extreme values upon the mean and skewness of the data due to the small incidence of extremely high incomes.

WHAT ARE THEIR HOUSING ACCOMMODATIONS?

As shown in Exhibit V-4, the reduced-sized household has the most homogeneous set of housing accommodations; 92.5 percent live in detached single-family units. In contrast, the augmented households' accommodations are diversified, with apartment units representing the largest single type, or 42.9 percent of the total.

The data also shows that for all types of residences the anticipated change will occur within five years. However, proportionally, the largest *potential* turnover within this time period will occur in two- to four-family units.

As shown in Exhibit V-5, there is a distinct difference in the size accommodations among the three sets of respondents. The largest proportion of reduced-sized households are living in the largest units (four or more bedrooms), while the majority of augmented households are in the smallest units (one and two bedrooms). In comparison, over 70 percent of the stable-sized households live in units of three or more bedrooms.

More increasing households are living in older units than are decreasing households — 56 percent and 29.9 percent respectively. This is also the case for the newer units and can be attributed to the incidence of increasing households in Princeton University housing. The greatest single proportion of decreasing households are living in homes 11-20 years old.

The greatest proportion of decreasing households are owners, while increasing households generally are renters or holders of Princeton University contracts (primarily rental contracts, although a few are for mortgage arrangements — 83.2 percent, 47.3 percent and 33.8 percent respectively). Anticipated household changes will occur sooner for renters and Princeton-contract holders than for owners; that is, faster for increasing than decreasing households.

EXHIBIT V-3

INCOME: DERIVED MEANS AND MEDIANS

Household size within the next ten years will:	Mean 1969	Median 1969	N
Remain the same	$21,723	$19,204	233
Decrease	26,403	23,999	83
Increase	16,614	12,870	70

Source: Present Residents Survey — Summer 1970 — n=501
(Non-responses Excluded)

EXHIBIT V-4

POTENTIAL RESHAPED HOUSEHOLDS BY TYPE OF RESIDENCE

	TYPE OF RESIDENCE							
HOUSEHOLD SIZE WITHIN THE NEXT TEN YEARS WILL:	Detached Single Family		2-3-4 Family		Apartment		Total	
	Number	Percent	Number	Percent	Number	Percent	Number	Percent
Remain the same	211	73.5	32	11.1	44	15.3	287	100.0
Decrease	98	92.5	2	1.9	6	5.7	106	100.0
Increase	21	30.0	19	27.1	30	42.9	70	100.0
Total	330	71.3	53	11.4	80	17.3	463	100.0

Source: PRS — Summer 1970 — n=501 (Non-responses Excluded)

A CLOSER LOOK AT HOUSING DEMAND

EXHIBIT V-5

POTENTIAL RESHAPED HOUSEHOLDS BY TOTAL NUMBER OF BEDROOMS

Within the Next 5 to 10 Years Will the Size of Your Household:

NUMBER OF BEDROOMS	Remain the Same?		Decrease?		Increase?		Total Number	Average Percent
	Number	Percent	Number	Percent	Number	Percent		
Zero	2	0.7	0	0.0	0	0.0	2	0.4
One	24	8.2	0	0.0	19	25.3	43	9.1
Two	56	19.2	6	5.6	27	36.0	89	18.8
Three	106	36.3	31	29.0	20	26.7	157	33.1
Four	104	35.6	70	65.4	9	12.0	183	38.6
Total	292	100.0	107	100.0	75	100.0	474	100.0

Source: PRS — Summer 1970 — n=501 (Non-responses Excluded)

RENT LEVELS AND HOUSING VALUES

The monthly contract rent level paid varies with each type of reshaped household. One out of every four augmented households is paying under $99; another quarter is paying less than $149. In contrast, only 6.7 percent of the decreasing households are paying under $149.

These differences are similar to those existing among the incomes of the respective groups. The reduced-sized household is paying the most dollars for the largest units at the peak time of their housing requirements; the increasing household is in the reverse situation. The households which do not anticipate any changes are those theoretically in equilibrium.

Contrary to the previous findings, the owners' median house values do not vary as strikingly as do rents. While there is the expected difference between home values for the decreasing and increasing households, the differential is not large. Furthermore, there is little divergence between the decreasing and stable-sized household.

EXHIBIT V-6

MEDIAN MONTHLY RENT LEVELS

Household size within the next ten years will:	Rent Level	N
Remain the same	$165.32	74
Decrease	234.00	15
Increase	131.64	55

Source: PRS — Summer 1970 (Non-responses Excluded)   sponses Excluded)

EXHIBIT V-7

MEDIAN HOUSING VALUES

Household size within the next ten years will:	Selling Price	N
Remain the same	$50,807	171
Decrease	50,305	76
Increase	47,668	16

Source: PRS — Summer 1970 (Non-responses Excluded)   sponses Excluded)

A CLOSER LOOK AT HOUSING DEMAND

The similar proportional distribution of housing values among all three groups and the low differential among median selling prices reflects the fact that there is a limited housing stock available to potential buyers at any one time. Furthermore, the choice of purchasing a home on the part of increasing households seems to be related to their higher incomes in comparison with the rest of their contemporaries.

From the previous analysis it is possible to distinguish social profiles for each segment of the reshaped household market. The decreasing household represents 22.6 percent of the total present resident population. Members of these households have lived in Princeton longer than members of the increasing households, are married, middle-aged and have a median family size of 3.2. The educational level is high (a college degree), and the bulk of respondents work in a professional or managerial capacity. The median income of this group is $23,999. The reduced-sized household typically has an owner living in a single-family home with four or more bedrooms. The house has a median value of $50,305.

The augmented household is characterized by its low age and high potential mobility. These households represent 15.8 percent of the total resident population. The respondents are young and are both married and single. This is reflected in their short residency within the community — over 70 percent have been in Princeton for less than five years. The median household size is two; over 50 percent have no children. The educational level is high, a fraction more than a college degree, and the majority work in a professional capacity. Over 20 percent of the augmented households are graduate students. The median income is $12,870, barely half that of the reduced-sized households. The increasing families are predominately renters or holders of Princeton contracts (rental units) of one- and two-bedroom apartments and are paying a monthly median rent of $131.64.

HOUSING DEMAND OF THE RESHAPED HOUSEHOLD

Will a reshaped household adjust its housing accommodations to changes in family size and concomitant housing requirements? Will the community experience a shifting of residents within, or will the changing households leave Princeton, and, if so, how many?

These are some of the questions that will be dealt with in this section. This section considers the future housing demands of adjusting families, records their preferences, and notes the housing deficiencies within the community which they feel would inhibit their future plans.

THE MOBILITY OF THE RESHAPED HOUSEHOLD

When asked whether the change in household size would cause the family to remain in Princeton or move away, the bulk of respondents said they wanted to stay in Princeton. More than three out of four gave this response, while only 23.3 percent indicated that they would move away. This latter category is a little more heavily represented in the Borough, but the differences are not major. Obviously Princeton has a very loyal citizenry; however, will they be able to match their loyalty to alternate housing accommodations?

Greater mobility is evident among increasing households, renters, Princeton-contract holders, and residents in two- to four-family homes and apartments. The single-family homeowners are more stationary regardless of changes in household size. Over 50 percent of those who planned to move are renters living in two- to four-family units or apartments.

The movers are also living in the oldest units; 65.7 percent of these persons live in units over 20 years old as compared to 31.3 percent for those who will remain. The selling prices of homes owned by potential movers vary from $15,000 to $100,000; however, the largest proportion fall within the $31,000 to $51,999 range.

HOUSING REQUIREMENTS: SIZE, TENURE, TYPE

The proportion of reshaped households indicating a desire for larger accommodations is 32 percent,* for smaller accommodations 22.6 percent, while similar accommodations were mentioned as necessary by 43.4 percent. It is the Borough residents who are going to need larger facilities; 45.7 percent of the Borough's reshaped households said they expected to need increased space, while only 22.9 percent of the Township respondents indicated a need for larger facilities. Notice, however, that the proportion of movers into smaller accommodations is approximately the same in both cases, around the 25 percent mark. Once again, Borough residents are going to be under considerable pressure in finding appropriate size accommodations.

The large proportion of decreasing households requiring the same size accommodations (78.9 percent) warns of a situation of inertia in which many people are reluctant to move, and stay on in a dwelling that provides an excess of space theoretically necessary for their family needs. This is most prevalent among single-family homeowners; 85.5 percent of all those desiring the same amount of space are living in single-family homes; 78.9 percent are owners. Interestingly, over one-fifth of the increasing households state that their housing requirements will remain the same. These households may have larger accommodations than the bulk of their contemporaries.

*Although the graduate student population randomly occurred in the PRS, only three graduate student households reported that they would need larger accommodations.

A CLOSER LOOK AT HOUSING DEMAND

Families who want larger units are presently renters or Princeton-contract holders, living in two- to four-family units or apartments. The smaller units are typically required by owner residents of single-family homes. Only a small proportion of renters require smaller units.

Thirty-six percent of all respondents desiring different accommodations said they would become renters, while 54 percent expressed a desire to own a home. The bulk of homeowners requiring different accommodations would like to remain owners. Furthermore, 48.3 percent of the present renters and 76.5 percent of the Princeton-contract holders want to become owners. Although these last two tenure changes are significant, it is important to note that 51.7 percent of the renters would like to continue to rent. While both types of reshaped households want to become owners, this is more prevalent among increasing families; 45.5 percent of the decreasing compared to 26.7 percent of the increasing households desire rental units. The desire to rent is slightly higher in the Borough than in the Township. The shift from renter to owner occurs among those presently living in two- to four-family units and apartment houses, while the reverse, owner to renter, is most prevalent among single-family-home residents.

When potential renters were asked what type of housing they would like to rent, 36 percent mentioned single-family units, 44 percent chose garden apartment units, and only 12 percent indicated an interest in middle- or high-rise units. A relatively small number, only 8 percent of the total, were interested in the townhouse type of development.

The limited high-rise or townhouse response may be much more an indication of lack of availability or even familiarity of potential consumers with this type of amentiy than a distaste for them per se. Township people have a slightly greater interest in middle- or high-rise apartments and townhouses than do Borough residents. Fifty percent of the Borough renters are looking forward to living in garden apartments.

The shift in types of residence for the potential renters is greatest among those shifting from single-family homes to garden apartments, and, conversely, from apartments to single-family homes.

PERCEPTION OF HOUSING DEFICIENCIES

Do members of reshaped households feel that there are housing deficiencies within the Princeton housing market that will inhibit their future plans? If so, what are these deficiencies, and residents of which sector are under the most pressure to maintain their present dwelling or move away from the community to fulfill their housing requirements?

As shown in Exhibit V-8, more reshaped households feel that there are housing deficiencies within Princeton that would inhibit future plans than do stable-sized households. Specifically, 46.6 percent of the

EXHIBIT V-8

PERCEPTION OF HOUSING DEFICIENCIES BY POTENTIAL RESHAPED HOUSEHOLDS

Specific Housing Deficiencies in Princeton as Inhibitors of Future Plans:	Household Size Within the Next 10 Years Will:							
	Remain the Same		*Decrease*		*Increase*		*Total*	
	Number	Percent	Number	Percent	Number	Percent	Number	Percent
INCIDENCE								
Yes	85	31.4	48	46.6	42	63.6	175	39.8
No	186	68.6	55	53.4	24	36.4	265	60.2
Total	271	100.0	103	100.0	66	100.0	440	100.0
TYPE								
Single Family	31	42.5	15	38.5	13	35.1	59	39.6
Garden Apartment	30	41.1	18	46.2	21	56.8	69	43.3
High/Medium Rise	9	12.3	4	10.3	3	8.1	16	10.7
Town House	3	4.1	2	5.1	0	0.0	5	3.4
Total	73	100.0	39	100.0	37	100.0	149	100.0
OCCUPANCY METHOD								
Rental	54	75.0	23	63.9	27	73.0	104	71.7
Cooperative	5	6.9	5	13.9	3	8.1	13	9.0
Ownership	13	18.1	8	22.2	7	18.9	28	19.3
Total	72	100.0	36	100.0	37	100.0	145	100.0

EXHIBIT V-8 (Cont'd.)

PERCEPTION OF HOUSING DEFICIENCIES BY POTENTIAL RESHAPED HOUSEHOLDS

Specific Housing Deficiencies in Princeton as Inhibitors of Future Plans:	Remain the Same		Household Size Within the Next 10 Years Will:				Total	
			Decrease		Increase			
	Number	Percent	Number	Percent	Number	Percent	Number	Percent
COST								
(Monthly/House Value)								
Under $100/Under $12,000	9	11.4	5	11.6	5	12.8	19	11.8
$100-135/$12,000-$14,499	24	30.4	7	16.3	12	30.8	43	26.7
$136-174/$17,500-$24,999	34	43.0	21	48.8	12	30.8	67	41.6
$175-249/$25,000-$39,999	7	8.9	7	16.3	7	17.9	21	13.0
$250-399/$40,000-$59,999	4	5.1	3	7.0	3	7.7	10	6.2
$400-600/$60,000-$85,000	1	1.3	0	0.0	0	0.0	1	0.6
Total	79	100.0	43	100.0	39	100.0	161	100.0

Source: PRS — Summer 1970 — n=501 (Non-responses Excluded)

decreasing households and 63.6 percent of the increasing households had this feeling.

The typical set of Princeton housing deficiencies mentioned by the reshaped household appears to be the rental of a garden apartment for $136-174 per month.

The lack of single-family homes is directly related to the cost of these units rather than their absence. There seems to be a deficient number of available homes costing between $17,500 and $24,999.

It is important to note the low incidence of requests for the cooperative form of residency among decreasing households. The small size may signify unfamiliarity more than distaste for this form of residency.

PRESENCE OF DISSATISFACTION

Dissatisfaction among the reshaped households accounts for 35 percent of those dissatisfied within the community. A higher proportion of increasing households are discontented than decreasing households — 17.3 percent of the increasing households as opposed to 7.5 percent of the decreasing households. The major reason among increasing households is lack of space or structural deficiencies. The decreasing households typically voiced a desire for more land or a different house style.

Estimates on the number of reshaped households in the overall Princeton community are based on the results of the PRS. These estimates represent the lower limit, or conservative number of reshaped households due to the elimination of non-responses from the active population.

As shown in Exhibit V-9, the number of households whose size will change within the next ten years is 2,400, or 38 percent of the total number of Princeton households. Increasing household size is more frequent in the Borough, while the Township has a greater proportion of the decreasing households. This is not surprising because the Borough contains a larger number of two-family and multiple-family dwelling units [3] which are characteristic of the life style of young couples and expanding families.

The transiency of a substantial proportion of the population is reflective of the reshaping process. Almost one-quarter of these households, 23.4 percent, say they will move away from the community. Again, this mobility is more pronounced in the Borough, and among renters and holders of Princeton contracts. The single-family homeowner is the most resistant toward moving due to his commitment to and investment in the community. Although his needs may change, he is most able to accommodate these within his present circumstances.

This 23.4 percent represents a projected mobility figure for those leaving the community. However, to judge adequately the demands upon

A CLOSER LOOK AT HOUSING DEMAND

EXHIBIT V-9

POTENTIAL RESHAPED HOUSEHOLDS BY PRINCETON MUNICIPALITY

| | Within the Next 5 to 10 Years Will the Size of Your Household: | | | | | | | |
| | Remain the Same | | Decrease | | Increase | | Total | |
	Number	Percent	Number	Percent	Number	Percent	Number	Percent
Princeton Township	181	62.2	70	24.1	40	13.7	291	100.0
Pyramid Households	2269		879		500		3648	
Princeton Borough	111	60.7	37	20.2	35	19.1	183	100.0
Pyramid Households	1610		536		506		2652	
Total	292	61.6	107	22.6	75	15.8	474	100.0
Pyramid Households	3879		1415		1006		6300	

Source: PRS — Summer 1970 — n=501 (Non-responses Excluded)

the local housing market, it is essential to know the future mobility of the reshaped households *within* the community. It is to be assumed that all those who expressed a need for larger or smaller accommodations will move within or from the community. This represents 56.6 percent of the entire reshaped population, 39.8 percent of whom said they would move away, leaving 64 sample households as intra-Princeton movers, or a pyramided figure of 793 households. This latter figure represents 32.8 percent of the total potential reshaped households, and 12.6 percent of the households in the community.

Specific housing demands among reshaped households desiring different accommodations pivot about three forces: 1) the desire for homeownership on the part of young couples now renting and expecting larger families; 2) the continued desire for homeownership on the part of presently homeowning decreasing households; and 3) the desire to continue renting on the part of many decreasing households. As expected, the nature of the dwelling unit size varies with the projected family size change.

Of those wanting different accommodations, more Borough households prefer to rent than do Township households. Among these potential renters, the favored type of residence is the garden apartment. However,

EXHIBIT V-10

DEMAND FOR RENTAL UNITS BY POTENTIAL
RESHAPED HOUSEHOLDS DESIRING DIFFERENT ACCOMMODATIONS

| Type of Residence | Demand Measured by Number of Households | | | | | |
| | *Township* | | *Borough* | | *Total* | |
	Number	Percent	Number	Percent	Number	Percent
Single Family	4	36.4	5	35.7	9	36.0
Pyramid #		69		77		146
Garden Apartment	4	36.4	7	50.0	11	44.0
Pyramid #		69		108		177
Mid-High Rise	2	18.2	1	7.1	3	12.0
Pyramid #		35		15		50
Town House	1	9.1	1	.7.1	2	8.0
Pyramid #		17		15		32
Total	11	100.0	14	100.0	25	100.0
Pyramid #		190		215		405

Source: PRS — Summer 1970 — sub n=182 (Non-responses Excluded)

A CLOSER LOOK AT HOUSING DEMAND

a substantial percent would like to rent single-family homes, a phenomenon well documented in the Princeton community.

Projecting these rental demands for the total community, Exhibit V-10, presents the demand among potential reshaped households.

From this brief restatement of the trends among the potential reshaped households, it is possible to say that the potential shifting of housing accommodations as a consequence of family size change is only half that of the theoretical expectations. The tendency to maintain larger or smaller units than what is "necessary" is most probably influenced by the income characteristics of the household under question, and, secondly, by the limitations of the housing stock available at any one time. Reinforcing the latter statement is the fact that deficiencies within the Princeton housing market as inhibitors of future plans were cited by 50 percent of the potential reshaped households.

NOTES

1. Lansing, John B, Clifton, Charles Wade, Morgan, James N.: *New Homes and Poor People: A Study of Chains of Moves* (Institute for Social Research, University of Michigan, Ann Arbor, Michigan, 1969) p. 32.

2. Harvard University, Department of City and Regional Planning, Graduate School of Design: *SYMAP* (Harvard University, Laboratory of Computer Graphics, Cambridge, Massachusetts, 1963) p. 3.

3. *Supra,* p. 48.

Chapter VI
THE UNDERHOUSED

The underhoused population is defined as: 1) the poorly housed; 2) those who are overcrowded, or subject to intense land development different from other portions of the local residential community; or 3) those who are "locked into" neighborhoods because of racial *or* economic pressure. In the last case, residents may not desire or can not afford to maintain their parcels in a condition comparable to that of the standard housing stock.

The purpose of this section is to describe the socioeconomic and housing characteristics of Princeton's three underhoused areas, and to assess the needs of this population and the potential for improvement. A brief comparison of the underhoused areas and overall Princeton community is also presented.

An area containing poor housing conditions was defined, as specified under contract, for study by the research team by the Princeton Regional Planning Board. A set of three separate sub-areas was then established to provide a convenient method for data analysis.

Sub-area 1 (Witherspoon area) traverses the Borough boundaries into the Township, while Sub-area 2 (Linden Lane area) is completely within the Township and Sub-area 3 (Tree Street area) within the Borough. The Borough on the whole, contains 56 percent of the total number of underhoused dwelling units (Exhibit VI-1).

The entire underhoused area contains approximately 816 dwelling

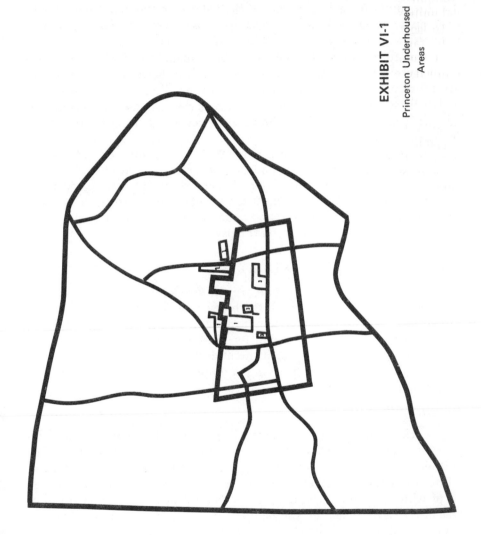

EXHIBIT VI-1

Princeton Underhoused
Areas

units (excluding housing projects), from which a 12 percent sample, involving 100 door-to-door interviews, was chosen. The number of interviews conducted within each sub-area and on each street was determined by a weighting procedure based on the proportion of the total number of dwelling units in each area and on each street in the underhoused area (Exhibit VI-2). Once the sub-area sample sizes were determined, individual units were randomly selected from each street.

To isolate potential differences in the responses and possible underlying factors contributing to and determining the nature of each sub-area, computer cross-tabulations were run for all variables by area and ethnicity. Analysis of the data by sub-areas reveals basic variations that are provocative, and which dramatize the ethnic differences purposely included in the area study.

Frequency distributions and percentages were derived for the responses to each question, in addition to cross-tabulations of specific variables to determine the major characteristics of four basic parameters: 1) ownership and tenantry; 2) rent-income ratios; 3) resident satisfaction or dissatisfaction, and housing desires; 4) desire and/or capacity for home improvement on the part of homeowners.

THE SOCIOECONOMIC PORTRAIT

Here we will describe and compare the socioeconomic characteristics and housing accommodations of the households within the three sample sub-areas. Comparative references are made with the inner core of Newark to highlight similarities and differences between underhoused areas. It is important to remember that the underhoused of Princeton must be viewed in relation to the Princeton community rather than to areas of major central city blight.

ETHNICITY

The ethnic composition presented in Exhibit VI-3 describes the division between black and white populations in the three sub-areas. The Witherspoon area is predominately black with a small proportion of white residents. Conversely, the Linden Lane area is primarily comprised of white of Italian descent, with a small proportion of nonwhites of Oriental origin. Based on the sample, the Tree Street area is entirely composed of white residents.

LENGTH OF RESIDENCE IN PRINCETON
AND AGE COMPOSITION

The underhoused areas as a whole are predominately composed of long-time Princeton residents, with a minority of newer residents. Fifty-five

EXHIBIT VI-2

SAMPLE SELECTION FOR PRINCETON UNDERHOUSED SURVEY

Witherspoon Area			Linden Lane Area			Tree Street Area		
Street	No. D.U.	Sample No.	Street	No. D.U.	Sample No.	Street	No. D.U.	Sample No.
Birch Avenue	98	12	Clearview Street	24	3	Bank Street	28	3
Green Street	25	3	Ewing Street	50	6	Chestnut Street	46	6
Harris Road	25	3	Linden Lane	38	5	Greenview Street	12	2
Henry Street	16	2				Humbert Street	25	3
John Street	61	7				Moran Street	20	2
Leigh Avenue	113	14				N. Tulane Street	9	1
Lytle Street	26	3				Pine Street	33	4
MacLean Street	15	2				Spruce Street	46	6
Quarry Street	15	2						
Race Street	6	1						
Shirley Court	12	1						
Witherspoon Lane	8	1						
Witherspoon Street	65	8						
Subtotals	485	59	Subtotals	112	14	Subtotals	219	27
Total	816	100						

Source: Underhoused Survey — Summer 1970.

EXHIBIT VI-3

ETHNIC COMPOSITION BY AREA

	Black		White		Other Nonwhite		Total	
	Number	Percent	Number	Percent	Number	Percent	Number	Percent
Witherspoon Area	50	84.7	9	15.3	0	0.0	59	100.0
Linden Lane Area	0	0.0	12	85.7	2	14.3	14	100.0
Tree Street Area	0	0.0	27	100.0	0	0.0	27	100.0
Total	50	50.0	48	48.0	2	2.0	100	100.0

Source: Underhoused Survey — Summer 1970 — n=100

percent of the respondents have lived in Princeton for 21 years or more, and less than 20 percent have been there for less than 5 years (Exhibit VI-4).

There is a significant difference among areas. The Witherspoon area contains the greatest proportion of long-time residents, whereas the Tree Street area has attracted newer residents. The bulk of the Linden Lane residents have resided in Princeton for 11 to 20 years.

The age distribution (Exhibit VI-5) highlights one of the most salient characteristics of communities with older sections containing poorer housing conditions — that of the elderly. Thirty-four percent, or one out of every three, of the household heads in the underhoused area are 65 or over. This tendency is more pronounced among the residents of the Witherspoon area, while the age distribution is more evenly divided in the other two areas. The Tree Street area, which has a large number of new residents, also has the highest proportion of 21- to 25-year-old heads of household.

The importance of this age distribution cannot be overstated. As is discussed later, the young are more likely to be motivated toward home maintenance and improvement; the elderly's lack of funds and initiative act as serious inhibitors of such action.

EXHIBIT VI-4
DURATION OF RESIDENCE IN PRINCETON BY AREA

| AREA | LENGTH OF RESIDENCE | | | | | |
	Under 1 Year	1-5 Years	6-10 Years	11-20 Years	21+ Years	Total
Witherspoon Area	1[1]	5	3	8	41	58
Linden Lane Area	1	1	2	6	4	14
Tree Street Area	3	8	3	3	10	27
Total	5	14	8	17	55	99
Witherspoon Area	1.7[2]	8.6	5.2	13.8	70.7	100.0
Linden Lane Area	7.1	7.1	14.3	42.9	28.6	100.0
Tree Street Area	11.1	29.6	11.1	11.1	37.0	100.0
Total	5.1	14.1	8.1	17.2	55.6	100.0

Source: Underhoused Survey — Summer 1970 — n=100 (Non-responses Excluded)
[1] Number
[2] Percent

EXHIBIT VI-5

AGE COMPOSITION BY AREA

AREA	AGE BRACKETS					
	21-25	26-35	36-49	50-64	65 & Over	Total
Witherspoon Area	3[1]	9	11	11	23	57
Linden Lane Area	0	3	3	4	4	14
Tree Street Area	3	5	6	6	7	27
Total	6	17	20	21	34	98
Witherspoon Area	5.3[2]	15.8	19.3	19.3	40.4	100.0
Linden Lane Area	0.0	21.4	21.4	28.6	28.6	100.0
Tree Street Area	11.1	18.5	22.2	22.2	25.9	100.0
Total	6.1	17.3	20.4	21.4	34.7	100.0

Source: Underhoused Survey — Summer 1970 — n=100 (Non-responses Excluded)
[1]Number
[2]Percent

HOUSEHOLD COMPOSITION AND SIZE

Fifty-three percent of all the underhoused households do not have any children under 18 years of age living at home. The second most common form of household composition is the married couple with one child under 18 years old. As would be expected from the age distribution, there is a substantial proportion of widowed persons — 16 percent.

Further analysis of the data reveals subtle differences among the areas. Although the Witherspoon area has the largest elderly population, it also houses the greatest proportion of children and large families. While the latter total is only seven of 47 households with four or more children, six of these are within the Witherspoon area. In contrast, the Linden Lane area has the highest proportion of households without children (under 18 years of age) at home, and the Tree Street area has the smallest. The Tree Street area is also characterized by a substantial proportion of one-member households.

A "modified extended family" situation, i.e., where relatives are living in the home instead of only parents and dependent children,[1] as in the "elementary family," is peculiar to the Witherspoon area. While families in the other areas have other persons living with them, all of these cases represent children over 18 years old, roomers or companions.

EDUCATION

The educational level of the household heads in the underhoused area is lower than that of the overall Princeton community as found in the PRS. The median education for the former is a high school diploma, compared to a college degree for the latter. However, in contrast to the educational level within the Newark inner core, the underhoused of Princeton hold a greater proportion of high school, college or graduate degrees. [2]

Looking at specific area variations, we find that 46 percent of the Witherspoon area, 43 percent of the Linden Lane area and 33 percent of the Tree Street area heads of household have less than a high school education. The Tree Street area has the highest proportion of residents with some form of higher education, while the Witherspoon area has the least. The difference between these areas is due to the number of graduate students and teaching professionals living in the Tree Street area, and the high proportion of elderly in the Witherspoon section. A large proportion of the Linden Lane area residents are elderly or middle-aged, many of whom migrated from Italy where they received little or no formal schooling. Nevertheless, it is important to note that not all of the underhoused have had little education. One out of five has completed four years of college or more, and of these one-fourth are black residents.

INCOME

As shown in Exhibit VI-6, the Witherspoon area has the highest percentage of low-income families. Almost 17 percent of the total number of families interviewed in that area earn under $3,000 a year; this compares with 14.3 percent and 11.1 percent for the Linden Lane and the Tree Street areas respectively. It is important to note that ten out of the 15 families with incomes below $3,000 a year are headed by a retired person. The area income breakdowns also reflect income differences along ethnic lines: in the Underhoused sample, twice as many blacks as whites earned under $3,000 a year.

Comparatively, the proportion of low-income families in Princeton is much smaller than that of the Newark core — 15 percent versus 24 percent. [3] Yet the higher white income factor was also found in Newark. [4]

The total family median income for the entire underhoused area is $7,845; the mean is $8,549 per year. Below is a chart contrasting the means and medians derived for each sub-area. As shown, the Witherspoon area has the lowest mean and median; the Linden Lane area has the highest.

EXHIBIT VI-6

TOTAL HOUSEHOLD INCOME BY AREA

	Under $3,000	$3,000- 5,999	$6,000- 9,999	$10,000- 14,999	$15,000- 19,999	$20,000- 24,999	$25,000- 29,999	$30,000 And Over	No Response/ Don't Know	Total
Witherspoon Area	10[1]	6	17	8	2	0	0	0	16	59
Linden Lane Area	2	3	2	5	1	1	0	0	0	14
Tree Street Area	3	5	7	6	2	0	0	1	3	27
Total	15	14	26	19	5	1	0	1	19	100
Witherspoon Area	16.9[2]	10.2	28.8	13.6	3.4	0.0	0.0	0.0	27.1	100.0
Linden Lane Area	14.3	21.4	14.3	35.7	7.1	7.1	0.0	0.0	0.0	100.0
Tree Street Area	11.1	18.5	25.9	22.2	7.4	0.0	0.0	3.7	11.1	100.0
Total	15.0	14.0	26.0	19.0	5.0	1.0	0.0	1.1	19.0	100.0

Source: Underhoused Survey — Summer 1970 — n=100 (Non-responses Included)
[1] Number
[2] Percent

EXHIBIT VI-7

INCOME: DERIVED MEANS AND MEDIANS

	Mean 1969	Median 1969	N
All	8,123	7,768	81
Witherspoon Area	7,081	7,293	43
Linden Lane Area	9,571	9,999	14
Tree Street Area	9,979	8,284	24

Source: Underhoused Survey — Summer 1970 — (Non-responses Excluded)

OCCUPATION AND PLACE OF WORK

Eliminating the retired and student population from the sample, unemployment among the poorly housed in Princeton is very low. One household out of the 100 respondents was reported to be on welfare, while 7 others said they were unemployed housewives. For the 56.1 percent of the total sample who are employed, the most predominant occupations are in the professional and technical, or laborer categories.

When comparing white-collar, blue-collar and service categories, some striking differences are evident among the areas. While the Witherspoon area is characterized by a high proportion of service workers and white-collar employees, 42.4 percent and 39.3 percent respectively, Linden Lane area's employment is split between blue-collar and service workers with a small proportion of white-collar work. In contrast, 61.5 percent of the Tree Street area's household heads are employed in white-collar work.

Besides looking at the characteristics of the employed, it is also important to look at the industrial distribution of the underhoused workers. In the Witherspoon and Linden Lane areas employers are the service industries, accounting for one out of every three jobs. In the Tree Street area, the educational institutions employ two out of every five respondents. Self-employment plays a more significant role in the Witherspoon area than in other areas; such activity involves 18.8 percent of the employed in the Witherspoon area, as opposed to 10 percent for the Linden Lane area and 7.1 percent for the Tree Street area.

The job location of employed workers in the underhoused areas is similar to the distribution found in the entire Princeton area. In both cases, major employment is within the Borough and the Township. A small percentage of respondents commute to New York City or Philadelphia. There is little area differentiation, except that fewer respondents in the Tree Street area worked locally.

As shown in Exhibit VI-8, each area is characterized by a different combination of housing types. The Linden Lane area is the most homogeneous, composed entirely of detached single-family houses, while the Witherspoon and Tree Street areas contain a wider range of housing types, including two- to four-family units* and apartments. The Witherspoon area is dominated by single-family units, while three out of five units in the Tree Street area are two- to four-family homes. There is a small percentage of larger multifamily units in the underhoused area.

A comparison along ethnic lines shows that a greater proportion of blacks than whites live in detached single-family units.

The median age of all dwelling units in the underhoused area is over 40 years. The Witherspoon and Tree Street areas are typified by this median, with a few exceptions in the Witherspoon area, where one out of five of the sampled units was built 20 to 40 years ago. However, the Linden Lane area diverges substantially from this median. In that area, 100 percent of the sampled units were built 10 to 20 years ago, and approximately 43 percent of these respondents were the first occupants of their homes. The age characteristics of the dwelling units are similar for all types of residence with the exception of the apartment units which are 21 to 40 years old.

Three out of every five dwelling units in the underhoused sections of Princeton are owner-occupied; only 38 percent of the dwelling units are rental units. Exhibit VI-9 shows variations among the areas. The Witherspoon and Linden Lane areas are characterized by a predominance of owner-occupied units, the latter being the most homogeneous. In contrast, 59.3 percent of the Tree Street area respondents are renters.

There is very little black/white differentiation with regard to tenure, except that a higher proportion of blacks are homeowners (Exhibit VI-9). Although this is a reversal of the situation typically found in underhoused areas, it can be attributed to three factors: the longevity of the residents in Princeton; the small number of incomes below $3,000 (this excludes retired individuals who bought their homes a long time ago); and the lack of rental units available within the area.

The two- to four-family home is the most widely found type of rental residence in the underhoused areas; however, there is also a significant proportion of detached single-family home rentals — 21.1 percent. This is slightly lower than the equivalent figure for these rentals in the entire Princeton area.

---

*A two- to four-family unit is defined as all structures with or without separate entrances housing two, three or four households.

EXHIBIT VI-8

TYPE OF RESIDENCE BY AREA

	Detached Single House		2-3-4 Family House		Apartment House		Total	
	Number	*Percent*	*Number*	*Percent*	*Number*	*Percent*	*Number*	*Percent*
Witherspoon Area	38	64.4	17	28.8	4	6.8	59	100.0
Linden Lane Area	14	100.0	0	0.0	0	0.0	14	100.0
Tree Street Area	10	37.0	16	59.3	1	3.7	27	100.0
Total	62	62.0	33	33.0	5	5.0	100	100.0

Source: Underhoused Survey — Summer 1970 — n=100

EXHIBIT VI-9
FORM OF TENURE BY AREA AND ETHNICITY

	Own		Rent		Total	
	Number	*Percent*	*Number*	*Percent*	*Number*	*Percent*
AREA						
Witherspoon Area	39	66.1	20	33.9	59	100.0
Linden Lane Area	12	85.7	2	14.3	14	100.0
Tree Street Area	11	40.7	16	59.3	27	100.0
Total	62	62.0	38	38.0	100	100.0
ETHNICITY						
Black	32	64.0	18	36.0	50	100.0
White	29	60.4	19	39.5	48	100.0
Other Nonwhite	1	50.0	1	50.0	2	100.0
Total	62	62.0	38	38.0	100	100.0

Source: Underhoused Survey — Summer 1970 — n=100

Age of a housing unit is not the overriding variable in determining whether it is owned or rented. Although there is a higher proportion of rental units over 40 years old, the bulk of all units in the underhoused area is within this category.

RENT LEVELS

The average renter is paying a median rent of $122.75 per month for a two-bedroom unit in a two- to four-family structure. The apartment renter has the smallest monthly costs of all renters and resides in the smallest units. He pays approximately $90.50 for a one- or two-bedroom unit. In contrast, the single-family home renter is paying the highest monthly rentals — $149 for a home with three or more bedrooms. Further data analysis reveals variation among the areas as shown in Exhibit VI-10.

The conversion of the rent costs into rent-income ratios, i.e., the percentage of total annual income expended for annual rent costs, shows some important characteristics about these areas. Exhibit VI-11 presents the tabulation of the percent of gross annual income spent on contract rent within each income class. In every class there is a tendency for households to cluster in rent-income brackets. A finding typical of many such studies is that "the proportion of income spent on rent is not constant but declines, on the average, as income increases."[5] All those earning under $3,000 annually are expending over 30 percent of their incomes

A CLOSER LOOK AT HOUSING DEMAND

EXHIBIT VI-10

MONTHLY RENT LEVELS BY AREA

	$ 1-99	$100-149	$150-199	$200-249	$250-299	Total	Median
Witherspoon Area	8[1]	11	0	0	1	20	
Linden Lane Area	0	0	2	0	0	2	
Tree Street Area	1	9	3	1	1	15	
Total	9	20	5	1	2	37	
Witherspoon Area	40.0[2]	55.0	0.0	0.0	6.7	100.0	$122.75
Linden Lane Area	0.0	0.0	100.0	0.0	0.0	100.0	108.08
Tree Street Area	6.7	60.0	20.0	6.7	6.7	100.0	*
Total	24.3	54.1	13.5	2.7	5.4	100.0	135.07

*Sample size too small for generalization
Source: Underhoused Survey — Summer 1970 — sub n=38 (Non-responses Excluded)
[1] Number
[2] Percent

EXHIBIT VI-11

AVERAGE RENT-INCOME RATIOS BY INCOME BRACKET

RENT-INCOME RATIOS	Under $3,000	$3,000-5,999	$6,000-9,999	$10,000-14,999	$15,000-Over	Total
Less Than 10%	0[1]	0	0	0	2	2
10-14%	0	0	3	3	1	7
15-19%	0	0	0	1	0	1
20-29%	0	1	9	2	0	12
30% +	7	3	0	0	0	10
Total	7	4	12	6	3	32
Less Than 10%	0.0[2]	0.0	0.0	0.0	80.0	6.3
10-14%	0.0	0.0	25.0	50.0	20.0	21.9
15-19%	0.0	0.0	0.0	16.7	0.0	3.1
20-29%	0.0	25.0	75.0	33.3	0.0	37.5
30% +	100.0	75.0	0.0	0.0	0.0	31.2
Total	100.0	100.0	100.0	100.0	100.0	100.0

Source: Underhoused Survey — Summer 1970 — sub n=38 (Non-responses Excluded)
[1] Number
[2] Percent

for rent. Those earning over $15,000 a year are spending less than 15 percent of their income for rent. Similar results were found in the Gershen Associates Report *Examination of Moderate and Low Income Housing Accommodations.* [6]

Rent-income ratios* by area present a different picture than that in Exhibit VI-11, one that tends to obscure the previous findings. Note the difference of 4 percent between the average rent-income ratio of the Witherspoon and Tree Street areas — 21 percent and 17 percent respectively. However, these figures should be compared with the corresponding costs for the nation and for Northern New Jersey. The former is approximately 15 percent,[7] the latter, 16.1 percent for renters.[8] In both cases, the ratio for the Princeton underhoused is higher.

Recalling the ethnic differences between the Witherspoon and Tree Street areas, black renters are expending a higher percentage of their annual income for housing than are white renters.

HOUSING VALUES[†]

Although the annual mean incomes of both renters and owners are approximately the same — $8,060 and $8,166 respectively— a greater proportion of owners than renters earn $10,000 or more per year. Homeowners tend to be older than renters; the owner's median age is 61, compared to 39 for renters. A greater proportion of owners than renters have lived in Princeton at the same address for ten years or more.

The purchase price of the homes within the underhoused area in Princeton is a function of the age of the owner, time differentials and price fluctuations in the housing market. The lowest purchase prices found were in the Witherspoon and Tree Street areas, where the median prices were approximately $10,000. The median purchase price for the Linden Lane area was considerably higher, $17,332. These median prices also reflect the respective ages of the homes in each area. It should be recalled that the newest homes, those 11 to 20 years old, are in the Linden Lane area.

As would be expected from the preponderance of long-time residents and elderly homeowners in the underhoused area, 71.1 percent of all homeowners have no mortgage and own their homes outright. This is most pronounced in the Witherspoon and Tree Street areas. Respondents holding mortgages are paying a median monthly payment of $122. There is little area differentiation (Exhibit VI-12).

*The rent-income ratio for Area 2 is insignificant due to the small number of renters within this area and their disparate incomes.

†Acknowledging the difficulty of equating monthly mortgage payments or housing value with monthly rent payments, the owner's housing costs will be discussed separately. However, it is important to note first some of the basic differences between owners and renters, possibly accounting for their housing accommodations differential.

A CLOSER LOOK AT HOUSING DEMAND

EXHIBIT VI-12

MONTHLY MORTGAGE PAYMENTS BY AREA

	Under $100		$101-150		$151-200		No Mortgage		Total	
	Number	Percent	Number	Percent	Number	Percent	Number	Percent	Number	Percent
Witherspoon Area	2	5.4	5	13.5	2	5.4	28	75.7	37	100.0
Linden Lane Area	2	16.7	3	25.0	1	8.3	6	50.0	12	100.0
Tree Street Area	1	9.1	0	0.0	1	9.1	9	81.8	11	100.0
Total	5	8.3	8	13.3	4	6.7	43	71.7	60	100.0

Source: Underhoused Survey — Summer 1970 — sub n=62 (Non-responses Excluded)

Comparing the median annual income of those owners holding mortgages with those not holding them, we find a substantial difference — $10,050 as opposed to $6,499. Again there is no area variation.

EXHIBIT VI-13

SIZE OF HOUSEHOLD BY TOTAL NUMBER OF BEDROOMS

NUMBER OF BEDROOMS	One	Two	Three	Four	Five	Six	Seven	Eight to Ten	Total
One	3[1]	6	0	0	0	0	0	0	0
Two	2	14	4	4	6	1	0	0	31
Three	4	11	6	13	4	5	1	3	47
Four or More	0	3	2	6	1	0	1	0	13
Total	9	34	12	23	11	6	2	3	100
One	33.3[2]	17.6	0.0	0.0	0.0	0.0	0.0	0.0	9.0
Two	22.2	41.2	33.3	17.4	54.5	16.7	0.0	0.0	31.0
Three	44.4	32.4	50.0	56.5	36.4	83.3	50.0	100.0	47.0
Four or More	0.0	8.8	16.7	26.1	9.1	0.0	50.0	0.0	13.0
Total	100.0	100.0	100.0	100.0	100.0	100.0	100.0	100.0	100.0

Source: The Underhoused Survey — Summer 1970 — n=100
[1] Number
[2] Percent

EXHIBIT VI-14

QUALITY OF EXTERNAL APPEARANCE BY FORM OF TENURE

	QUALITY OF EXTERNAL APPEARANCE							
FORM OF TENURE	Poorer Than Neighbors		Same As Neighbors		Better Than Neighbors		Total	
	Number	Percent	Number	Percent	Number	Percent	Number	Percent
Own	5	8.1	35	56.5	22	35.5	62	100.0
Rent	16	42.1	20	52.6	2	5.3	38	100.0
Total	21	21.0	55	55.0	24	24.0	100	100.0

Source: Underhoused Survey — Summer 1970 — n=100

In sum, most of the underhoused residents in Princeton own their housing—often free of mortgages. The elements of age as well as income stringencies may limit their ability to make further investment in their holdings.

SIZE OF DWELLING VERSUS NEED

As shown in Exhibit VI-13, most families within the underhoused area have a sufficient number of bedrooms. The smaller households comprised of two or less persons may even be considered as overhoused in relation to their stage in the family life cycle. [9] However, for 10 percent of the underhoused sample there is not a sufficient number of bedrooms available; these are the larger families, with six to ten persons who live in units with two or three bedrooms.

The median number of bedrooms and persons per household for the underhoused area is three. The Linden Lane area has a median of two bedrooms per unit. Other than this, there is little area variation.

The median number of bedrooms is, however, a function of type of residence. Detached single-family homes have a median of three bedrooms, as compared to two bedrooms for two- to four-family units and one for apartments.

QUALITY OF DWELLING UNIT

Defining the quality of a dwelling unit is difficult because it involves a variety of subjective elements. However, four observations were made dealing with the exterior conditions and construction, and the state of maintenance.

As shown in Exhibit VI-14, the owner-occupied units are in better condition, externally, than the rental units. Forty-two percent of all rental units are classified "poorer than neighbors" compared to 8 percent for owner-occupied units. A higher percentage of owner-occupied than rental units are classified "better than neighbors." Similiar findings were reported for Newark in *The Tenement Landlord:*

> It is the single-parcel owner, who by a very wide margin, has the smallest proportion of poorly-kept and the highest proportion of well-kept parcels....

> Regardless of area, resident ownership is the keystone of good maintenance. [10]

Almost all dwelling units in the underhoused areas are of frame construction with "reasonable to good siding." The greatest proportion of frame constructed units with "bad siding" are in the Witherspoon area.

Looking at the area variations, we find that major differences occur between the Linden Lane area and the Witherspoon and Tree Street areas. The latter areas are composed of dwelling units varying in quality, while the Linden Lane area is the most homogeneous. Seventy-eight percent of the units in the Linden Lane area are classified as "in good condition" and having the "same" external quality as their neighbors. A comparison of the street block with the general area* reveals that in all cases, the street blocks of the Linden Lane area are the "same" as the general area, implying little superficial difference between this area and the blocks outside of the underhoused area.

In contrast, the poorest conditions appear in the Witherspoon area, where one out of every four units is classified as "poorer than neighbors" and as being in poor condition. The Tree Street area also has one out of four units classified as "poorer than neighbors." The street blocks within the Witherspoon and Tree Street areas are mixed, with equivalent proportions of similar, better and poorer blocks.

It is possible to distinguish three separate socioeconomic sub-area profiles. The Witherspoon area is primarily composed of black residents who have lived in Princeton for a long time. The largest single proportion of respondents are elderly. This area also contains the highest percentage of children under 18 years old. The majority of households consist of a married couple, although many are headed by a widowed person. The bulk of the employed heads of households are employed as service workers, and the median total family income is $7,293 per year. Housing accommodations are a mixture of types, although detached single-family units are dominant. The average resident owns a three-bedroom unit, which was initially purchased for a median price of $10,250. Seventy-five percent of the owners have no mortgage.

Almost all residents of the Linden Lane area are of white Italian descent and have lived in Princeton for over 20 years. This area is the most homogeneous of the three, with very few internal socioeconomic differences. Most households are headed by a married male, with few children under 18 years of age. The heads of the households are primarily blue-collar or service workers and earn an annual median income of $9,999. The area is composed entirely of detached single-family units 10 to 20 years old, all of which are owner-occupied. Many of the present residents are the initial occupants of their homes. The median size home has two bedrooms and was purchased for $17,332.

The Tree Street area contains an array of residents and housing types. It is composed entirely of white residents, both old and young, married, widowed and single. Long-time residents, as well as a significant propor-

*General area is defined as frontage across the street and several blocks in all directions.

tion of newer residents, are living there. The head of the household has the greatest amount of education of all subarea residents and earns his living as a professional. The median annual income of this subarea is $8,284. The housing units are of a mixed variety, but two- to four-family units predominate and are occupied by renters paying a median rent of $135.07 per month for a two-bedroom unit. The majority of the units are 40 years or older. Eighty-two percent of the homeowners have no mortgages and purchased their homes for a median price of $9,499.

RESIDENT HOUSING DISSATISFACTION

This section includes a description of the frequency and degree of dissatisfaction in each underhoused subarea, an analysis of the causes of dissatisfaction, and a comparison of subarea dissatisfaction and pockets of random dissatisfaction within Princeton. This latter data was secured as a result of the PRS.

FREQUENCY AND DEGREE OF DISSATISFACTION

As shown in Exhibit VI-15, the bulk of the underhoused residents are satisfied with their housing accommodations. One out of four is dissatisfied. Dissatisfaction is most closely related to form of tenure and income rather than age or education. Sixty percent of the dissatisfied are renters; 40 percent are owners. Exhibit VI-16 presents the degree of satisfaction by income. As can be seen, the bulk of satisfied respondents earn between $6,000 and $14,999 per year. In contrast, the major source of dissatisfaction occurs in the lower income brackets — those earning under $10,000 per year.

Dissatisfaction also varies with area. The Witherspoon area residents are the most dissatisfied, while the Tree Street area respondents expressed the least discontent. The former area also displays the greatest degree of dissatisfaction; 5.2 percent are *very* dissatisfied. This extreme case is peculiar to the Witherspoon area and emphasizes the differences of dissatisfaction between black and white residents. In contrast, residents of the Linden Lane area exhibit the greatest degree of satisfaction; 35.7 percent of these respondents were very satisfied.

SPECIFIC CAUSES OF DISSATISFACTION

In response to an open-ended question concerning the reasons for discontent among dissatisfied residents, the most frequently mentioned responses were as follows:

Lack of space	21.7 percent
Rent too high	17.4 percent
Landlord doesn't do needed repairs	26.1 percent

EXHIBIT VI-15

DEGREE OF SATISFACTION BY AREA

	Very Satisfied		Satisfied		Dissatisfied		Very Dissatisfied		Total	
	Number	Percent	Number	Percent	Number	Percent	Number	Percent	Number	Percent
Witherspoon Area	5	8.6	37	63.8	13	22.4	3	5.2	58	100.0
Linden Area	5	35.7	6	42.9	3	21.4	0	0.0	14	100.0
Tree Street Area	4	14.8	18	66.7	5	18.5	0	0.0	27	100.0
Total	14	14.1	61	61.6	21	21.2	3	3.0	99	100.0

Source: Underhoused Survey — Summer 1970 — n=100 (Non-responses Excluded)

EXHIBIT VI-16

SATISFACTION WITH PRESENT HOUSING ACCOMMODATIONS BY TOTAL HOUSEHOLD INCOME

	Under $3,000	$3,000-5,999	$6,000-9,999	$10,000-14,999	$15,000-19,999	$20,000-24,999	$25,000-29,999	$30,000 And Over	No Response/ Don't Know	Total
Very Satisfied	1[1]	1	5	4	1	0	0	0	2	14
Satisfied	110	7	16	14	2	0	0	1	11	61
Dissatisfied	4	6	2	1	2	1	0	0	5	21
Very Dissatisfied	0	0	3	0	0	0	0	0	0	3
Total	15	14	26	19	5	1	0	1	18	99
Very Satisfied	7.1[2]	7.1	35.7	28.6	7.1	0.0	0.0	0.0	14.3	100.0
Satisfied	16.4	11.5	26.2	23.0	3.3	0.0	0.0	1.6	18.0	100.0
Dissatisfied	19.0	28.6	9.5	4.8	9.5	4.8	0.0	0.0	23.8	100.0
Very Dissatisfied	0.0	0.0	100.0	0.0	0.0	0.0	0.0	0.0	0.0	100.0
Total	15.2	14.1	26.3	19.2	5.1	1.0	0.0	1.0	18.2	100.0

Source: Underhoused Survey – Summer 1970 – n=100 (Only Non-responses to Income Included)
[1] Number
[2] Percent

Inability to maintain tax payments or complaints that taxes are too high were not major reasons for dissatisfaction except in the Linden Lane area. Isolated responses dealt with general neighborhood dissatisfaction or lack of specific equipment, e.g., air conditioning, within the dwelling unit.

Specific reasons for dissatisfaction differ between renters and owners. The former stress high rents and landlord inattention to repairs, while the latter emphasize annoyances of noise, lack of air conditioning, high taxes and lack of space. Only on the dimension of lack of space do these two groups agree.

Causal analysis reveals basic differences among the areas. The major reason for dissatisfaction within the Witherspoon area is that the landlords do not attend to needed repairs; second to this is the lack of space. Landlord inattention is reflected in the existence of poorly maintained units within this area as was mentioned in the preceding topic. In contrast, two out of the three residents dissatisfied in the Linden Lane area stated that they were unable to keep up the taxes, or that the taxes were too high. The reasons for dissatisfaction in the Tree Street area were mixed and general in nature. Although not recorded as a specific source of dissatisfaction, many residents in the Tree Street area complained about the lack of garage or parking space for their cars. This defect arises from the age of the buildings in that area, the majority of which were built before the auto boom era.

When asked about possible sources of action regarding their dissatisfaction, 52.6 percent said they felt they could do nothing, while only 15.8 percent said they felt they could move. The former response is concentrated in the Witherspoon area, the latter in the Linden Lane area.

POORLY HOUSED AREA OF DISSATISFACTION
VERSUS POCKETS OF RANDOM DISSATISFACTION

A comparison of dissatisfaction within the underhoused area and a random sampling of the entire Princeton community reveals overlapping pockets of dissatisfaction. The major areas of dissatisfaction within the Borough are found in Voting Districts Six and Seven, which correspond almost entirely with the Witherspoon area (Exhibit VI-17). In these voting districts 40 percent and 39.1 percent of the respective respondents are dissatisfied with their housing accommodations. At this point it should be recalled that residents of the Witherspoon area exhibited the most dissatisfaction of all underhoused subareas. Another incidence of random dissatisfaction occurs in Township Voting District Six, corresponding to a portion of the Linden Lane area.

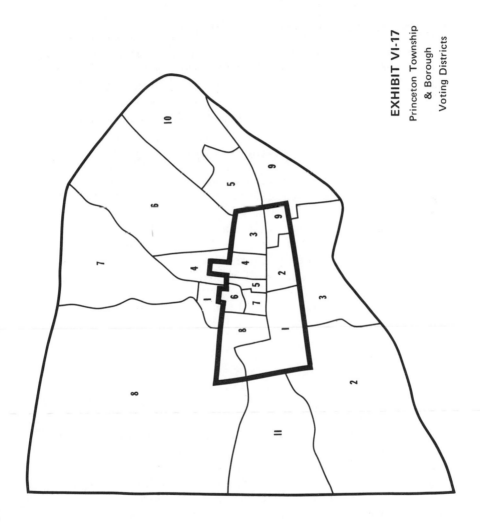

EXHIBIT VI-17
Princeton Township
& Borough
Voting Districts

Areas of overlapping housing satisfaction are also evident. The bulk of Borough Voting District Four and Township Voting District Four, portions of which correspond to the Linden Lane and Tree Street areas respectively, record high proportions of satisfaction.

HOUSING DESIRES OF THE UNDERHOUSED

The housing desires of residents of underhoused areas were abstracted from questions concerning plans for future moves, and the desired type of dwelling units, tenure and amount of space. This section will look at these future needs, make area comparisons, and present a profile of the potential mover. Another sub-section considers the home ownership potential of present renters.

POTENTIAL MOBILITY AMONG THE POORLY HOUSED

As shown in Exhibit VI-18, almost one out of every three households within the underhoused area indicated plans for moving within the next six years. This figure varies among sub-areas. Proportionally, the Witherspoon area exhibits the least potential mobility, with 25.4 percent answering that they had plans to move; the Tree Street area represents that highest mobility potential, with 44.4 percent answering positively. The latter case reflects the area's mixed household composition. The high mobility factor in the Tree Street area complements the high potential of family size change (especially increases) within Voting District Four as reflected in the results of the PRS.

WHAT ARE THE UNMET NEEDS?

The greatest percentage of potential movers, or 38.7 percent, would like the same type of dwelling units as they now have. One out of every four persons in this category is presently living in a detached single-family home. Over one out of every two persons living in a two- to four-family unit cite a desire to live in a detached single-family unit. The preference for garden apartments was surprisingly small, only 6.5 percent, or two households out of the 31. It is noteworthy that there was no desire for two- to four-family units, while 51.6 percent of the potential movers live in this type of dwelling unit. Another important, though small, recurring factor is that two out of the three persons mentioning the "other" category said they wanted to live in a senior citizens housing project.

Potential movers show a preference for home ownership; 56.6 percent wished to own their own homes as opposed to 48.4 percent who wish to rent. There are few differences between present owners and renters although the differential among areas is pronounced. The bulk of the Linden Lane and Tree Street areas would prefer to become renters, while the potential movers in the Witherspoon area desire home ownership.

The greatest demand among the potential movers is for more space. This tendency differs by area and by form of tenure. A higher proportion of renters than owners want more space. Many of the latter desire less space. More space is desired by the potential movers in the Witherspoon area as opposed to less space for those in the Linden Lane and Tree Street areas.

Specific unmet needs of the potential movers in the underhoused area reflect certain characteristics of their present environment. "Movers" in the Witherspoon area stress the need for better housing conditions and interior features, while Linden Lane "movers" want more land, ranch homes and garages.

PROFILE OF THE POTENTIAL MOVER

As shown in Exhibit VI-18, the potential mover in the underhoused area would probably be a renter, under 35 years of age, who works as a white-collar employee and earns $10,000 or more a year. He would probably reside in the Tree Street area. While there are many possible combinations of mover characteristics, the above profile represents the most likely case. Fifty percent of all those who had moving plans are under 35 years of age, 67.7 percent are renters, 43.3 percent are white-collar workers, and 46.6 percent earn over $10,000 a year. The elderly are the most resistant towards moving, as are the homeowners and those earning under $5,999 a year. These residents are trapped in their present dwelling units, regardless of housing desires or satisfactions, because of their age or low incomes. Fifty percent of the dissatisfied within the underhoused area plan to move, while half of these, or 25.3 percent of the satisfied, plan to move.

Fifty-two percent of the potential movers live in two- to four-family units, and the same proportion want to live in detached single-family units. As the number of bedrooms in the present dwelling units increases, the potential for mobility decreases.

RENTERS: HOMEOWNERSHIP GOALS

Buying a home is an important goal for over half of the renters in the underhoused area. Eliminating the Linden Lane area from the comparison because of the small incidence of renters, 60 percent of the Witherspoon area renters as opposed to 43.8 percent of the Tree Street area renters feel that home ownerhip is important. Those under 35 and those earning between $6,000-$9,999 a year feel most strongly about home ownership.

EXHIBIT VI-18

MOVING PLANS DURING THE NEXT SIX YEARS BY AREA AND FAMILY CHARACTERISTICS

AREA AND FAMILY CHARACTERISTICS	Plans to Move In Next Six Years		No Plans To Move		Total	
	Number	Percent	Number	Percent	Number	Percent
AREA						
All	31	31.0	69	69.0	100	100.0
Witherspoon Area	15	25.4	44	74.6	59	100.0
Linden Lane Area	4	28.6	10	71.4	14	100.0
Tree Street Area	12	44.4	15	55.6	27	100.0
N=100						
AGE						
Under 35	15	65.2	8	34.8	23	100.0
35-64	12	29.3	29	70.7	41	100.0
65 and over	3	8.9	31	91.1	34	100.0
N=98 (Non-responses Excluded)						
OWNS OR PAYS RENT						
Pays Rent	21	55.3	17	44.7	38	100.0
Owns or is Buying	10	16.1	52	83.9	62	100.0
N=100						

EXHIBIT VI-18 (Cont'd.)

MOVING PLANS DURING THE NEXT SIX YEARS BY AREA AND FAMILY CHARACTERISTICS

AREA AND FAMILY CHARACTERISTICS	Plans to Move In Next Six Years		No Plans To Move		Total	
	Number	Percent	Number	Percent	Number	Percent
OCCUPATION						
White Collar	13	56.5	10	43.5	23	100.0
Blue Collar	4	33.3	8	66.7	12	100.0
Service Work	6	30.0	14	70.0	20	100.0
Retired, Student, or Unemployed	7	16.3	36	83.7	43	100.0
N=98 (Non-responses Excluded)						
TOTAL FAMILY INCOME PER YEAR						
Under $3,000	3	20.0	12	80.0	15	100.0
$3,000-5,999	2	14.3	12	85.7	14	100.0
$6,000-9,999	10	38.5	16	61.5	26	100.0
$10,000-14,999	8	42.1	11	57.9	19	100.0
$15,000 and over	3	42.9	4	57.1	7	100.0
N=81 (Non-responses Excluded)						

Source: Underhoused Survey — Summer 1970

Sixty percent of the potential buyers feel that they will buy within the next five years, although only 35 percent of these respondents had definite plans to buy within Princeton. A greater proportion of potential movers had definite plans *not* to buy within Princeton.

The reasons cited for negative replies to the question concerning moving within the next five years and buying within Princeton were characteristic of the areas. Those in the Witherspoon area stated that the taxes and homes were too expensive in Princeton, while the Tree Street area respondents cited the lack of permanent job plans. (The latter cases were graduate students.) The higher educational achievement of the renters in the Tree Street area allows a wider range of potential mobility and choice, whereas the low incomes and educational achievement of the Witherspoon area residents limit both mobility and choice.

HOME OWNERSHIP AND THE CAPACITY FOR SELF-HELP HOME IMPROVEMENTS

What, if any, are the inhibitors of home maintenance and improvement in the underhoused areas of Princeton? What influence do taxes and the fear of tax reassessment have? What improvements would be made in an atmosphere free of tax increases? These are some of the issues considered in this section. Comparisons will be made with responses generated from a Newark study designed to answer similar questions.

TAXES AND HOMEOWNERSHIP

To uncover the resident's view of the problems associated with home ownership, maintenance and improvement, all homeowners were asked: "There are many problems in maintaining and improving properties. In the case of your home, how would you rate the following categories in order of importance to you? 1) neighborhood considerations; 2) mortgage costs; 3) tax levels; 4) tax reassessment; 5) housing code and inspection requirements. Exhibit VI-19 presents the results of this question tabulated by area. An inverse rank weighting system was used for presentation. The factor cited by each homeowner as most important was given a weight of five, the second most important was given a weight of four, and so on, until the fifth factor was equated with one. The sum of the weights was then divided by the total number of responses.

Although there are area variations, the major inhibitor of home maintenance and improvement is the tax level, while housing code and inspection requirements are least important. Tax reassessment is ranked equally among all areas; however, its impact is not as dynamic as the tax level. The importance of taxes was also found in the case of small parcel owners in the inner core of Newark: "while of great importance to all groups, their greatest impact (tax levels) is upon small holders..."[11]

A CLOSER LOOK AT HOUSING DEMAND

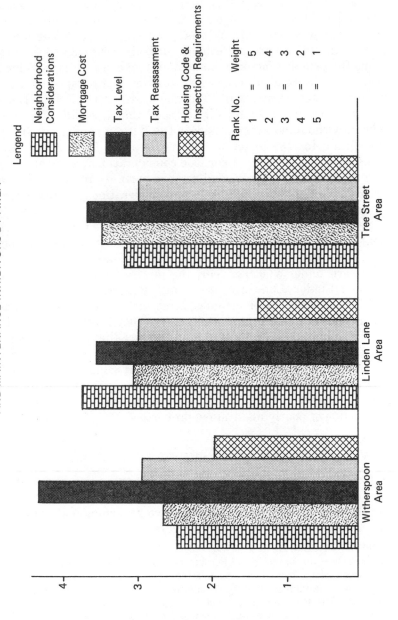

EXHIBIT VI-19

OWNER'S RANK ORDERING OF IMPROVEMENT
AND MAINTENANCE INHIBITORS BY AREA

Lengend

Neighborhood
Considerations

Mortgage Cost

Tax Level

Tax Reassassment

Housing Code &
Inspection Requirements

Rank No.		Weight
1	=	5
2	=	4
3	=	3
4	=	2
5	=	1

Witherspoon
Area

Linden Lane
Area

Tree Street
Area

The Witherspoon and Tree Street areas exhibit similar graphic profiles but a different ordering of the priorities of maintenance and improvement problems. The Witherspoon area presents the most distinct picture of all three areas. Residents of both areas ranked the tax level as being the primary factor in home maintenance and improvement, while there is a difference in the second ranking. Witherspoon area residents cited tax assessments, while mortgage costs were cited by Linden Lane area owners. It is worthwhile to recall that the bulk of elderly homeowners without mortgages reside in the Witherspoon area, thus partially accounting for the difference between areas. In contrast, the Linden Lane owners specify neighborhood considerations as the primary factor, and the tax level as the second most important problem of home ownership. Comparatively, neighborhood considerations are ranked lowest for those owners in the Witherspoon area.

Several implications can be drawn from these area differences. Resident owners in the Witherspoon area, the elderly with low incomes, find that their largest burden is taxes. Because most of the elderly in this area earn under $3,000 a year, the pinch of taxes is most acute. Conversely, Linden Lane area residents, who are generally middle-aged individuals with larger incomes, stress amenities or neighborhood considerations as most important. This tendency is reinforced by the Italian ethnic composition of the area, and the fact that many residents do not speak English. These factors act as a drawstring around the area.

Another point worthy of mention is that while housing code and inspection requirements were cited as the least significant problem, this figure is highest in the Witherspoon area, the area containing the highest proportion of poorly maintained properties.

OWNER'S KNOWLEDGE OF
NONREASSESSABLE IMPROVEMENTS

Exhibit VI-20 presents the owner's responses to a series of questions about the tax impact of a variety of improvements. The data is presented by Borough and Township as these two governing bodies have different tax assessment policies.*

*Phone conversations were held on August 4, 1970, with Mr. Robson and Mr. Paterson respectively of the Township and Borough tax offices. While the former office adheres to a more standardized form of reassessments (i.e., a standard guide book), the Borough handles each case as an individual action. This latter practice is also influenced by the age and condition of the house under question. Borough principles dictate that any improvements which will increase the value of the home necessitates home reasessment. It is also important to note that the Township requires fewer building permits than does the Borough. The former does not require permits for electrical wiring, water heater and central heating improvements, whereas the latter does. The examples cited by the Borough official are generalizations and may vary.

A CLOSER LOOK AT HOUSING DEMAND

EXHIBIT VI-20

OWNER KNOWLEDGE OF NON-REASSESSABLE IMPROVEMENTS
BY TOWNSHIP AND BOROUGH

	Princeton Township		Princeton Boro		Total	
	Number	Percent	Number	Percent	Number	Percent
Repairing Porches, etc.						
Yes, will be reassessed	13	36.1	10	38.5	23	37.1
No reassessment	15	41.7	11	42.3	26	41.9
No Response/Don't Know	8	22.2	5	19.2	13	21.0
Total	36	100.0	26	100.0	62	100.0
Electrical Wiring						
Yes, will be reassessed	2	5.6	3	11.5	5	8.1
No reassessment	26	72.2	20	76.9	46	74.2
No Response/Don't Know	8	22.2	3	11.5	11	17.7
Total	36	100.0	26	100.0	62	100.0
Water Heater						
Yes, will be reassessed	3	8.3	2	7.7	5	8.1
No reassessment	28	77.8	21	80.8	49	79.0
No Response/Don't Know	5	13.9	3	11.5	8	12.0
Total	36	100.0	26	100.0	62	100.0
Central Heat						
Yes, will be reassessed	7	19.4	2	7.7	9	14.5
No reassessment	22	61.1	21	80.8	43	69.4
No Response/Don't Know	7	19.4	3	11.5	10	16.1
Total	36	100.0	26	100.0	62	100.0
Outside Refacing						
Yes, will be reassessed	21	58.3	10	38.5	31	50.0
No reassessment	9	25.0	12	46.2	21	33.9
No Response/Don't Know	6	16.7	4	15.4	10	16.1
Total	36	100.0	26	100.0	62	100.0

Source: Underhoused Survey — Summer 1970 — sub n=62 (Non-responses Included)

First observations reveal variations in responses for individual improvements and in some differences between Borough and Township residents. Note that there is a substantial proportion of "No Response/ Don't Know" answers which increases the percentage of residents possibly inhibited by tax fears.

Similar proportions of Borough and Township owners feel they would be reassessed for porch and step repairs and replacements. Tax authorities in the municipalities say that porch and step repairs are improvements not reassessable in the Borough, but reassessable in the Township.

With respect to internal improvements, including electrical wiring, water heater and central heating improvements, both sets of respondents are aware that such changes are not subject to reassessment. There is little variation between the groups except that a greater proportion of the Township residents think they will be reassessed for central heating improvements. For all three types of improvement, changes can be made without reassessment in both the Township and Borough.

A substantial proportion of residents in both the Township and Borough are aware of the tax reassessable nature of outside refacing. Fifty percent of all owners answered positively. However, Township owners were more aware in this case than were Borough owners. According to tax officials in both areas, this improvement would subject the property to tax reassessment.

A number of homeowners pointed out that they might not get reassessed for a specific improvement at the time of that improvement, but that is was likely that their assessment would increase with periodic city tax reassessments.

These findings lead to the conclusion that reassessment policies tend to defeat home improvements which would most readily enhance the appearance of the whole community.

Further analysis of the data which reveals basic variations among areas is presented in Exhibit VI-21. Linden Lane area homeowners are the most apprehensive about internal improvements, although no reassessments are made in these cases. In comparison, Witherspoon area residents are most aware that external improvements are reassessable.

TAX RELIEF POTENTIAL

Homeowners were asked: "What improvements would you make in this property if you were sure of not getting a boost in taxes?" The results appear in Exhibit VI-22. In all cases, except that of the Linden Lane area, over 50 percent of the owners said they would not make improvements. As would be expected, two out of three of these replies were made by elderly respondents.

The lack of area variation is partially explained by the reason found in the aversion to make improvements despite tax guarantees. Forty-three percent of the respondents in the Tree Street area indicated that their house already had all the necessary repairs done. This rose to 100 percent in the Linden Lane and Witherspoon areas respectively.

Respondents also cite a lack of money and old age as reasons for not improving their homes. However, one set of responses is peculiar to the

EXHIBIT VI-21
OWNER KNOWLEDGE OF NON-REASSESSABLE IMPROVEMENTS BY AREA

	Area 1		Area 2		Area 3		Total	
	Number	Percent	Number	Percent	Number	Percent	Number	Percent
Repairing Porches, etc.								
Yes, Will be Reassessed	18	46.2	2	16.7	3	27.3	23	37.1
No Reassessment	12	30.8	9	75.0	5	45.5	26	41.9
No Response/Don't Know	9	23.1	1	8.3	3	27.3	13	21.0
Total	39	100.0	12	100.0	11	100.0	62	100.0
Electrical Wiring								
Yes, Will be Reassessed	3	7.7	2	16.7	0	0.0	5	8.1
No Reassessment	28	71.8	8	66.7	10	90.9	46	74.2
No Response/Don't Know	8	20.5	2	16.7	1	9.1	11	17.7
Total	39	100.0	12	100.0	11	100.0	62	100.0
Water Heater								
Yes, Will be Reassessed	2	5.1	2	16.7	1	9.1	5	8.1
No Reassessment	32	82.1	9	75.0	8	72.7	49	79.0
No Response/Don't Know	5	12.8	1	8.3	2	18.2	8	12.9
Total	39	100.0	12	100.0	8	100.0	62	100.0
Central Heat								
Yes, Will be Reassessed	6	15.4	3	25.0	0	0.0	9	14.5
No Reassessment	27	69.2	7	58.3	9	81.8	43	69.4
No Response/Don't Know	6	15.4	2	16.7	2	18.2	10	16.1
Total	39	100.0	12	100.0	11	100.0	62	100.0
Outside Refacing								
Yes, Will be Reassessed	21	53.8	6	50.0	4	36.4	31	50.0
No Reassessment	13	33.3	3	25.0	5	45.5	21	33.9
No Response/Don't Know	5	12.8	3	25.0	2	18.2	10	16.1
Total	39	100.0	12	100.0	11	100.0	62	100.0

Source: Underhoused Survey — Summer 1970 — Sub n=62 (Non-responses Included)

EXHIBIT VI-22

TAX RELIEF POTENTIAL HOME IMPROVEMENTS BY AREA

	Addition To House	Exterior Major	Interior Major	Exterior Minor	Interior Minor	None	Total
What Improvements Would You Make If You Were Sure Of Not Getting A Boost in Taxes?							
Witherspoon Area	8[1]	2	1	4	3	19	37
Linden Lane Area	5	1	1	1	0	4	12
Tree Street Area	2	1	0	1	0	7	11
Total	15	4	2	6	3	30	60
Witherspoon Area	21.6[2]	5.4	2.7	10.8	8.1	51.4	100.0
Linden Lane Area	41.7	8.3	8.3	8.3	0.0	33.3	100.0
Tree Street Area	18.1	9.1	0.0	9.1	0.0	63.7	100.0
Total	25.0	6.7	3.3	10.0	5.0	50.0	100.0

Source: Underhoused Survey — Summer 1970 — sub n=62 (Non-responses Excluded)
[1] Number
[2] Percent

Tree Street area. Residents here said they were unable to make additions because of zoning restrictions. While only two owners cited this reason for not making improvements, it is still noteworthy because the owners express a desire to expand and improve their housing but are unable to because of limitations imposed by the intensity of existing land development.

Conversely, 15 out of the 30 owners who replied positively said they would put an addition onto their home. With the exception of the Linden Lane area, there is no significant variation between the areas. In the Linden Lane area, a larger proportion of the owners responded positively, with 62.5 percent desiring home additions.

OTHER INHIBITORS OF HOME IMPROVEMENT

Another obstacle toward home improvement is the inability of owners to secure a long-term mortgage. Would receipt of a long-term mortgage increase the number of owners who make improvements? To research this, homeowners were asked: "Would you improve this property if given a long-term mortgage?" The results were substantially negative; 64.5 percent of the homeowners said they would not make improvements.

Again there is little area differentiation, except that there was a greater degree of uncertainty in the Linden Lane area.

The reasons for the negative answers reflect significant characteristics of the underhoused area. Fifty percent of the respondents gave the same reason as given for the negative replies to the tax potential question — essentially that there were no improvements needed. However, the next largest response centered on the disclination toward another mortgage. This answer was peculiar to Witherspoon area residents, and implies that repayment of past mortgages had been tedious and difficult, and that owners do not want to incur another debt.

Furthermore, those who did not want to improve their property if given a long-term mortgage also said they would not make improvements if given a tax advantage. In contrast, it is noteworthy that five out of ten dissatisfied owners said they would improve their property in both of the above cases.

CONCLUSIONS

That old age acts as an inhibitor of home improvements is quite clear. The reluctance of the elderly to make any further repairs because of lack of funds, desire and/or necessity has also been well documented. At the same time, continued ownership is often the least expensive form of housing for the elderly.[12]

Fear of tax level increases rather than tax reassessment is dominant in the minds of the underhoused respondents. While the great majority of residents are homeowners, their incomes, especially those of the elderly, are generally below $10,000 a year. Home ownership and the burden of high taxes may overstrain some households.

A large proportion of the underhoused dwelling units are in good and, in some cases, excellent condition. Repairs and improvements have been performed continuously whenever necessary. This is reflected in the large incidence of persons answering that "there are no repairs to be made or that all had been done."

Home improvements are not automatically increased by tax-free guarantees or the granting of long-term mortgages. The pockets of the worst housing are those occupied by renters. Questions such as those considered here should be asked of absentee landlords, although it is likely that they respond as have homeowners.

It is the fear of neighborhood impact and even its corollary, failure to secure tenants willing to pay for the improvements, which inhibits improvements. Guarantees against tax increases, even if they were forthcoming and believed, do not necessarily generate a larger rent roll in themselves.[13]

The underhoused area represents a variety of housing conditions and characteristics. Recalling the definition of an underhoused area given in this chapter's background, it is now possible to correlate each segment of the definition with a particular area or areas.

There are pockets of poor housing within the Witherspoon area. Those overcrowded or subjected to an intensity of land development are also found in this area, although this condition is more pronounced in the Tree Street area. All areas are characterized by households "locked into" present residences and neighborhoods because of either economic or racial pressure. This last example is accentuated by the concentration of elderly within the areas. Commonly the market value of a house owned by an elderly person is less than its value as a place to live.

> Typically these properties are old homes, often located in areas no longer considered to be desirable residential areas and frequently run down and neglected because of the physical and financial inability of their owners to maintain them. Thus, these assets often are difficult to convert to cash and when sold do not yield enough to provide suitable new housing.[14]

Comparatively, underhoused area residents are less educated, hold a greater proportion of blue-collar jobs, and have smaller family incomes than other Princeton residents. There is a wide gulf between the median incomes of these groups, $7,700 and $17,500 respectively. Accommodations in the underhoused area reflect the residents' lower financial power and the older physical character of the area. While single-family houses predominate, one-third of all units are two- to four-family structures. This latter proportion is much higher than that found in the remaining community's housing stock.

Good conditions in the housing stock are dependent upon the presence of a resident homeowner; deteriorating housing is concentrated among renters. The neglect in maintenance and improvement is further evidenced by the tenants' voiced dissatisfactions and desires for better housing.

Reviewing the characteristics of the underhoused in relation to the overall Princeton community emphasizes the gap in buying power, and needs and desires which account for the various patterns of housing accommodations. It is obvious that the characteristics of the Princeton community as a whole are at the extreme end of the continuum of socioeconomic and housing traits. This is true even when a comparison is made with other affluent suburbs. But the underhoused do not represent the opposite end of this continuum. Instead, hard-core central city slums such as those found in Newark are characteristic of this extreme. Princeton's underhoused area is somewhere in the middle.

The large proportion of resident homeowners is an important asset to the underhoused area. Yet the problems involving maintenance and improvement pivot around the age of the owners, and incidence of absentee landlords. Fear of tax increases and tax reassessment of home improvements act as inhibitors of such steps. Policy should be addressed to these factors.

When asked what actions the Planning Board would take as a result of this study, 52 percent of the responses were positive, with residents saying they expect more housing or increased concern. The negative replies (paperwork and no action) were concentrated among the black population, reflecting a smaller degree of faith in their ability to be reached through public action initiated by the Planning Board.

This sub-study distinguishes the difference between the underhoused population and the resident population as personified within "The Affluent Suburb" chapter. The socioeconomic characteristics and concomitant immobility of the underhoused limit, if not completely inhibit, their ability to meet current bid prices dictated by the local market forces.

NOTES

1. Fox, Robin: *Kinship and Marriage* (Penguin Books, Baltimore, Maryland, 1967), p. 14.

2. Burchell, Robert W., James W. Hughes, George Sternlieb: *Housing Costs and Housing Restraints:* Newark, New Jersey (Center for Urban Social Science Research, Rutgers University, 1970), pp. 35-36.

3. *Ibid.*, p. 37.

4. *Ibid.*, p. 37.

5. Rapkin, Chester: "Rent-Income Ratio" in *Urban Housing*, edited by Wheaton, Milgram and Meyerson (The Free Press, New York, 1966), p. 169.

6. *Examination of Moderate and Low Income Accommodations*, Alvin Gershen Associates, June 15, 1967, p. 6.

7. *Housing and Urban Development Trends*, Annual Summary, May 1970 (U.S. Department of Housing and Urban Development, Washington, D.C.), p. 49.

8. *Consumer Expenditures and Income, Northern New Jersey, 1960-1961,* BLS Report No. 337-63 (U.S. Department of Labor, Bureau of Labor Statistics, December 1963), p. 13.

9. *Supra,* p. 117.

10. Sternlieb, George: *The Tenement Landlord* (Rutgers University, New Brunswick, N.J., 1966), p. 176.

11. Sternlieb, *op. cit.,* p. 212.

12. Niebanck, Paul L.; *The Elderly in Older Urban Areas* (Institute for Environmental Studies, University of Pennsylvania 1965), p. 56.

13. Sternlieb, *op. cit.,* p. 223.

14. U.S. Senate, The Subcommittee of Housing for the Elderly, "Housing for the Elderly," in *Urban Housing,* edited by Wheaton, Milgram and Meyerson (The Free Press, New York, 1966), p. 223.

Chapter VII
THE MUNICIPAL EMPLOYEES

Perhaps the most difficult area of housing need is that generated by the burgeoning middle class. The private market alone has been called upon in the great majority of cases to ferret out and answer this difficult area of individual and group need.*

Yet it is essentially the middle class in Princeton, possbily as a forerunner of a national trend, for which the market has ceased to provide sufficient housing. There have been requests that the enabling elements of extra-market subsidy be applied to aid the local elements of a struggling middle class. In most instances this has been directed to specific segments of the community's municipal employee population.

If housing is to be provided either for a particular group or within a specific economic range, it becomes necessary to know the socioeconomic characteristics of those for whom it is being provided, the type and price of shelter the group now occupies, whether assistance is deemed appropriate or necessary by the potential clients and, possibly, if it can be measured, an indication of attitude of the group for which the effort is

---

*The provision of F.H.A. financing which helped fuel the middle-income housing boom of post World War II days is no longer an adequate bridge between the middle incomed and construction costs.

EXHIBIT VII-1

MUNICIPAL EMPLOYEE SAMPLE STRUCTURE

SAMPLE STRUCTURE

Municipal Employee Group	Population	Sample	Percent Sample	Weighting	Adjusted Sample	Adjusted Percent Sample	Population Residence Outside/Inside Community	Sample Residence Outside/Inside Community
Teachers[1]	342	39	11.5	2	78	23	180 / 162	22 / 17
Police	54	13	24	1	13	24	20 / 34	6 / 7
Other White Collar Staff[2]	84	18	22	1	18	22	46 / 38	10 / 8
N, n, n(Adj.)	482	70			109			

[1] Includes all instructional staff, senior administrative personnel at *local* schools, and school related specialists i.e. psychologists, librarians, speech therapists.
[2] Includes all white collar personnel at local municipal offices plus an additional segment found specifically in the Regional School Board offices.

Source: Municipal Employees Survey — Summer 1970

to be made. In a nutshell, this is the charge given to this section.

The municipal employee survey consisted of 70 in-depth interviews with three groups of municipal employees, sampled according to their specific representation in the overall employee population (Exhibit VII-1). Three groups were chosen; teachers, police and "other" white-collar municipal staff.† Each group received an adjusted sample of approximately 23 percent of their local total, further subdivided in relation to existing community residence/non-residence ratios.

In pursuit of the charge, the intent was to measure not only housing-related social and economic dimensions but, in addition, to survey employee attitudes toward housing, jobs and the community of their employ.

The results which follow are contained in four subsections: socio-economic characteristics, housing, opinions on residence and the attitude of municipal employees.

THE SOCIOECONOMIC PROFILE

PLACE OF RESIDENCE

By far the most popular municipal employee residences in the areas which surround the Princeton community are those immediately to Princeton's southeast or southwest (Exhibit VII-2). Seventy-two percent of the teachers, all of the policemen and 90 percent of the white-collar staff who were surveyed and found to live outside of Princeton, chose one of these two areas. In over half of the cases the reason specified was either single-family housing value or the availability of multifamily rentals.

The communities to the south and east, i.e., Cranbury, East Windsor, West Windsor, Plainsboro, Hightstown, Skillman and Jamesburg offered in 1960 [1] a housing base similar to Princeton's (5,000 dwelling units), yet this base has increased at four times Princeton's rate over the period 1960 to 1966. [2]

To the south and west, Lawrence, Pennington, Hopewell Township, Ewing, Trenton and Hamilton offer a substantial housing stock of 68,000 dwelling units, [3] to which an additional 10,500 units have been added over the period 1960 to 1966. [4]

In both areas, multifamily development has taken place at the rate of at least 50 percent of all housing units put in place since 1960. [5] This has

†Blue-collar staff were eliminated from the survey due to a desire to concentrate the sample in areas where the economic gap between potential housing costs and municipal employee salaries was the least. It should be noted, however, that the percentage of blue-collar workers living within the community is on a par with other groupings of municipal employees.

EXHIBIT VII-2

PLACE OF RESIDENCE BY MUNICIPAL EMPLOYEE TYPE

EMPLOYEE TYPE	Franklin, Rocky Hill, So. Brunswick, East Brunswick	Hightstown, Cranbury, E. Windsor, W. Windsor, Plainsboro, Skillman, Jamesburg	Lawrence, Pennington, Hopewell Township, Ewing, Trenton, Hamilton	Hopewell Borough, Montgomery Township, Amwell, Flemington	Princeton Borough	Princeton Township	Penn.	Other Distant N. J.	Total
Teachers	6[1]	14	18	2	18	16	2	2	78
Police	0	2	4	0	3	4	0	0	13
Other White Collar Staff	0	5	4	1	2	6	0	0	18
Total	6	21	26	3	23	26	2	2	109
Teachers	7.7[2]	17.9	23.1	2.6	23.1	20.5	2.6	2.6	100.0
Police	0.0	15.4	30.8	0.0	23.1	30.8	0.0	0.0	100.0
Other White Collar Staff	0.0	27.8	22.2	5.5	11.1	33.4	0.0	0.0	100.0
Average	5.5	19.3	23.9	2.8	21.1	23.9	1.8	1.8	100.0

Source: Municipal Employee Survey — Summer 1970 — n=70 — Teacher sub n x 2

[1] Number
[2] Percent

supplemented the middle-income market to an extent far in excess of Princeton's. In 1969 a newly constructed 120-unit development in East Windsor carried an average rent of $151 per month for a two-bedroom unit. [6] This was approximately 70 percent of the cost for comparable but more dated units in Princeton Borough at the same time. [7]

Few (8.3 percent) municipal employees seek areas either to Princeton's northeast or to its northwest. Even fewer (3.7 percent) seek other more distant New Jersey areas or the suburban communities of neighboring Pennsylvania. The ideal place for the non-resident appears to be outside the inflated Princeton housing market, so reducing cost, yet sufficiently close to permit reasonable commuting schedules. This finding was supported by a survey conducted by the Princeton Regional Education Association in which 50 percent of the non-Princeton-residing local teachers were surveyed and reported an average commuting distance to 12 to 13 miles and a range, in 95 percent of the cases, of between 5 and 22 miles.

LENGTH OF RESIDENCE

Length of stay within the current community of residence is relatively low for municipal employees (Exhibit VII-3). Both police and white-collar staff had residence medians of below four years. Only teachers were slightly less transient, with a median of 6.3 years.

This apparently high transiency, almost double that in the Princeton community itself, may be attributed to the high non-primary labor force participation in the case of teachers and white-collar staff and to the relative youth of both local police units. In the former instance, the nomadic following of the employment of the head of the household contributes to transiency; whereas in the latter, recent or contemplated marriage and the accompanying changes in shelter requirement produces a similar effect.

There also appeared to be a noticeable "settling" period evident among the bulk of more senior municipal personnel. These people, experiencing the latter stages of the reshaped household, could not afford the luxury of excess space and were either ridding themselves of this burden or converting it to income-providing rental space. In many cases this adjustment also contributed to "group" transiency figures.

MARITAL STATUS

There were no great differences in the marital status of specific segments of the municipal employee population, between resident and non-resident elements, or between the group as a whole and that of the Princeton community (Exhibit VII-3). Minor differences show the marital status of the teachers to be very close to figures representing the com-

EXHIBIT VII-3
LENGTH OF RESIDENCE IN COMMUNITY AND MARITAL STATUS
MUNICIPAL EMPLOYEES AND PRINCETON COMMUNITY
RESIDENCE — 1970

| | **LENGTH OF RESIDENCE** | | | |
| | Municipal Employees | | | |
	Tea Teachers	*Police*	*Other White Collar Staff*	*Municipal Employees*
Median in Community (Years)	6.3	3.8	3.7	4.7

| | Princeton Residents | | |
	Princeton Borough	*Princeton Township*	*Princeton Community*
Median in Community (Years)	9.0	8.0	8.3

| | **MARITAL STATUS** | | | |
| | Municipal Employees | | | |
	Teachers	*Police*	*Other White Collar Staff*	*Municipal Employees*
Single	12.8	15.4	16.7	13.8
Married	79.5	84.6	72.2	78.9
Divorced/Widowed	7.7 (2.6D) (5.1W)	0.0	11.1 (5.6D) (5.5W)	7.3 (2.7D) (4.6W)
Total	100.0	100.0	100.0	100.0

| | Princeton Residents | | |
	Princeton Borough	*Princeton Township*	*Princeton Community*
Single	16.2	9.8	12.4
Married	64.4	81.8	74.7
Divorced/Widowed	19.4 (4.2D) (15.2W)	8.4 (4.2D) (4.2W)	12.9 (4.3D) (8.6W)
Total	100.0	100.0	100.0

Source: Present Resident/Municipal Employee Surveys — Summer 1970)

EXHIBIT VII-4

**MARITAL STATUS AND RESIDENCE OF TEACHERS IN THE PRINCETON REGIONAL SCHOOL
SYSTEM — 1966 AND 1970**

| | THOSE LIVING IN PRINCETON | | | | THOSE LIVING OUTSIDE PRINCETON | | | | TOTAL | |
| | Married | | Single | | Married | | Single | | | |
SEX	Number	Percent	Number	Percent	Number	Percent	Number	Percent	Number	Percent
Male										
1966[1]	21	(17.2)	8	(6.6)	86	(70.5)	7	(5.7)	122	(100.0)
1970[2]	23	(21.3)	10	(9.3)	65	(60.1)	10	(9.3)	108	(100.0)
Female										
1966	102	(49.5)	17	(8.3)	69	(33.5)	18	(8.7)	206	(100.0)
1970	106	(45.3)	23	(9.8)	76	(32.5)	29	(12.4)	234	(100.0)

[1] Results of League of Women Voters Survey — Winter 1966-67 — p. 6-7
[2] Princeton Regional Schools Staff Directory 1969-70 — p. 1-28

Source: Municipal Employee Survey — Summer 1970

EXHIBIT VII-5

TOTAL HOUSEHOLD INCOME BY MUNICIPAL EMPLOYEE TYPE

EMPLOYEE TYPE	HOUSEHOLD INCOME						
	Under $10,000	$10,000- 15,999	$16,000- 20,999	$21,000- 30,999	Over $31,000	No Response/ Don't Know	Total
Teachers	4[1]	26	16	26	4	2	78
Police	2	8	2	1	0	0	13
Other White Collar Staff	4	5	5	4	0	0	18
Total	10	39	23	31	4	2	109
Teachers	5.1[2]	33.3	20.5	33.3	5.1	2.6	100.0
Police	15.4	61.5	15.4	7.7	0.0	0.0	100.0
Other White Collar Staff	22.2	27.8	27.8	22.2	0.0	0.0	100.0
Average	9.2	35.8	21.1	28.4	3.7	1.8	100.0

Source: Municipal Employee Survey — Summer 1970 — n=70 (Non-responses Included) —
Teacher sub n x 2

[1] Number
[2] Percent

munity mean. Police evidence slightly higher marital homogenity, and white-collar staff include a greater proportion of young singles.

In the case of teachers, detailed results obtained using the Princeton Regional School Staff Directory for 1969-70 are not too dissimilar from those obtained via a survey conducted by the Princeton League of Women Voters three years ago.[8] Their analysis here provides insight into residency choice and marital status not available for the other two groups of municipal employees (Exhibit VII-4). Of the increasing proportion of single teachers, Princeton, as opposed to "outside Princeton," appears to be attracting a proportionate share of males, yet only about half of the respective increase in single females. Perhaps the ability of single males to reside in inferior yet economical quarters in Princeton's underhoused areas largely accounts for this difference.

FAMILY INCOME

The median family income of municipal employees is unusually high ($16,980, Exhibit VII-5), as close to 60 percent of the teachers and 33 percent of the white-collar staff surveyed are two-income families. In the case of teachers, this is almost twice the percentage of dual wage earners in the local Princeton community.

While the dual working role is a common phenomenon in the early and latter stages of marriage, during the child-rearing period the family usually must rely solely upon the primary income. The monthly housing expenditure reflects this dependence on one income as is evidenced by a *$15,000* difference in median *housing value* between municipal employees and Princeton community residents. The difference between median *family incomes* for municipal employees and other Princeton residents is only *$520* a year.

Thus, the $12-$14,000 median for *head-of-household's* income is what the municipal employee relies upon for regular income and draws on for recurring housing expenditures. While this salary median is a representative figure of the various aspects of municipal employ, it currently is only 75 percent of the median in evidence in the Princeton community.

SIZE OF HOUSEHOLD

Municipal employee household size is approximately 3 percent smaller than that currently found in the Princeton community (Exhibit VII-6). To a large extent this figure is kept low by the small size of teaching families, 64 percent of whom reported household sizes of two or less. Police, who have household sizes and numbers of children approximately one greater than teachers, are still only 20 percent above the local community mean.

As one might surmise, public school usage by municipal employees is also less than that found in the community as a whole (Exhibit VII-7). Teachers and white-collar staff contribute approximately 0.6 children per household to the local school system, while police double this figure. At this rate, the municipal employee mean of 0.65 children per household is still 10 percent less than that currently found in the local population.

MUNICIPAL EMPLOYEE HOUSING

The underlying dimensions of the Princeton municipal employee's housing environment are ascertained principally via the Municipal Employee Survey. Of the defining elements, two in particular provide the firmest basis of differentiation — housing type and housing cost. These two parameters are the elements initially examined in this section. Other important housing dimensions do exist, however, and these are subsequently considered. Housing satisfaction in terms of particular accommodations, the basic rationale for residence selection in terms of community, and the current propensity for the reshaped household are all

EXHIBIT VII-6

MEDIAN INCOMES AND MEAN HOUSEHOLD SIZE OF MUNICIPAL EMPLOYEES AND PRINCETON COMMUNITY RESIDENTS — 1970

| | *FAMILY INCOME* | | | |
| | Municipal Employees | | | |
	Teachers	*Police*	*Other White Collar Staff*	*Municipal Employees*
Median Income	$18,500	$13,375	$16,000	$16,980
		Princeton Residents		
	Princeton Borough		*Princeton Township*	*Princeton Community*
Median Income	$13,290		$21,075	$17,500

| | *HOUSEHOLD SIZE* | | | |
| | Municipal Employees | | | |
	Teachers	*Police*	*Other White Collar Staff*	*Municipal Employees*
Mean Household Size	2.87	3.76	2.94	3.00
		Princeton Residents		
	Princeton Borough		*Princeton Township*	*Princeton Community*
Mean Household Size	2.81		3.35	3.14

Source: Present Resident/Municipal Employee Surveys — Summer 1970

integral components of the overall housing picture. Consideration of all these factors provides a synthesis of the municipal employees' residential milieu.

TYPE OF HOUSING

The residential composition of the greater Princeton community, as established in the section on housing supply, reveals that 75 percent of total housing units are in single-family dwellings, 8.5 percent in two-family and 16.5 percent in multifamily accommodations. Exhibit VII-8 shows almost an identical pattern of housing types used by municipal employees — 77.1 percent reside in single-family dwellings, 5.5 percent

EXHIBIT VII-7

NUMBER OF CHILDREN UNDER AGE 18 AND PUBLIC SCHOOL USAGE — MUNICIPAL EMPLOYEES AND PRINCETON COMMUNITY RESIDENTS — 1970

	NUMBER OF CHILDREN UNDER AGE 18			
	Municipal Employees			
	Teachers	*Police*	*Other White Collar Staff*	*Municipal Employees*
Per Household Mean	0.64	1.69	1.05	0.84
	Princeton Residents			
	Princeton Borough		*Princeton Township*	*Princeton Community*
Per Household Mean	0.80		1.30	1.11

	PUBLIC SCHOOL USAGE			
	Municipal Employees			
	Teachers	*Police*	*Other White Collar Staff*	*Municipal Employees*
Per Household Mean	0.56	1.22	0.61	0.65
	Princeton Residents			
	Princeton Borough		*Princeton Township*	*Princeton Community*
Per Household Mean	0.55		0.89	0.75

Source: Present Resident/Municipal Employee Surveys — Summer 1970

in dwellings containing two, three and four housing units and 17.4 percent in apartment house accommodations. Thus, despite slight variations between category percentages, the existing composition of the Princeton housing market is identical to the residential housing preferences of the Princeton municipal employee.

Also of remarkable similarity is the breakdown of residential types within the municipal employee subpopulations. For each of three categories, i.e., teachers, police and white-collar staff, the percentage of residential forms used vary, at the most, by 1 percent. Viewing this same subject by community/non-community residence shows a concentration of apartment dwellers in the non-Princeton areas. This at first blush

EXHIBIT VII-8

TYPE OF RESIDENCE BY MUNICIPAL EMPLOYEE TYPE

EMPLOYEE TYPE	TYPE OF RESIDENCE			
	Single Family House	2-3-4 Family House	Apartment House	Total
Teachers	60[1]	4	14	78
Police	10	1	2	13
Other White Collar Staff	14	1	3	18
Total	84	6	19	109
Teachers	76.9[2]	5.1	17.9	100.0
Police	76.9	7.7	15.4	100.0
Other White Collar Staff	77.8	5.6	16.7	100.0
Average	77.1	5.5	17.4	100.0

Source: Municipal Employee Survey — Summer 1970 — n=70 — Teacher sub n x 2
[1] Number
[2] Percent

suggests that there is an imbalance in the local market showing either a preponderance of rental units in other communities or a shortage of these units in Princeton. Previous research bears out the existence of both situations.

FINANCIAL CHARACTERISTICS

Although great similarities by type are evident in the above comparisons, serious variations are evident when the financial structure of municipal employee housing is compared to the Princeton community. While the median housing value for the residences of the municipal employees exceeds $35,000, the corresponding figure for the average Princeton resident is $50,000 (Exhibit VII-9).

This disparity of more than $15,000, if assigned to the municipal employee, would reflect an increase of over 43 percent in total current housing cost for this population subgroup. Translated into monthly mortgage payments, the Princeton employee pays $193 a month while Princeton residents as a whole pay $248. Although this difference is only 28.5 percent, it should be recalled that double the proportion of Princeton residents live in homes with no mortgage than do municipal employees. The decrease in mortgage magnitudes may possibly be explained in terms of

EXHIBIT VII-9

FINANCIAL CHARACTERISTICS OF MUNICIPAL EMPLOYEE DWELLING UNITS

MEDIAN VALUES — 1970

EMPLOYEE TYPE/PRINCETON COMPARISON

FINANCIAL INDICATORS	Teachers	Police	Other White Collar Staff	Municipal Employees	Princeton Community	Municipal Employee Increase Over What Currently Paying
Housing Value	$35,640	$32,500	$36,250	$35,400	$50,590	43%
Gross Rent[1]	$ 140	$ 125	$ 88	$ 131	$ 174	33%
Mortgage Payments	$ 207	$ 172	$ 182	$ 193	$ 248	28.5%

[1] Renters are in small proportion — n (3-16) may be too small to generalize

Source: Municipal Employee Survey — Summer 1970

larger initial down payments by Princeton residents, or perhaps an earlier period of mortgage commitment. (The average Princeton resident, with a much greater longevity in terms of place of residence, may have incurred a mortgage before the surge of interest rates in the late 1960s and/or have substantially amortized it.) No matter what the specific reasons, the fact remains that municipal employee who seeks home ownership within the Princeton community would experience a vast housing cost increase for accommodations comparable to those outside Princeton.

The same situation applies to those municipal employees classified as renters. While the average employee pays $131 in rent, the corresponding community resident pays $174, an incremental difference of $43 in absolute terms, or 33 percent. Again, considering comparative residential facilities, the municipal employee who specifically seeks Princeton as his community of residence would experience a substantial increase in rental payments.

In both the rental and home ownership categories considerable cost differences exist between the average municipal employee and the Princeton community resident. There are also noticeable differences between the costs assumed by the various types of municipal employees. Basically these differences parallel those previously noted in family incomes. Teachers with higher family incomes pay more for housing than do white-collar workers and police. These slight variations in housing cost by municipal employee profession are the same for municipal workers who live in and out of the Princeton community. A great disparity remains, however, between the municipal employee and the average Princeton resident. This situation is reflected for each sub-group of municipal worker whether considered in isolation or in total.

RESIDENTIAL SATISFACTION

Two principal dimensions of the municipal employee housing picture have been compared to the corresponding components of that of the Princeton community. By type, little difference was exhibited. On the other hand, cost differentials were found to be significant. Residential satisfaction, considered here, shows results of the latter type. In Chapter I of this report it was established that almost 88 percent of the respondents to the PRS exhibited satisfaction with their current housing, i.e., a dissatisfaction rate of 12 percent. Turning to Exhibit VII-10, those municipal employees residing within the Princeton community reveal dissatisfaction at a rate of almost 21 percent, while only 10 percent of similar employees living outside show dissatisfaction.

A CLOSER LOOK AT HOUSING DEMAND

EXHIBIT VII-10

HOUSING SATISFACTION BY COMMUNITY RESIDENCE

	RESIDENCE		
	Princeton Residence	Non-Princeton Residence	Total Number Average Percent
Satisfied	39[1]	54	93
Dissatisfied	10	6	16
Total	49	60	109
Satisfied	79.5[2]	90.0	85.6
Dissatisfied	20.5	10.0	14.4
Total	100.0	100.0	100.0

Source: Municipal Employee Survey — Summer 1970 — n=70 — Teacher sub n x 2
[1] Number
[2] Percent

Overall the 14.4 percent municipal employee dissatisfaction mean is not too dissimilar from the 12.4 percent figure found within the Princeton community. Yet this combined figure should not obscure the dissatisfaction of the municipal employees living in the Princeton community compared to those living outside. Such feelings demand close scrutiny prior to policy considerations concerning employee residential location. Perhaps the following analysis will assist in elucidating the various causative agents.

RATIONALE FOR COMMUNITY SELECTION

An interesting bifurcation of results is evident when examining community selection rationale (Exhibit VII-11). Those municipal employees who reside in Princeton said their rationale for community selection was because of the local environment or local attachment (these latter characteristics measured by "place of birth or early rearing"). Over 59 percent expressed these two reasons. Conversely, the non-Princeton residents' reasons for selection was commonly because of financial considerations, with almost 47 percent strictly expressing a concern for housing value. This compares to a percentage of zero for the corresponding reason by the employee who resides in Princeton.

EXHIBIT VII-11

REASON FOR SELECTING COMMUNITY OF RESIDENCE BY COMMUNITY RESIDENCE

| | Housing Value | Local Environment | *REASON FOR COMMUNITY SELECTION* | | | | | |
			Place of Birth Or Early Rearing	Commuting Convenience	School System	Municipal Requirement	Other	Total
Princeton Residence	0[1]	13	16	14	4	2	0	49
Non-Princeton Residence	28	4	11	11	3	1	2	60
Total	28	17	27	25	7	3	2	109
Princeton Residence	0[2]	26.5	32.6	28.6	8.2	4.1	0	100.0
Non-Princeton Residence	46.7	6.7	18.3	18.3	5.0	1.7	3.3	100.0
Average	25.7	15.5	24.7	22.9	6.4	2.8	1.8	100.0

Source: Municipal Employee Survey — Summer 1970 — n=70 — Teacher sub n x 2
[1] Number
[2] Percent

EXHIBIT VII-12

MUNICIPAL EMPLOYEE HOUSING SELECTION PROFILE

*If 100 Municipal Employees Newly
Entering the Public Job Market Were
Seeking Housing Locally:*

25	Would *not* look for housing in Princeton because they already lived there. (All would reside in Princeton)
13	Would *not* look for housing in Princeton because for personal reasons they would prefer not to live in Princeton. (All would settle elsewhere)
13	Would *not* look for housing in Princeton because they knew housing would not be available at prices they could afford. (All would settle elsewhere)
22	Would look for housing in Princeton and be disappointed because of its specific non-availability. (All would settle elsewhere)
13	Would look for housing in Princeton, occasionally find what they were looking for yet in most instances find much better housing value elsewhere. (Seven would settle elsewhere)
14	Would look for housing in Princeton, find suitable quarters and remain within the community. (All would reside in Princeton)

Source: Municipal Employee Survey — Summer 1970

Thus the financial dimension, highlighted previously in terms of Princeton/non-Princeton housing costs, again makes its presence powerfully felt. Consequently, this is one of the principal causes of the housing dissatisfaction noted above.

Exhibit VII-12 portrays the magnitude and direction of the housing selection decision should 100 new municipal employees of characteristics similar to the sample come to the local housing market. Two points to be noted here are: 1) If existing figures are valid a significant percentage of potential municipal employees already live in Princeton and require

EXHIBIT VII-13

THE MUNICIPAL EMPLOYEE RESHAPED HOUSEHOLD

	Static Households	Increasing Households	Decreasing Households	Total
	Municipal Employees			
Percent of Total Households	69.7	20.2	10.1	100.0
	Princeton Community			
Percent of Total Households	61.6	15.8	22.6	100.0

Source: Municipal Employee Survey — Summer 1970

no new housing; 2) other than these, only one out of every four would wind up living within the community.

THE RESHAPED HOUSEHOLD

When the municipal employee reshaped household is viewed (Exhibit VII-13), one finds a reverse percentage of municipal employee households that are in the family expansion stage of the life cycle (increasing households) than is evident in the corresponding category of Princeton community households. This may be an indication of increased space necessities of this employee subgroup and, again, a possible contributory element to the exhibited dissatisfaction. In total, younger household structures appear to be associated with municipal employees (90 percent static or expanding) than they do with local community residents (77 percent static or expanding). This again points to the phenomenon of the largest space requirements being associated with those least able to afford it.

In summation, it is possible to take a position with regard to the municipal employee housing situation in much the same fashion as was done with their household characteristics. With the possible exception of the reshaped household, very little difference exists between the needs of this group and those of the population at large. The overriding difference, which, not incidentally, is reinforced by locational preference, is one of economics. A 30 percent gap exists between the housing that is available locally and the ability of the municipal employee to pay for it. This is clearly exhibited between community and municipal employee cost means and further in a cost differential within the municipal employee subgroup between those who do and those who do not choose to live in Princeton.

THE MUNICIPAL EMPLOYEE VIEW

ON LIVING WITHIN THE COMMUNITY OF THEIR EMPLOY

When municipal employees were asked whether they *should* live within the community of their employ, less than 60 percent believed that this was necessary. Responses from teachers, police and white-collar staff were essentially the same; however Princeton resident and non-resident replies were slightly different. Of the municipal employees currently residing in Princeton, almost 70 percent thought that living and working in the same community was a healthy situation. Of those who live outside, this same degree of certainty was expressed by only slightly over half of the respondents (Exhibit VII-14).

EXHIBIT VII-14

MUNICIPAL EMPLOYEE TYPE BY THE NECESSITY TO RESIDE WITHIN THE COMMUNITY OF THEIR EMPLOY

EMPLOYEE TYPE	Do You Think { Teachers / Police / Municipal Workers } Should Live Within The Community In Which They Work?			
	Yes	No	Mixed Feelings	Total
Teachers	44[1]	30	4	78
Police	7	5	1	13
Other White Collar Staff	11	6	1	18
Total	62	41	6	109
Teachers	56.4[2]	38.5	5.1	100.0
Police	53.8	38.5	7.7	100.0
Other White Collar Staff	61.1	33.3	5.6	100.0
Average	56.9	37.6	5.5	100.0

Source: Municipal Employee Survey — Summer 1970 — n=70 — Teacher sub n x 2
[1]Number
[2]Percent

The results expressed here are not unlike those found by the Princeton Regional Educational Association in a similar survey in 1969:

The opinion that it would be a good idea for teachers to have the opportunity not the obligation to live in Princeton was expressed by *80 percent* of the non-resident primary wage earners. That opinion was shared by a *majority* of the teachers who live in Princeton as well as non-resident teachers who are secondary wage earners. [9]

Our municipal employee survey attempted to refine the answers somewhat, by calling for a structured conclusion on the part of the person interviewed. This was attempted with the question "Is it necessary for municipal employees to live within the community of their employ?" rather than a policy-evoking question such as "Do you think municipal employees should have the opportunity, not the obligation, to live in Princeton?" The former type of question, as previous figures indicate, commands a slightly smaller following, yet hopefully this lack of support is replaced by a stronger indication of feeling on policy.

ON WHETHER THEIR NINE TO FIVE JOB IS AFFECTED BY NON-RESIDENCE

When the three groups of municipal employees were asked whether municipal job performance was affected by non-community residence 85 percent of the police and 65 percent of the teachers and white-collar staff resoundingly answered "no"! (Exhibit VII-15).

This apparent inconsistency with previous percentages expressing favorable attitudes toward living in the community of their employ will be explained in the section concerning municipal employee views on extra-job responsibility. Suffice it to say here, that there is a distinction made between after-hour activities and the regular work-day duties of municipal employees. Municipal employees are not affected by community non-residence in the performance of their normal working day duties. However, after-hour activity in Princeton will be curtailed by non-residence.

Returning once again to the nine to five regular working period, police felt that they could actually be more impartial in the bulk of their routine calls or summons-issuing assignments if they lived outside the community. Teachers felt in many cases that living outside has no effect on class performance, yet offered the benefit of a respite from both the activity of the working day and the noticeable pressure of the encroaching academic environment. Finally, white-collar workers said that, barring certain positions, municipal employ was no different than any other

EXHIBIT VII-15

THE EFFECTS OF NON-RESIDENCE ON WORKING DAY JOB EFFECTIVENESS BY MUNICIPAL EMPLOYEE TYPE

| | Do You Think Living Outside of Princeton Limits The Effectiveness of a { Teacher / Policeman / Municipal Worker } ? | | | | |
	Yes	No	Depends Upon The Individual	Undecided	Total
Teachers	28[1]	48	2	0	78
Police	2	11	0	0	13
Other White Collar Staff	5	13	0	0	18
Total	35	72	2	0	109
Teachers	35.9[2]	61.5	2.6	0.0	100.0
Police	15.4	84.6	0.0	0.0	100.0
Other White Collar Staff	27.8	72.2	0.0	0.0	100.0
Average	32.1	66.1	1.8	0.0	100.0

Source: Municipal Employee Survey — Summer 1970 — n=70 - Teacher sub n X 2

[1] Number
[2] Percent

organizational or industrial job and that, in their case, job responsibility terminated with the working day and could be performed equally well regardless of place of residence.

These feelings were brought out in further cross-tabulations by Princeton/non-Princeton residence. In both residence areas, only 32 percent of the respondents stated that place of residence and job effectiveness were linked to any substantial degree, and there appeared no evidence that municipal employees currently residing in the Princeton community actively supported their locational decision for reasons of job effectiveness.

ON THE RESPONSIBILITIES AND COMMITMENT OF A MUNICIPAL WORKER

Specific ideas concerning responsibilities and the degree of commitment of municipal workers were solicited from the three groups of mu-

EXHIBIT VII-16

RELATIONSHIP TO PRINCETON AS A COMMUNITY BY MUNICIPAL EMPLOYEE TYPE

| | | *RELATIONSHIP TO PRINCETON* | | | | | |
| | | *Employee With Many Extracurricular Activities* | | | | | |
EMPLOYEE TYPE	Employee 9.5	Concerned Yet Inactive Member Of Its Working Populace	Profes-sion-ally Related	Non-Profes-sion-ally Related	Both	An Active Aid To Community Leadership	Total
Teachers	10[1]	10	20	8	24	6	78
Police	3	5	0	1	3	1	13
Other White Collar Staff	4	3	1	6	3	1	18
Total	17	18	21	15	30	8	109
Teachers	12.8[2]	12.8	25.6	10.3	30.8	7.7	100.0
Police	23.1	38.5	0.0	7.7	23.1	7.7	100.0
Other White Collar Staff	22.2	16.7	5.6	33.3	16.7	12.5	100.0
Average	15.6	16.5	19.3	13.3	27.5	7.3	100.0

Source: Municipal Employee Survey — Summer 1970 — n=70 - Teacher sub n X 2

[1] Number
[2] Percent

nicipal employees. The responses showed little geographic significance compared to the differences accruing along professional lines. Teachers, perhaps due to structured extracurricular requirements, appear to be heavily involved with the community of their employ. This is apparent both for those who live outside as well as for those inside Princeton.

Exhibit VI-16 indicates that only 26 percent of the teachers surveyed said that their total job responsibility fell within the nine to five working period or that they were concerned, yet inactive, members of the local populace.

Police (especially patrolmen) felt that their main involvement with the community was during their working day or shift period. Over 61 percent reported general inactivity beyond the normal working period and in most cases classified themselves as concerned yet relatively inactive citizens. Police reported a much more favorable reaction to returning home and being sufficiently distant to be "off call" than to being within the community of their employ and participating in local rescue squad or volunteer fire department activities.

White-collar workers were found somewhere between the police and teacher extremes. The bulk of these people have the least mandatory professional attachment to the community, yet in a few instances their specific jobs contain significant post-working day responsibilities. Administrators, municipal engineers, public works supervisors, social workers, recreation directors, etc., are generally on call and in many cases spend substantial periods of "free" time in municipal business.

Frequently this professional attachment, as in the case of teachers, leads to other community oriented non-professional activities. To this group add municipally employed wives of active local citizens and subtract the clerks, engineering assistants, librarians, etc., whose jobs require little if any post-working day allegiance, and you arrive at a very mixed group. Yet this group, which claims in 40 percent of the cases that it is relatively inactive, evidences three times the rate of its nearest competitor in *non-professional* extracurricular activity.

An interesting situation arises when the question of the existence of extra-job responsibility (beyond the 9 to 5 working period) is put to the three groups (Exhibit VII-17). Teachers, who appear to be the most actively involved in post-job community activities, were the last ones to say that this form of municipal allegiance should be considered a "job responsibility" (75 percent). Police, who reported themselves as relatively inactive, are the leading force in the recognition of an "extra-job" responsibility (85 percent). White-collar workers, again probably due to their diversity, simply fall between the two other municipal employee extremes.

These descrepancies may possibly be explained by the job Princeton requires of these municipal employees, as opposed to that required by other communities. With the possible exception of the narcotics problem and instances of local student unrest, Princeton has a relatively low crime rate and even lower incidence of serious crime. Princeton is a comparatively safe environment for both police and local citizenry. The oft-repeated value of having a policeman living down the street still prevails as an unchallenged goal, yet the necessity for its fulfillment is not locally evident. With the limitations of local housing economics and a low crime rate, an off-duty, non-investigative arrest is rare although most police feel they have a natural post-job responsibility to be near the community.

Teachers feel a definite professional challenge in choosing to work within the Princeton community. In most instances they attempt to be

EXHIBIT VII-17

FEELINGS CONCERNING EXTRA-JOB RESPONSIBILITY BY MUNICIPAL EMPLOYEE TYPE

Do You Believe That There Exist Other Responsibilities To The Community By Whom You Are Employed That Extend Beyond The Regular 9 To 5 or Shift Work Period?

	Yes	No	Depends Upon The Job	Total
Teachers	58[1]	20	0	78
Police	11	2	0	13
Other White Collar Staff	14	4	0	18
Total	83	26	0	109
Teachers	74.4[2]	25.6	0.0	100.0
Police	84.6	15.4	0.0	100.0
Other White Collar Staff	77.8	22.2	0.0	100.0
Average	76.1	23.9	0.0	100.0

Source: Municipal Employee Survey — Summer 1970 — n=70 - Teacher sub n X 2

[1] Number
[2] Percent

well prepared for scheduled class sessions and are more than willing to meet with students during periods beyond the normal working day. Based on interviews, it appears, however, that this post-job counseling is more frequently sought by Princeton parents than it is by parents in other communities. While teachers will devote extra time professionally if called upon, by no means do they wish this to be classified a routine or recurring "professional duty."

Since there were varied attitudes concerning extra-job responsibility within the municipal employee professions, attempting to ascertain whether this was effected by place of residence did not follow traditional breakdowns. Only those municipal employees who recognized the existence of extra-job responsibility were sought as respondents to this somewhat limited subject (Exhibit VII-18). From these individuals the strongest support for the necessity of community residence was recorded to date. Close to 70 percent stated that community residence materially affected their ability to pursue extra-job responsibilities.

This topic, although considered last, serves to tie the basic subject matter of this section together. If one were to summerise the impact of

EXHIBIT VII-18

EXTRA-JOB RESPONSIBILITIES BY THE EFFECT OF NON-COMMUNITY RESIDENCE

Do You Believe That There Exist Other Responsibilities To The Community By Whom You Are Employed That Extend Beyond The 9 to 5 Or Shift Work Period?	Does Living Outside The Community Hinder These Responsibilities?		
	Yes	No	Total
Yes	58[1]	25	83
No	0	26	26
Total	58	51	109
Yes	69.9[2]	30.1	100.0
No	0.0	100.0	100.0
Average	53.2	46.8	100.0

Source: Municipal Employee Survey — Summer 1970 — n=70 - Teacher sub n X 2

[1] Number

[2] Percent

Exhibits VII-14 through VII-18, it would be that Princeton, though unable to offer housing at acceptable prices to its municipal workers, appears not to be suffering from a reduced individual performance during the working day. There appears to be no massive support within the municipal employee group itself for either the necessity for community residence or its positive effect on job performance.

With regard to "extra-job responsibility," there appears, however, to be an identifiable loss. Princeton benefits, though, from those municipal workers who are so involved professionally that their non-professional attachments also are directed to the community of their employ. Due to a relatively low local crime rate and a community-wide educational interest, the teacher rather than the policeman is sought for assistance after the normal working day. It is interesting to note, however, that more policemen than teachers feel that this extra duty is a definite part of their job responsibility, and would be receptive, though would probably not volunteer, for additional extra-job assignments. Part of this attitude is evidenced in the police's recent youth and narcotics activities, and may prove to be the best current indicator of the results of their previous under-utilization.

Of those municipal workers who believe that extra-job responsibility is material, a solid block has been formed behind the need for community residence. The decision to be made here concerns the value to be placed upon this goal. Is there sufficient evidence that in municipal response this is a necessary asset and not just a "folksy" convenience? Finally, does the cost of pursuing this goal endanger the pursuit of the required daily performance of each of these municipal servicing agents?

THE ATTITUDE OF THE MUNICIPAL EMPLOYEE

The attitude of municipal employees, within the limits of this study, must be viewed via very crude measurement instruments. The approach employed here is the direct questionnaire. In this case, municipal employee attitudes are categorized according to responses to questions dealing with both their social and physical environments. Attitudes are analyzed principally in relation to housing and desire to live within the community.

IS THE COMMUNITY OF LOCAL EMPLOY
A PRESTIGIOUS ONE?

This question was asked of municipal employees in an effort to characterize the meaning of Princeton to the municipal employee and possibly bring to the surface any existing latent hostility. "Prestigious community," a frequently employed realty description of Princeton was used as the initial stimulus.

The responses to this question by municipal-employee type were quite varied. Teachers gave the term "prestige" when related to Princeton its least academic and most negative meaning (Exhibit VII-19). Close to 57 percent of the teachers surveyed stated that the prestige of Princeton either was nonexistent, or frequently took the form of local snobbishness. Approximately 20 percent recognized its existence in the form of wealth or affluence, and only a slightly larger percentage associated prestige with academia or Princeton University.

To white-collar workers, moreover, the "prestige of Princeton" was definitely academic. A significant proportion of this group (39 percent) also had trouble in recognizing its existence locally, yet a clear majority (44 percent) identified it and subsequently associated it with the University.

Police had still another interpretation of local prestige. Almost without question they associated its local presence with wealth or affluence. To police, if Princeton received any type of national reputation, it would be in terms of the economic achievements of its local populace.

EXHIBIT VII-19

THE MEANING OF THE PRESTIGE OF PRINCETON BY
MUNICIPAL EMPLOYEE TYPE

	What is the First Thing Which Comes to Mind When Someone Mentions the "Prestige" of Princeton?			
Employee Type	Wealth or Affluence	The University or Academia	Snobishness or Distaste	Non-Existence or Untruth	Total
Teachers	16[1]	18	20	24	78
Police	8	4	0	1	13
White Collar Staff	3	8	3	4	18
Total	27	30	23	29	109
Teachers	19.5[2]	23.1	25.6	30.8	100.0
Police	61.5	30.8	0.0	7.7	100.0
White Collar Staff	16.7	44.4	16.7	22.2	100.0
Average	24.8	27.5	21.1	26.6	100.0

Source: Municipal Employee Survey — Summer 1970 — n=70 - Teacher sub n X 2 .

[1] Number

[2] Percent

The recognition or non-recognition of the prestige of Princeton, as well as its three interpretations, provide an interesting view of the overall community. Any hostility evidenced was in most cases found within the teacher subgroup. This generally took the form of a distaste engendered by an inattention to children by parents concerning non-academic matters. In some cases teachers felt that local affluence was a casual agent leading to parent inattentiveness which subsequently caused significant permissiveness in local youth. It was their opinion that Princeton had gone past the norm with regard to this matter.

IS PRINCETON A GOOD PLACE
TO BE A MUNICIPAL WORKER?

In 95 percent of the cases municipal workers responded affirmatively to this question. The only negative responses were received from teachers, who felt that parents were too concerned with the academic success

EXHIBIT VII-20

REASONS WHY PRINCETON IS A GOOD PLACE TO BE A MUNICIPAL WORKER IN BY MUNICIPAL EMPLOYEE TYPE

| | *Princeton Provides a Satisfactory Working Environment Because of:* | | | | | |
	The Attitude of Its Populace	Its Abundance of Physical Facilities	The Education Level of Its Populace	The Attitude of Surrounding Co-Workers	No Response/ Don't Know	Total
Teachers	24[1]	16	28	4	0	72
Police	5	6	2	0	0	13
White Collar Staff	5	5	4	3	1	13
Total	34	27	34	7	1	103
Teachers	33.3[2]	22.2	38.9	5.6	0.0	100.0
Police	38.5	46.2	15.4	0.0	0.0	100.0
White Collar Staff	27.8	27.8	22.2	16.7	5.6	100.0
Average	34.3	25.3	33.1	6.4	0.9	100.0

Source: Municipal Employee Survey – Summer 1970 – n=70 – Teacher sub n x 2

[1] Number
[2] Percent

of their children, and as such unduly burdened the teacher with post-working day counseling while shortchanging the child in other areas.

This response, however, was by far the exception and not the rule. In most instances, teachers, as well as all other municipal employees, lauded Princeton as a place of employment, specifically because of either the attitude or the education stimulation of its local populace (Exhibit VII-20). Teachers, police and engineers alike stated that they enjoyed "rising to the occasion" of their specific jobs, which were made challenging particularly by the interest expressed by community members. To a somewhat lesser extent, the abundance of physical facilities was mentioned, and in this category was included the safety element attested to by local police. Of overwhelming significance here are not the individual reasons but rather the singular affirmation of satisfaction expressed by Princeton municipal workers.

LOCAL HOUSING CONCERN

While reacting positively to the local populace in terms of providing favorable working atmosphere, municipal workers returned to earth when appraising the extent of local concern for their unfulfilled housing needs. On this point, there was no internal variation between municipal employee subgroups (Exhibit VII-21). Seventy-five percent of all workers stated that there was no concern evident locally for municipal employee housing. It should be noted that this is not a blanket condemnation of the Princeton populace but rather a realistic appraisal of the need for such action and its past lack of input.

Municipalities such as Irvington, and Jersey City, New Jersey, have recently been publicized for their significant percentages of municipal employees who live outside the community of their employ. [10] In these communities, municipal employees face a housing situation diametrically opposed to the one found in Princeton. Municipal employees can afford to live within the community, but for personal reasons choose to live outside. (In Princeton, municipal employees generally cannot afford to live in the community and by default must live outside.)

While much less publicized, equal percentages of Princeton municipal employees live outside their community. Contrary to local belief, in many instances this is also by choice. Regardless of the situation, however, the basic problem is no less real, and plausible remedies no less evasive.

In the previous chapter additional light has been cast on at least one aspect of the subject. In Princeton it has been found that municipal employees must increase present expenditures by 25 to 30 percent either to purchase housing or rent locally. No case has been found for increased

EXHIBIT VII-21

PRINCETON POPULACE CONCERN WITH MUNICIPAL EMPLOYEE
HOUSING BY MUNICIPAL EMPLOYEE TYPE

	Do you Think That the Princeton Populace is Concerned About Municipal Workers Housing/Lack of Housing Within the Community?					
	Yes Abun-dantly	Yes Super-ficially	No	Undecided	No Response/ Don't Know	Total
Teachers	10 [1]	2	58	6	2	78
Police	2	1	10	0	0	13
White Collar Staff	4	1	12	1	0	18
Total	16	4	80	7	2	109
Teachers	12.8 [2]	2.6	74.4	7.7	2.6	100.0
Police	15.4	7.7	76.9	0.0	0.0	100.0
White Collar Staff	22.2	5.5	66.8	5.5	0.0	100.0
Average	14.7	3.7	73.3	6.4	1.9	100.0

Source: Municipal Employee Survey — Summer 1970 — n=70 - Teacher sub n X 2

[1] Number
[2] Pencent

nine to five employee effectiveness as a result of community residence. There is no massive support (among municipal employees) for the necessity of residency, and, finally, there appear to be no significant attitude differences accruing along residence breakdowns which supersede those found along professional lines.

The only apparent loss to the community due to the non-residency of its municipal employees is a resultant lack of extracurricular participation. To the degree that the purcuit of these extracurricular activities becomes a high priority community goal, the problem of residency choice of municipal workers grows in its importance.

One factor appears to transcend the economic differences of a Jersey City or an Irvington and those of Princeton. Housing dissatisfaction is significantly higher for those who are required to live locally, than it is for those who pursue residency according to the market.

A CLOSER LOOK AT HOUSING DEMAND

NOTES

1. *New Jersey Census of Housing 1960* — Research Report #140 (New Jersey Department of Conservation and Economic Development, November 1965), pp. 18-19.

2. *New Jersey Housing and Dwelling Units 1960-1966* — Research Report #148 (New Jersey Department of Conservation and Economic Development, November 1965), pp. 40-43.

3. *New Jersey Census of Housing 1960, op. cit.,* pp. 18-19.

4. *New Jersey Housing and Dwelling Units 1960-1966, op. cit.,* pp. 40-43.

5. *New Multi-Family Dwellings in New Jersey 1967 and Other Years* (State of New Jersey Department of Community Affairs), 1967, pp. 33-36.

6. *Ibid.,* p. 34.

7. See the realty page of *The Princeton Packet* (Weekly — September to December 1967).

8. "Units on Housing — Teacher Survey" (60 Percent Sample) (League of Women Voters, Winter 1966-1967), p. 6.

9. "A Survey of Teacher Opinion" (Princeton Regional Educational Assoication, February 20, 1970), Summary Sheet, p. 2.

10. Hays, Daniel: "Cops, Firemen Living Out of Town Checked" (The Newark Evening News, September 30, 1970), p. 17; Meridith G. Thomas: "Six Firefighters Are Suspended" (The Newark Evening News, October 6, 1970), p. 28.

SUMMARY OF FINDINGS

Present Residents

— Identifiable and different class concentrations are found in both the Borough and Township. The Township is an exclusive home for the highly paid business executive or senior researcher, while the Borough provides a representative portion of its housing to the lower income service worker, domestic, laborer and student.

— There appears to be a uniform recognition of an insufficient supply of local rental units. The recognition of this factor tends to transcend all economic and tenurial groups.

— Housing dissatisfaction throughout the community is relatively slight. The dissatisfaction which does occur is found primarily among Borough lower-middle-class residents.

Housing and Land Inventory

— Princeton Borough's residential usage at extant permissible densities has reached 90 percent of capacity. Princeton Township is currently at 75 percent of its zoned housing potential.

— Princeton's current housing stock consists of 7,300 units of which approximately 75 percent are single-family units.

— From 1960 to 1970 little growth has been evidenced in the Borough. The Township's residential growth, although reduced both absolutely and relatively from the past decade, continues.

— Median dwelling unit construction cost in the Princeton community has doubled over the last ten years. The magnitude of this increase has been contributed to jointly by inflation and the increased housing desires of the Princeton buyer.

— Limited available land and the dominance of individual ownership outside the commercial core will preserve the existing character of the Borough's housing stock. Significant amounts of developable land held by various categories of receivers throughout the Township provide extensive alternatives for future development.

The Local Employers

— Surrounding local employers generate two-thirds of the total demand upon Princeton's housing stock. Finance insurance and real estate and educational and research firms are key to the major portion of this demand.

— Firms attracted to the area specifically because of the resources of Princeton are using other communities to house the vast majority of their personnel.

— Housing assistance in any form is generally not provided by local employers, nor is the local housing situation presently considered a limiting factor in job expansion.

— In order to maintain present usage ratios in the light of internal expansion and expectations of future competition, annual local housing construction will have to increase five-fold.

— The realities of the local market will generate more limited use of Princeton's stock by local employers and an increasing homogenity of the ultimate users.

The Newcomers

— There is an absence of low and moderate income families in the newcomer population, which leads toward an increasingly homogeneous wealthy community. The few low and moderate income families are renters concentrated among the Princeton University affiliates.

- The high purchase price of homes and lack of sufficient rental units is an inhibiting factor for the potential low and moderate income mover.

- There is a high degree of intra-versus extra-Princeton mobility. Almost one-third of the newcomer households previously lived in Princeton, while the remaining households represent a diverse pattern of previous locations.

- The most frequent cause of housing mobility is a job change, more so among renters than owners.

- The influence of Princeton University is clearly reflected in the high incidence of Princeton-contract holders among the newcomer renters.

The Reshaped Household

- Changes in household size within the next ten years will affect 38 percent of the households in Princeton. The majority of these potential changes will be decreases rather than increases in family size.

- Proportionally, the household of increasing size is more frequent in the Borough than Township, while the Township has a greater share of decreasing households.

- The reshaping process will cause 56.6 percent of local reshaped households to move into different housing accommodations. Forty percent of these expressed an intention to move away from the community.

- Mobility is greatest among increasing households who are predominately renters of two- to four-family units and apartments.

- Both sets of households desire home ownership and single-family units. Rental properties are desired primarily by decreasing families who are presently renting.

- There is a tendency among decreasing households to maintain larger units than what is "necessary" for their needs in relation to family size. This characteristic is strongly related to single-family home ownership.

- Deficiencies within the Princeton housing market as inhibitors of future plans were cited by 50 percent of the potential reshaped households.

The Underhoused

- One-half of the underhoused households are black, the bulk of whom are resident owners.

— The majority of the underhoused in Princeton own their own housing — often free of mortgages.

— The aged are a significant proportion of the owners. Regardless of the availability of financing, they are uninterested in home improvement investments.

— Incomes in the underhoused area are concentrated below $10,000 per year.

— The proportion of income spent on rent decreases as income increases; however, one-third of the sample renters spend 30 percent or more of their income for rent.

— Accommodations in the underhoused area reflect the residents' modest financial power and the older physical character of the area.

— Good housing conditions are dependent upon resident home ownership; deteriorating housing, accounting for 20 percent of the sample units, is concentrated among the rental units.

— Residential dissatisfaction is closely related to form of tenure and income.

— Financing help in itself will not generate rehabilitation.

— A major inhibitor of home maintenance and improvement is the uncertainty of local tax administration and rate increases. Fear of reassessment, especially on external improvements, dominates this uncertainty.

The Municipal Employee

— Approximately one-half of the Princeton municipal employee population currently resides outside the local community.

— Those who live outside the community do so specifically for housing value. Those who reside inside Princeton have lived there prior to price inflation or more recently sought out the community for its aesthetic or social environment.

— Housing dissatisfaction related to physical space, housing type or form of tenure is twice as prevalent among resident as non-resident municipal employees.

— Head of household's income for municipal workers as a group and Princeton residents generally differs by more than 25 percent.

— Municipal employee housing expenditures reflecting head of household's income are 30 percent less than those of Princeton residents.

— A majority of municipal employees believe community residence is desirable; however, very little support is given to the positive effect of local residence on nine to five job performance.

— Non-community residence has its most severe effect on the post-job community activities of municipal workers. This is Princeton's most severe loss in its current inability to house its municipal working force.

APPENDICES

Appendix 1:
METHODOLOGY

CHAPTER I: THE AFFLUENT SUBURB

Current social and economic characteristics of the Princeton populace were determined by a probability sample of 501 interviews. The sample was termed the Present Residents Survey (PRS) and was drawn from the Suburban Trenton New Jersey Bell Telephone Directory (February 1970), utilizing a specific proportion of singly listed 924 or 921 residential numbers.

In an effort to gain a perspective of 1970 residential Princeton the study attempted to sample the permanent resident households of both Township and Borough. This methodology excluded undergraduate and graduate dormitory residents of the three Borough educational institutions (Princeton University, Westminster Choir College, Princeton Theological Seminary). All faculty and married and single non-dormitory students residing in Princeton were considered, however, as part of the universe to be sampled.

This encompassed households including members of the Institute for Advanced Study or Defense Analysis, Princeton University's graduate student projects and the residences on Stockton Street maintained by the Seminary.

Employing this methodology resulted in a 60/40 division in favor of the Township. This is approximately the same as the relationship of total Township and Borough populations indicated by the 1970 Census.

Of a potential number of 819 Princeton households so selected, 501 interviews were successful. The difference between the attempted and completed sample is presented in Exhibit I-A. Basically it is the attempted sample minus refusals, "not at homes" (after four call backs) and a miscellaneous category consisting of non-residential numbers, disconnections and a few aborted interviews due to the inability to converse in a common language.

EXHIBIT I-A

ANALYSIS OF PRESENT RESIDENTS TELEPHONE SURVEY
PRINCETON BOROUGH AND TOWNSHIP - 1970

Numerical Summary

Phone call completions (total No. of successful interviews)		501
Completions on first attempt	390	
Completions via call back	111	
Phone call non-completions		318
Refusals	120	
Disconnects	26	
No response after four call backs	107	
Other	65	
Inability to understand language		
Professional phone not indicated by directory		
Princeton listing yet non-Princeton address		
Phone call attempts		819

Percentage Breakdown

Completions based on attempts		61
Completed on first attempt	48	
Completions via call back	13	
Non-completions based on attempts		39
Refusals	15	
Disconnects	3	
No response after four call backs	13	
Other	8	
Total		100

Source: Princeton Housing Study - Summer 1970

APPENDIX I

CHAPTER II: THE LAND AND
HOUSING INVENTORY

The land and housing inventory basically is an effort to determine the quantity and type of housing supplied locally over the past decade and the amount of land which remains for future development.

As an estimate of the quantity of housing supplied since 1960, building permits were tabulated in both the Township and Borough. Conversions and demolitions were respectively added to and substracted from newly put-in-place stock to calculate net residential gain. Construction costs over the given time period were placed in cohorts by year in an effort to supplement the analysis by tracing trends in the cost of new housing over time. Finally, 1960-1970 trends were projected to 1980 for a rough approximation of the future cost of local housing.

The land inventory involved surveying all vacant land in both municiplities after updating Borough and Township residential land use maps. To this land survey, after corrections were employed for wastage due to the floodway, road usage and platting inefficiencies, the existing zoning was applied in an effort to calculate each community's current residential holding capacity.

CHAPTER III: THE INSTITUTIONAL
EMPLOYERS

In attempting to ascertain the demand created by local institutional employers, those of the surrounding area were broken down by five of the eight Standard Industrial Classifications. (Agriculture, construction and mining were not utilized in the former cases due to lack of local growth, and in the latter, with the exception of the Kingston Trap Rock Quarry, due to local nonexistence.)

Six basic modular types were formulated from the five SIC categories: Large Manufacturing; Small Manufacturing; Transportation, Communication and Utilities; Finance, Insurance and Real Estate; Wholesaling and Retailing; and, finally, the Service Industry.

For each modular type an employment profile was developed; a survey of their current utilization of local housing was taken; and an indication of future growth and anticipated new competition obtained.

The population from which selected firms were taken was composed of those employers who physically reside within the boundaries of the Princeton community and additionally, of those who are within a ten mile radius to the north, south and east, and five miles to the west.

Fifty firms were then selected primarily by size and purpose as representative of six modular categories. A series of interviews with the personnel director of each firm was conducted. A minimum of six each were conducted with Princeton's non-institutional modular types, while the remainder (approximately 32) heavily documented the community's industrial life blood, i.e., its service and research firms.

CHAPTER IV: NEW HOMEOWNER/RENTER

In this portion of the study Princeton's rental, new construction and resale markets were closely scrutinized. One hundred of the most recent home buyers and renters were interviewed to answer such questions as: Who are they? Where are they from? What type of residence do they need?

Names of new homeowners over the period 1969-1970 were obtained from the Mercer County tax records and subsequently segregated according to the listed sale price of the housing transaction. A 20 percent sample was taken from each price category until the contracted 50 unit quota had been reached. These homeowners were then contacted by telephone and interviewed utilizing an instrument of approximately 40 questions. This questionnaire employed similar segments as did those for the present residents, municipal employees and underhoused sections of the study so comparisons could be made if desired.

Similarly, 50 new renters over the same one-year period were interviewed via an identical instrument; however, the structuring of the sample was somewhat less pure. Originally the study group sought to obtain lists of new users from the New Jersey Bell Telephone Company and the Public Service Gas and Electric Company. These lists were not made available, however, and new lists had to be compiled from a combination of cross-tabbing out "renters — residing in Princeton under a year" and additional information obtained from local realty agencies. Given this limitation, renters in small private homes, in most cases whose dwelling was not on the commerical market (a fairly common occurrence in Princeton), were under-represented in the sample.

CHAPTER V: THE RESHAPED HOUSEHOLD

The prevalence of the reshaped household in Princeton was projected from the probability sample. Once these households were isolated and further classified as those of either the reduced-size or augmented variety, the socioeconomic profiles and housing requirements were scrutinized and compared to those of the larger, resident population. Specific areas of potential transiency (i.e., the geographical location of reshaped households) were mapped and analyzed utilizing the SYMAP program.

CHAPTER VI: THE UNDERHOUSED

The underhoused areas within Princeton were specifically delineated by members of the Princeton Regional Planning Board. Three specific areas were chosen as being representative of the basic definition of an underhoused population.

Housing in the three main areas was inventoried on a block-by-block basis. The sample size, set at one hundred by contract, was apportioned among the areas in such fashion that 12 percent of the housing stock in each area was surveyed.

Door-to-door interviews employing a questionnaire were conducted and a superficial inspection made of both interior and exterior condition of the parcel. Via this methodology 59 parcels were sampled in the Witherspoon area, 14 parcels in the Linden Lane area, and 27 parcels in the Tree Street area.

The interviews and inspections sought to isolate the social, economic and housing profiles of specific community subsectors and additionally to determine the presence/non-presence of housing dissatisfaction and its causal influences.

CHAPTER VII: THE
MUNICIPAL EMPLOYEE

A representative sample (approximately 23 percent) of permanent Borough and Township employees were interviewed in depth to determine their feelings concerning job and extra-job responsibility, residence within the community of their employ, the attitude and interest of the Princeton populace and housing deficiencies incurred as a result of the Princeton municipalities as a place of current livelihood.

Municipal employees as a whole were subdivided into categories of teachers, police and other white-collar staff. Borough and Township personnel as well as Princeton residents and non-residents were sampled proportionately. Seventy interviews were undertaken, comprising 40 teachers, 13 policemen and 17 administrative personnel. Each interview was conducted utilizing an instrument of approximately 25 questions. Copies of the questionnaires are available at cost from the Rutgers Center for Urban Policy Research.

Appendix II:

MISCELLANEOUS NOTES

A NOTE ON SYMAP

SYMAP is a computer program for producing maps which graphically depict spatially disposed quantitative and qualitative information. It is suited to a broad range of applications, and is provided with numerous options to meet widely varying requirements.

Raw data of every kind when given to the computer may be manipulated in any manner desired. By assigning values to the coordinate locations of data points or data zones one or more of three types of maps may be produced.

TYPES

The Contour Map

The contour map consists of closed curves known as contour lines which connect all points having the same numeric value or height. Contour lines emerge from a datum plane at selected levels which are determined from the scale of the map and the range of the data. Between any two contour lines a continuous variation is assumed.

The Conformant Map

The conformant map is best suited for data, either qualitative or quantitative whose areal limits are of significance, and whose representation as a continuous surface is inappropriate. Each data zone is enclosed by a boundary conformant to some predefined spatial unit. The entire spatial unit is given the same value, and symbolism is assigned according to its numeric class.

The Proximal Map

The proximal map is very similar in appearance to the conformant map. However, the spatial units are defined by nearest neighbor methods from point information. Each character location on the output map is assigned the value of the data point nearest to it. Boundaries are assumed along the line where the values change.

PROCEDURES

In the Princeton study each household was given a set of X and Y geographic coordinates and utilized as a data point. The Official Map of Township and Borough was chosen to provide both the enclosing boundaries and specific location of each data point.

Contours and proximal surfaces were developed for specific variables according to the particular visual effect desired. In some cases, due to lack of local development, the visual presentation was formulated upon only limited information. This is a weakness of the data point option chosen by the study group; however, in some measure it is compensated for by the numerous presentations available from this type of information (i.e., specific household data versus a mean or median for a geographical area). By using the sample data point map in conjunction with the presentation of key variables, specific cases of under-representation may be clearly isolated.

A NOTE ON POPULATION PROJECTION

One of the most important keys to understanding Princeton is a thorough analysis of its population. The population mix of the overall community is considerably more complex than a mere summing of current census totals for both municipalities would indicate. Thus, in an attempt to better understand the nature of the data and in so doing become more familiar with the subject of study, a population projection was undertaken utilizing the information obtained from the PRS.

PROCEDURES

As Exhibits II B to D indicate, the method employed was to obtain an estimate of the percentage of "good" (Princeton-residential) numbers drawn from a random selection of unrefined Princeton numbers, multiply this by the mean number of Princeton listings per page, and finally multiply this by the total number of pages devoted to residential listings. The figure obtained here was termed the "telephone population." To this were added local estimates (New Jersey Bell Telephone Company) of both non-user and non-published rates. The overall population was then divided between Township and Borough according to respondent's location obtained via both a completion and non-completion analysis.

A NOTE ON THE HOUSING DEMAND OF PRINCETON BASED EMPLOYERS

In the course of analyzing the results of this study, it was brought to the attention of the study group that it would be interesting to view housing

EXHIBIT II - B

PRINCETON POPULATION PROJECTION

	Calculating the "Good Number" Percentage
819	Number of singlely listed 924 or 921 numbers with Princeton addresses which were not apparently commercial nor specially Princeton listed.
-53	Number of attempted calls which were subsequently found to be professional phones or Princeton listed residential phones not actually within municipal limits. ("Bad" calls)
-8	Number of "not at homes" after four call backs adjusted by the "bad" call percentage (Not at homes are assumed "good" numbers other than being adjusted by the known percentage of "bad" calls) $(107)\ (0.077)\ =\ 8$
-2	Number of disconnects (assuming equal replacement) adjusted by the "bad" call percentage $(\ 26)\ (0.077)\ =\ 2$
756	The total number of Princeton residents households based upon 819 attempts
$\dfrac{756}{819}\ =\ 0.925$	The "good" number percentage

Source: Princeton Housing Study - Summer 1970

EXHIBIT II - C

PRINCETON POPULATION PROJECTION

The Telephone Household Population Estimate

The "good" number percentage	X	Mean number of Princeton listings per page	X	Total number of white pages devoted to residential listings
0.925	X	61.0	X	110

Telephone Household Population = __6200__

The Total Household Population Estimate

Telephone Household Population +	Non-Published Population +	Non-User Population
Telephone Household Population +	(Telephone)(Local Non-) (Population)(Published) (Percentage)	+ Telephone (Local Non- (User Per- centage)
6200 +	6200 (0.075)	+ 6200 (0.025)
6200 +	465	+ 155

Total Household Population = __6820__

Source: Princeton Housing Study - Summer 1970

---

demand created solely by the demands of employers located within the bounds of the Princeton community itself. This would be ideal to demonstrate, for instance, the ramifications of a community goal which might seek to provide "sufficient housing to meet the future needs of all Princeton based employers."

PROCEDURES

For this analysis, the growth means and housing utilization rates previously established for the local employer modules were maintained and Princeton's physical share of the surrounding employment market used to modify previously calculated total local housing demand.
Exhibit II-E, which follows, projects housing demand generated by Princeton employers according to these ratios. In effect, the previous local housing demand *increase* from 1970 to 1975 is adjusted by Princeton's representation is the surrounding employer population and the resulting figure added to the 1970 base.

It should be noted that local zoning will exclude the entrance of large manufacturing firms, yet small manufacturing related to commercial

EXHIBIT II - D

PRINCETON POPULATION PROJECTION

The Borough-Township Share (by %)

Population division evidenced via 501 completions	61.5	Township
	38.5	Borough
Population division evidenced via 255 refusals, disconnects, not at homes, and non-translatables	51.5	Township
	49.5	Borough
Weighted population division as a result of both a completion and a non-completion analysis	58.0	Township
	42.0	Borough

Borough-Township Estimate

Borough Population Estimate

Borough Share	X	Total Number of Households	X	Mean Household Size	+	Students in Group Quarters Under 452 or Non-Private Exchange
0.420	X	6820	X	2.81	+	3860
					=	11,920

Township Population Estimate

Township Share	X	Total Number of Households	X	Mean Household Size	+	Students in Group Quarters Under 452 or Non-Private Exchange
0.580	X	6820	X	3.34	+	300
					=	13,500

Source: Princeton Housing Study - Summer 1970

retail sources most likely will be permitted. All other employer categories are permitted land uses under local codes. There are also sufficient amounts of vacant land zoned for non-residential uses to accommodate projected levels of employer growth.

RESULTS

The Princeton housing demand figure of approximately 6,600 units reflects an increase in housing demand of approximately 47 percent of what was previously calculated for local employers (Princeton's firms and those of other neighboring communities affecting Princeton's housing market.) The 1970 to 1975 housing demand is still two and one-half times the 1970 to 1975 supply and, assuming a bidding up of housing costs, forbodes increasing affluence and homogeneity of population in both Borough and Township.

EXHIBIT II-E

HOUSING DEMAND OF THE PRINCETON BASED EMPLOYERS

METHODOLOGY LEADING TO A DEMAND CALCULATION

EMPLOYER MODULE	Housing Demand Increase Previously Projected for Module Owner	Renter	Princeton's Local Zoning Limits Growth to Internal or Internal Growth Plus Competition	Princeton's Representation in the Population of Local Firms Considered	Housing Demand Generated by Princeton Employers 1975-(a) Owner	Renter	Housing Demand Generated by All Employers 1970-(b) Owner	Renter	Housing Demand in 1975 with Princeton Employers Only (a+b) Owner	Renter
Small Manufacturing	36	0	Growth & Competition	0.58	21	0	26	0	47	0
Large Manufacturing	87	14	Growth Only	0.06	5	1	216	36	221	37
Transportation, Communication and Public Utilities	48	24	Growth & Competition	0.33	16	8	72	24	88	32
Finance, Insurance and Real Estate										
Banks	34	2	Growth & Competition	1.00	34	2	86	4	120	6
Other F.I.R.E.	72	0	Growth & Competition	0.45	32	0	180	0	212	0
Wholesale and Retail										
Wholesale	11	1	Growth & Competition	0.50	6	1	96	8	103	9
Retail	40	0	Growth & Competition	0.38	15	0	80	0	95	0
The Service Industry	2,220	1,160	Growth & Competition	0.48	1,070	557	2,640	1,360	3,710	1,917
Sub-Totals	12,548	1,200			1,199	569	3,396	1,432	4,596	2,001
Totals	3,748				1,768		4,828		6,597	

Source: Local Employers' Survey — Summer 1970

Appendix III
QUESTIONNAIRES

INSTITUTIONAL EMPLOYERS QUESTIONNAIRE

1. How long has your firm been located in Princeton?

Less than 1 year	1 (1)	_____
1-5 years	1 (2)	_____
6-10 years	1 (3)	_____
11-20 years	1 (4)	_____
20 years and over	1 (5)	_____
No Response/Don't Know	1 (9)	_____

(Skip 2)

2. What attracted you to this community?
(Primary Reason (3) — Secondary Reason (4))

Favorable tax structure	3, 4 (1)	_____
Lower production costs	3, 4 (2)	_____
Skilled manpower pool	3, 4 (3)	_____
Land availability	3, 4 (4)	_____
Nearness to competition	3, 4 (5)	_____

Accessibility to neighboring metropolitan areas	3, 4	(6) _____
Environment of the local community	3, 4	(7) _____
Other	3, 4	(8) _____
No Response/Don't Know	3, 4	(9) _____

3. What is the major function of your firm? i.e., What is your speciality?

Construction	5	(1) _____
Manufacturing	5	(2) _____
Transportation, Communication and Utility	5	(3) _____
Wholesale/Retail	5	(4) _____
Finance, Insurance, Real Estate	5	(5) _____
Services (research)	5	(6) _____
Other	5	(7) _____
No Response/Don't Know	5	(9) _____

4. How many people do you employ?

Full time (Male (6) — Female (7))

1 to 25	6, 7	(1) _____
26 to 99	6, 7	(2) _____
100 to 249	6, 7	(3) _____
250 to 999	6, 7	(4) _____
1,000 and over	6, 7	(5) _____
No Response/Don't Know	6, 7	(9) _____

Part time (Male and Female Combined)

1 to 25	8	(1) _____
26 to 99	8	(2) _____
100 to 249	8	(3) _____
250 to 999	8	(4) _____
1,000 and over	8	(5) _____
No Response/Don't Know	8	(9) _____

5. What percentage of your labor force is comprised of:

a. Professional, Technical and Kindred Workers

0	9	(1) _____
1-5	9	(2) _____
6-15	9	(3) _____
16-25	9	(4) _____

26-39	9	(5) _____
40-59	9	(6) _____
60-84	9	(7) _____
85-100	9	(8) _____
No Response/Don't Know	9	(9) _____

b. Managers, Officials and Proprietors

    Same Format as 5 (a)   10   (1-9) _____

c. Clerical and Kindred Workers (Sales)

    Same Format as 5 (a)   11   (1-9) _____

d. Craftsmen, Foremen and Kindred Workers

    Same Format as 5 (a)   12   (1-9) _____

e. Operators and Kindred Workers

    Same Format as 5 (a)   13   (1-9) _____

f. Service Workers

    Same Format as 5 (a)   14   (1-9) _____

g. Laborers and Private Household Workers

    Same Format as 5 (a)   15   (1-9) _____

                                                  (Skip 16)

6. What percentage of your labor force earns:

a. Below $4,000

0	17	(1) _____
1-5	17	(2) _____
6-15	17	(3) _____
16-25	17	(4) _____
26-39	17	(5) _____
40-59	17	(6) _____
60-84	17	(7) _____
85-100	17	(8) _____
No Response/Don't Know	17	(9) _____

b. $4,000-$6,999

    Same Format as 6 (a)   18   (1-9) _____

c. $7,000-$9,999

    Same Format as 6 (a)   19 (1-9) _____

d. $10,000-$15,999

    Same Format as 6 (a)   20 (1-9) _____

e. $16,000-$20,999

    Same Format as 6 (a)   21 (1-9) _____

f. $21,000-$30,999

    Same Format as 6 (a)   22 (1-9) _____

g. $31,000-$50,999

    Same Format as 6 (a)   23 (1-9) _____

                                (Skip 24)

7. What percentage of your employees live in:

a. Princeton (Township or Borough) (Skip to 8)

0	25	(1) _____
1-5	25	(2) _____
6-15	25	(3) _____
16-25	25	(4) _____
26-39	25	(5) _____
40-59	25	(6) _____
60-84	25	(7) _____
85-100	25	(8) _____
No Response/Don't Know	25	(9) _____

b. Five mile radius

    Same Format as 7 (a)   26 (1-9) _____

c. Ten mile radius

    Same Format as 7 (a)   27 (1-9) _____

d. New York or Philadelphia

    Same Format as 7 (a)   28 (1-9) _____

e. Other (Pennsylvania and Distant N.J.)

    Same Format as 7 (a)   29 (1-9) _____

8. What percentage of your employees who live in Princeton earn:

   a. Under $10,000

0	30	(1) _____
1-5	30	(2) _____
6-15	30	(3) _____
16-25	30	(4) _____
26-39	30	(5) _____
40-59	30	(6) _____
60-84	30	(7) _____
85-100	30	(8) _____
No Response/Don't Know	30	(9) _____

   b. $10,000-$15,999

      Same Format as 8 (a)   31 (1-9) _____

   c. $16,000-$20,999

      Same Format as 8 (a)   32 (1-9) _____

   d. $21,000-$30,999

      Same Format as 8 (a)   33 (1-9) _____

   e. $31,000-$50,999

      Same Format as 8 (a)   34 (1-9) _____

9. Have any of your employees mentioned a desire to live in Princeton?

Yes	35	(1) _____
No (Skip to 10)	35	(2) _____
No Response/Don't Know	35	(9) _____

9 (a). If "Yes" what percentage?

0	36	(1) _____
1-5	36	(2) _____
6-15	36	(3) _____
16-25	36	(4) _____
26-39	36	(5) _____
40-59	36	(6) _____
60-84	36	(7) _____
85-100	36	(8) _____
No Response/Don't Know	36	(9) _____

10. If more housing were available in Princeton, would your employees prefer to be:

Owners	37	(1)	_____
Renters	37	(2)	_____
Both	37	(3)	_____
No Response/Don't Know	37	(9)	_____

11. Does your company own any housing in Princeton for use by management or other personnel?

No (Skip to 12)	38	(1)	_____
Yes (Indicate who it is for_____)	38	(2)	_____
Both	38	(3)	_____
No Response/Don't Know	38	(9)	_____

11 (a). If "Yes," is the housing maintained on a rental or ownership basis?

Rental (How many?)	39	(1)	_____
Ownership (How many?)	39	(2)	_____
Both	39	(3)	_____
No Response/Don't Know	39	(9)	_____

11 (b). If "Yes," is there a waiting list for these homes?

Yes	40	(1)	_____
Owners	40	(2)	_____
Renters	40	(3)	_____
No	40	(4)	_____
No Response/Don't Know	40	(9)	_____

12. What percentage of your employees who live in Princeton:

a. Are owners?

0	41	(1)	_____
1-5	41	(2)	_____
6-15	41	(3)	_____
16-25	41	(4)	_____
26-39	41	(5)	_____
40-59	41	(6)	_____
60-84	41	(7)	_____
85-100	41	(8)	_____
No Response/Don't Know	41	(9)	_____

b. Are renters?

Same Format as 12 (a)   42   (1-9) _____

13. What percentage of your Princeton employees live in:

a. Single family detached houses?

0	43	(1) _____
1-5	43	(2) _____
6-15	43	(3) _____
16-25	43	(4) _____
26-39	43	(5) _____
40-59	43	(6) _____
60-84	43	(7) _____
85-100	43	(8) _____
No Response/Don't Know	43	(9) _____

b. 2-4 family houses?

Same Format as 13 (a)   44   (1-9) _____

c. Multi-family apartments

Same Format as 13 (a)   45   (1-9) _____

14. Do you think there is currently a shortage of housing in Princeton?

Yes	46	(1) _____
No (Skip to 15)	46	(2) _____
No Response/Don't Know	46	(9) _____

14 (a). If "Yes," in what type of structure?

Single family	47	(1) _____
Garden apartments	47	(2) _____
Mid-high rise	47	(3) _____
Townhouses	47	(4) _____
Other	47	(5) _____
Both one and two	47	(6) _____
2-3-4	47	(7) _____
All types	47	(8) _____
No Response/Don't Know	47	(9) _____

14 (b). If "Yes," by what type of occupancy method?

Rental	48	(1) _____
Cooperative/condominium	48	(2) _____
Ownership	48	(3) _____
Both rental and ownership	48	(4) _____
No Response/Don't Know	48	(9) _____

14 (c). If "Yes," in what rental (49) or purchase price (50) range?

Under $100 monthly	(Under $12,000)	49, 50	(1) _____
$100-135 monthly	($12,000-14,499)	49, 50	(2) _____
$136-174 monthly	($17,500-24,999)	49, 50	(3) _____
$175-249 monthly	($25,000-29,999)	49, 50	(4) _____
$250-399 monthly	($40,000-49,999)	49, 50	(5) _____
$400-599 monthly	($60,000-85,000)	49, 50	(6) _____
Over $600 monthly	(Over $85,000)	49, 50	(7) _____
Other		49, 50	(0) _____
No Response/Don't Know		49, 50	(9) _____

15. Do you think more of your competitiors will relocate to the Princeton area in the next five years?

Yes	51	(1) _____
No	51	(2) _____
Unsure	51	(3) _____
No Response/Don't Know	51	(9) _____

16. As you envision the next five years, do you think your firm will:

Expand	52	(1) _____
Decrease	52	(2) _____
Remain the same	52	(3) _____
No Response/Don't Know	52	(9) _____

16 (a). If "Expand" or "Decrease," by what percentage?

0	53	(1) _____
1-5	53	(2) _____
16-15	53	(3) _____
16-25	53	(4) _____
26-39	53	(5) _____

40-59 percent	53	(6) _____
60-84 percent	53	(7) _____
85-100 percent	53	(8) _____
No Response/Don't Know	53	(9) _____

17. Are there any housing deficiencies in Princeton which would inhibit your future plans?

Yes	54	(1) _____
No (Skip to 18)	54	(2) _____
No Response/Don't Know	54	(9) _____

18. What is the most serious housing deficiency by type of structure?

Single family home	55	(1) _____
Garden apartments	55	(2) _____
Mid-high rise	55	(3) _____
Townhouses	55	(4) _____
Other	55	(5) _____
Both one and two	55	(6) _____
2-3-4	55	(7) _____
All types	55	(8) _____
No Response/Don't Know	55	(9) _____

19. What is the most serious housing deficiency by occupancy method?

Rental	56	(1) _____
Cooperative/condominium	56	(2) _____
Ownership	56	(3) _____
Other	56	(4) _____
Both one and three	56	(5) _____
No Response/Don't Know	56	(9) _____

20. What is the most serious deficiency by monthly costs (57) or selling price (58)?

Under $100 monthly	(Under $12,000)	57, 58	(1) _____
$100-135 monthly	($12,000-14,999)	57, 58	(2) _____
$136-174 monthly	($17,500-24,999)	57, 58	(3) _____
$175-249 monthly	($25,000-29,999)	57, 58	(4) _____
$250-399 monthly	($40,000-49,000)	57, 58	(5) _____

$400-599 monthly	($60,000-85,000)	57, 58	(6) _____
Over $600 monthly	(Over $85,000)	57, 58	(7) _____
Other		57, 58	(8) _____
No Response/Don't Know		57, 58	(9) _____

21. Is there any housing deficiency which affects your hiring of "top notch" employees?

No	59	(1) _____
Yes	59	(2) _____
No Response/Don't Know	59	(9) _____

PRESENT RESIDENTS QUESTIONNAIRE

1. Do you live in Princeton Township or Princeton Borough?

Princeton Township	1	(1) _____
Princeton Borough	1	(2) _____

2. How long have you lived in Princeton?

Under 1 year	2	(1) _____
1-5 years	2	(2) _____
6-10 years	2	(3) _____
11-20 years	2	(4) _____
21 + years	2	(5) _____
No Response/Don't Know	2	(9) _____

3. How long have you lived at your present address?

Same	3	(1) _____
Less than 3 years	3	(2) _____
3-5 years	3	(3) _____
6-10 years	3	(4) _____
10 years and over	3	(5) _____
No Response/Don't Know	3	(9) _____

4. Comparing what you spend on housing now with what you were spending on housing at your previous residence, would you say you are spending much more on housing, now, a little more, a little less or a lot less?

Much more	4	(1) _____
Little more	4	(2) _____
Little less	4	(3) _____
Lot less	4	(4) _____
Same	4	(5) _____
No Response/Don't Know	4	(9) _____

5. What type of residence do you now live in?

Detached single family	5	(1) _____
2-3-4 family house	5	(2) _____
Apartment house	5	(3) _____
Other	5	(4) _____
No Response/Don't Know	5	(9) _____

6. Do you currently own or pay rent?

Own	6	(1) _____
Pay rent	6	(2) _____
Other	6	(3) _____
Princeton Contract	6	(4) _____
No Response/Don't Know	6	(9) _____

7. Approximately how old is your house?

Under 5 years	7	(1) _____
5 to 10 years	7	(2) _____
11 to 20 years	7	(3) _____
Over 20 years	7	(4) _____
No Response/Don't Know	7	(9) _____

8. How many bedrooms does your apartment/house have?

None	8	(1) _____
One	8	(2) _____
Two	8	(3) _____
Three	8	(4) _____
Four or more	8	(5) _____
No Response/Don't Know	8	(9) _____

Owners Only (Questions 9 and 10)

9. Could you tell me what the present selling price of your home is — I mean about what would it bring if you sold it today?

Under $15,000	9	(1) _____
$15-30,999	9	(2) _____
$31-50,999	9	(3) _____
$51-75,999	9	(4) _____
$76-100,000	9	(5) _____
Over $100,000	9	(6) _____
No Response/Don't Know	9	(9) _____

10. How much is your monthly mortgage payment including taxes? (If unable to answer "including taxes," take figure without taxes, but so note.)

Under $150	10	(1) _____
$151-200	10	(2) _____
$201-275	10	(3) _____
$276-400	10	(4) _____
$401-550	10	(5) _____
$551-750	10	(6) _____
Over $750	10	(7) _____
No Mortgage	10	(8) _____
No Response/Don't Know	10	(9) _____

Renters Only (Question 11)

11. How much is your monthly rent without utilities?

_____	_____	_____
11	12	13

No Response/Don't Know	14	(9) _____

12. As you envision the next 5 to 10 years, do you anticipate that the size of your household will: remain the same, decrease, or increase?

Remain the same	15	(1) _____
(Skip to Question 13)		
Decrease	15	(2) _____
Increase	15	(3) _____
No Response/Don't Know	15	(9) _____

12 (a). Why: (Write in answer — leave code blank.)

_____

_____ 16 _____

12 (b). When will this happen?

Within a year   17 (1) _____
1-5 years   17 (2) _____
6-10 years   17 (3) _____

No Response/Don't Know   17 (9) _____

12 (c). Will this change cause you to: remain in Princeton or move outside?

Remain in Princeton   19 (1) _____
Move outside   19 (2) _____
No Response/Don't Know   19 (9) _____

12 (d). Will you require larger or smaller accommodations?

Larger accommodation   20 (1) _____
Smaller accommodation   20 (2) _____
Same (Skip to Question 13)   20 (3) _____

No Response/Don't Know   20 (9) _____
(Skip to Question 13)

12 (e). Will you become a renter rather than owner?

Renter   21 (1) _____
Owner (Skip to 13)   21 (2) _____
Other (Skip to 13)   21 (3) _____

No Response/Don't Know   21 (9) _____
(Skip to 13)

12 (e-1). If renter, what type of housing?

Single family house   22 (1) _____
Garden apartment   22 (2) _____
Mid or high rise   22 (3) _____
Town house   22 (4) _____
Other   22 (5) _____

No Response/Don't Know   22 (9) _____

13. Are there specific housing deficiencies in Princeton which would inhibit any future plans?

Yes	23	(1) _____
No (Skip to 14)	23	(2) _____
No Response/Don't Know (Skip to 14)	23	(9) _____

13 (a). What is the most serious housing deficiency by type of structure? i. e., lack of:

Single family homes	24	(1) _____
Garden apartments	24	(2) _____
Mid or high rise	24	(3) _____
Town houses	24	(4) _____
Other	24	(5) _____
No Response/Don't Know	24	(9) _____

13 (a-1). List a possible secondary deficiency by number. (i. e., 1-4 or 9 for none.)

_____
25

13 (b). What is the most serious housing deficiency by occupancy method? i. e., lack of:

Rental units	26	(1) _____
Cooperatives/condominiums	26	(2) _____
Ownership units	26	(3) _____
Other	26	(4) _____
No Response/Don't Know	26	(9) _____

13 (b-1). List a possible secondary deficiency by number. (i. e., 1-3 or 9 for none.)

_____
27

13 (c). What is the most serious housing deficiency by monthly costs (excluding utilities) or current selling price? i. e., insufficient housing available at:

Under $100 monthly	(Under $12,000)	28	(1) _____
$100-135	($15,500-17,499)	28	(2) _____

$136-174	($17,500-24,999)	28	(3) _____
$175-249	($25,000-39,999)	28	(4) _____
$250-399	($40,000-59,999)	28	(5) _____
$400-600	($60,000-85,000)	28	(6) _____
Over $600	(Over $85,000)	28	(7) _____
No Response/Don't Know		28	(9) _____

13 (c-1). List a possible secondary deficiency by number. (i. e., 1-6 or 9 for none.)

_____
29

14. Are you satisfied with your present accommodations?

Yes	30	(1) _____
No	30	(2) _____
No Response/Don't Know	30	(9) _____

14 (a). If "No," why? _____

_____   _____   _____
31   32

15. If there were no housing shortage, would you like to stay in Princeton or would you like to move away?

Stay in Princeton	33	(1) _____
Move away	33	(2) _____
No Response/Don't Know	33	(9) _____

16. Are you anxious to stay in Princeton (move away), or doesn't it matter much to you?

Anxious to stay	34	(1) _____
Anxious to move away	34	(2) _____
Doesn't matter	34	(3) _____
Other_____	34	(4) _____
No Response/Don't Know	34	(9) _____

17. What is your present marital status?

Single	35	(1) _____
Married	35	(2) _____
Separated	35	(3) _____

Divorced	35	(4)	_____
Widowed	35	(5)	_____
Other	35	(6)	_____
No Response/Don't Know	35	(9)	_____

18. How many children (under age 18) do you have? (If 0 skip to 20)

_____
36

18 (a). What is the age of your youngest child?   _____ _____
37   38

19. How many of your children attend public school within the Borough/Township?

40

20. Do you have anyone else living in your home?

No (Skip to 21)	41	(1)	_____
Yes	41	(2)	_____
No Response/Don't Know	41	(9)	_____

20 (a). If "Yes," how many?

_____
42

20 (b). If "Yes," blood relationship and in-laws?

Father	43	(1)	_____
Mother	43	(2)	_____
Father-in-law	43	(3)	_____
Mother-in-law	43	(4)	_____
Both (any combination)	43	(5)	_____
Additional child under 18	43	(6)	_____
Domestic	43	(7)	_____
Other	43	(8)	_____
No Response/Don't Know	43	(9)	_____

21. What is the age of head of household?

Under 21	44	(1)	_____
21-25	44	(2)	_____
26-35	44	(3)	_____

QUESTIONNAIRES

36-49	44 (4) _____
50-64	44 (5) _____
65 and over	44 (6) _____
No Response/Don't Know	44 (9) _____

22. What is his/her (head of household) highest level of education?

Less than high school	45 (1) _____
High school	45 (2) _____
College (BA-BS)	45 (3) _____
Masters Degree	45 (4) _____
Ph. D. or equivalent	45 (5) _____
Other	45 (6) _____
No Response/Don't Know	45 (9) _____

23. What is the occupation of the head of household? (List specific job and title.) _____

_____   _____   _____

                                        46   47

24. Who is his/her (head of house) employer? (If self-employed so indicate.)

                    _____   _____

                    48   49

25. Does anyone else in the immediate household work for pay?

No	50 (1) _____
Yes	50 (2) _____
No Response/Don't Know	50 (9) _____

If "Yes," how many?   _____

                    51

26. What is the total household income?

Under $10,000	52 (1) _____
$10-15,999	52 (2) _____
$16-20,999	52 (3) _____
$21-30,999	52 (4) _____
$31-50,999	52 (5) _____

$51-75,999	52	(6) _____
$76-124,999	52	(7) _____
$125,000 and over	52	(8) _____
No Response/Don't Know	52	(9) _____

27. Voting District

    _____   _____
      53   54

UNDERHOUSED QUESTIONNAIRE

Case #_____
Street _____

1. How long have you lived in Princeton?

Under 1 year	1	(1) _____
1-5 years	1	(2) _____
6-10 years	1	(3) _____
11-20 years	1	(4) _____
Over 21 years	1	(5) _____
No Response/Don't Know	1	(9) _____

2. How long have you lived at your present address?

Same	2	(1) _____
Less than 3 years	2	(2) _____
3-5 years	2	(3) _____
6-10 years	2	(4) _____
10 years and over	2	(5) _____
No Response/Don't Know	2	(9) _____

3. Approximately how old is your apartment/house?

First occupants	3	(1) _____
Under 10 years	3	(2) _____
10 to 20 years	3	(3) _____

21 to 40 years	3	(4) _____
Over 40 years	3	(5) _____
No Response/Don't Know	3	(9) _____

4. Could you tell me how many bedrooms your apartment/home has?

None	4	(1) _____
One	4	(2) _____
Two	4	(3) _____
Three	4	(4) _____
Four or more	4	(5) _____
No Response/Don't Know	3	(9) _____

5. Do you currently own or pay rent?

Own (Go to Question 6)	5	(1) _____
Pay Rent (Go to Question 8)	5	(2) _____
Other _____	5	(3) _____
No Response/Don't Know	5	(9) _____

Owners Only (Questions 6 and 7)

6. Could you tell me approximately how much you paid for this house?

Under $7,000	6	(1) _____
$7,000-11,999	6	(2) _____
$12,000-15,999	6	(3) _____
$16,000-19,999	6	(4) _____
$20,000-29,999	6	(5) _____
$30,000-39,999	6	(6) _____
$40,000 and over	6	(7) _____
No Response/Don't Know	6	(9) _____

7. How much is your monthly mortgage payment, including taxes? (If unable to answer "including taxes," take figure without taxes, but so note.)

Under $100	7	(1) _____
$101-150	7	(2) _____
$151-200	7	(3) _____
$201-300	7	(4) _____
$301-400	7	(5) _____

$400 and over	7	(6) _____
No mortgage	7	(7) _____
No Response/Don't Know	7	(9) _____

Renters Only (Question 8)

8. How much is your monthly rent without utilities?

_____	_____	_____
8	9	10

No Response/Don't Know	(9) _____
	11

All Respondents

9. Are you very satisfied, satisfied, dissatisfied, or very dissatisfied with your present accommodations?

Very satisfied (Skip to Question 12)	12	(1) _____
Satisfied (Skip to Question 12)	12	(2) _____
Dissatisfied (Skip to Question 10)	12	(3) _____
Very dissatisfied (Skip to Question 10)	12	(4) _____
No Response/Don't Know (Go to Question 12)	12	(9) _____

10. Why? (Pertains to 12-3 and 12-4 only.)

_____
13

11. What do you think you could do about this?

_____ _____
14

12. Do you have plans to move within the next 6 years?

No (Go to Question 13)	15	(1) _____
Yes	15	(2) _____

12 (a). If you were to move what type of dwelling unit would you look for?

Same as present	16	(1) _____
Single family house	16	(2) _____
2-3-4 family house	16	(3) _____
Mid or high rise apartment house	16	(4) _____

Garden apartment 16 (5) _____

Other 16 (6) _____

No Response/Don't Know 16 (9) _____

12 (b). Would you like to buy or rent?

Buy 17 (1) _____

Rent 17 (2) _____

Nor Response/Don't Know 17 (9) _____

12 (c). Would you desire more, less, or the same amount of space as you are presently living in?

More 18 (1) _____

Less 18 (2) _____

Same 18 (3) _____

No Response/Don't Know 18 (9) _____

12 (d). What other things would you look for in a home and neighborhood, i.e., what are your housing desires?

Home _____ _____ _____
                                           19 20

Neighborhood _____ _____ _____
                                           21 22

Owners Only (Questions 13-19)

13. There are many problems in maintaining and improving properties. In the case of your home how would you rate the following categories in order of importance to you: (Rank 1-5, 1 being the most important)

Neighborhood consideration 23 _____

Mortgage cost 24 _____

Tax level 25 _____

Tax Reassessments 26 _____

Housing code and inspection requirements 27 _____

No Response/Don't Know 28 _____

13 (a). Are there any other factors which you find troublesome?

_____ _____
                                                                29

14. (Hand card No. 1 to owner and ask him or her to tell you which ones he knows by number, i.e., 1, 2, 3, 4, which ones can be made without reassessments.)

    a. Repairing porches, etc.

        Yes, will be reassessed   30   (1) _____
        No reassessment   30   (2) _____

        No Response/Don't Know   30   (9) _____

    b. Electrical wiring

        Yes, will be reassessed   31   (1) _____
        No reassessment   31   (2) _____

        No Response/Don't Know   31   (9) _____

    c. Water Heater

        Yes, will be reassessed   32   (1) _____
        No reassessment   32   (2) _____

        No Response/Don't Know   32   (9) _____

    d. Central heat

        Yes, will be reassessed   33   (1) _____
        No reassessment   33   (2) _____

        No Response/Don't Know   33   (9) _____

    e. Outside refacing

        Yes, will be reassessed   34   (1) _____
        No Reassessment   34   (2) _____

        No Response/Don't Know   34   (9) _____

15. What improvements would you make in this property if you were sure of not getting a boost in taxes? (List in order of preference.)

    a. _____   35   _____

    b. _____   36   _____

    c. _____   37   _____

        None   38   (1) _____

        No Response/Don't Know   38   (9) _____

15 (a). If "None," why?

_____   39   _____

16. Would you improve this property if given a long-term mortgage?

     Yes   40   (1) _____
     No   40   (2) _____

     No Response/Don't Know   40   (9) _____

16 (a). If "No," why not?

_____   41 _____

17. Do you know of any financial programs sponsored by the government for improvement for your property?

     Yes   42   (1) _____
     No   42   (2) _____

     No Response/Don't Know   42   (9) _____

17 (a). If "Yes," what are they?

_____   43   _____

18. What source would you turn to if you needed money to make improvements on your property?

     Savings bank   44   (1) _____
     Mortgage broker   44   (2) _____
     Finance company   44   (3) _____
     Personal loan, commercial bank   44   (4) _____
     Personal resources   44   (5) _____
     Second mortgage   44   (6) _____
     Bank w/o detail   44   (7) _____
     Other   44   (8) _____

     No Response/Don't Know   44   (9) _____

(Write Down Any Extra Information)

Renters Only (Questions 20 and 21)

19. Is buying a home an important goal for you?

     Yes (Go to Question 21)   45   (1) _____

No (Go to Question 22)   45   (2) _____

No Response/Don't Know   45   (9) _____
(Go to Question 22)

20. Do you think you will buy within the next five years?

      Yes (Go to Question 21-a)   46   (1) _____
      No (Go to Question 21-b)   46   (2) _____
      Maybe (Go to Question 21-b)   46   (3) _____

      No Response/Don't Know   46   (9) _____

20 (a). Do you plan on buying within Princeton?

      Yes (Go to Question 22)   47   (1) _____
      No (Go to Question 21-c)   47   (2) _____
      Maybe (Go to Question 21-c)   47   (3) _____

      No Response/Don't Know   47   (9) _____

20 (b). Why is this?

_____   48   _____

20 (c). If "No," why?

_____   49   _____

21. What is your present marital status?

      Single   50   (1) _____
      Married   50   (2) _____
      Separated   50   (3) _____
      Divorced   50   (4) _____
      Widowed   50   (5) _____
      Other   50   (6) _____

      No Response/Don't Know   50   (9) _____

22. How many persons live in this dwelling unit?

           _____   _____
           51   52

23. How many children under ages 18 do you have?   _____
                                                      53

24. Besides your spouse and children, is anyone else living in your home?

Yes	54	(1)	_____
No	54	(2)	_____
No Response/Don't Know	54	(9)	_____

24 (a). If "Yes," how many?

_____
55

24 (b). If "Yes," give relationship.

_____
56

25. What is the age of the head of household?

Under 21	57	(1)	_____
21-25	57	(2)	_____
26-35	57	(3)	_____
36-49	57	(4)	_____
College (2 yrs.)	58	(3)	_____
Secretarial school/Trade school (after high school)	58	(4)	_____
College (BA-BS)	58	(5)	_____
Masters Degree	58	(6)	_____
Ph.D or equivalent	58	(7)	_____
Other	58	(8)	_____
No Response/Don't Know	58	(9)	_____

27. What is the occupation of the head of household?
    (List specific job and title.)

_____

_____
59

28. Who is his/her (head of household) employer?
    (If self-employed, so indicate.) Where is this located?

_____

_____   _____
60   61

29. Does anyone else in the immediate household work for pay?

Yes	62	(1)	_____
No	62	(2)	_____
No Response/Don't Know	62	(9)	_____

30. Approximately what was your total family income for the last year?

Less than $3,000	63	(1) _____
$3,000-5,999	63	(2) _____
$6,000-9,999	63	(3) _____
$10,000-14,999	63	(4) _____
$15,000-19,999	63	(5) _____
$20,000-24,999	63	(6) _____
$25,000-29,999	63	(7) _____
$30,000 and over	63	(8) _____
No Response/Don't Know	63	(9) _____

(Record All Comments)

31. What action do you think will come about as a result of this study?

More housing	64	(1) _____
Increased concern	64	(2) _____
Paperwork	64	(3) _____
Nothing	64	(4) _____
Other	64	(5) _____
No Response/Don't Know	64	(9) _____

(To Be Answered after the Interview by Observation)

32. Residence:

Princeton Township	65	(1) _____
Princeton Borough	65	(2) _____

33. Type of Residence:

Detached single family	66	(1) _____
2-3-4 family house	66	(2) _____
Apartment house	66	(3) _____
Other _____	66	(4) _____

34. Construction:

Frame	67	(1) _____
Frame with reasonable to good siding	67	(2) _____
Frame with bad siding	67	(3) _____
Masonry	67	(4) _____
Other _____	67	(5) _____

35. Quality of external appearance:

    Poorer than neighbors   68   (1) _____
    Same as neighbors   68   (2) _____
    Better than neighbors   68   (3) _____

36. Quality of street blocks vs. area:

    Same as   69   (1) _____
    Better than   69   (2) _____
    Poorer than   69   (3) _____

37. General comments: (Surveyor's comments and evaluation of the dwelling unit in general.)

    _____   70   _____
    _____   71   _____

38. Race of respondent:

    Black   72   (1) _____
    White   72   (2) _____
    Other   72   (3) _____

Area # _____
77

Case # _____   _____   _____
        78   79   80

MUNICIPAL EMPLOYEES QUESTIONNAIRE

1. Where do you live?

    Franklin, Rocky Hill, South Brunswick, North Bruns-
    wick, East Brunswick   1   (1) _____
    Cranbury, East Windsor, West Windsor, Plainsboro,
    Hightstown, Jamesburg, Skillman   1   (2) _____
    Lawrence, Pennington, Hopewell Township, Ewing,
    Trenton, Hamilton   1   (3) _____

Hopewell Borough, Montgomery Township, Amwell,
Flemington   1   (4) _____
Princeton Borough   1   (5) _____
Princeton Township   1   (6) _____
Other Middlesex County   1   (7) _____
Pennsylvania   1   (8) _____
Other — Distant New Jersey   1   (9) _____

2. How long have you lived there?

Under 1 year   2   (1) _____
1 to 5 years   2   (2) _____
6 to 10 years   2   (3) _____
11 to 20 years   2   (4) _____
21 years and over   2   (5) _____

No Response/Don't Know   2   (9) _____

3. Do you work for Princeton Borough or Princeton Township?

Borough   3   (1) _____
Township   3   (2) _____
Both   3   (3) _____
Other   3   (4) _____

No Response/Don't Know   3   (9) _____

4. How long have you been employed by the above listed municipality(ies)?

Under 1 year   4   (1) _____
1 to 3 years   4   (2) _____
4 to 10 years   4   (3) _____
10 to 20 years   4   (4) _____
20 years and over   4   (5) _____

No Response/Don't Know   4   (9) _____

5. Throughout your tenure as a municipal employee, have you looked for housing locally in either the Borough or Township?

Yes (skip to 6)   5   (1) _____
No   5   (2) _____

No Response/Don't Know   5   (9) _____

5 (a). If "No," why not?

Cost of housing	6	(1)	_____
Availability of housing	6	(2)	_____
Already lived there	6	(3)	_____
Preferred not	6	(4)	_____
Travelling difficulty	6	(5)	_____
No Response/Don't Know	6	(9)	_____

6. What type of housing were you seeking?

a.
Rental	7	(1)	_____
Ownership	7	(2)	_____
Other	7	(3)	_____
No Response/Don't Know	7	(9)	_____

b.
Single family house	8	(1)	_____
1-4 family house	8	(2)	_____
Garden apartment	8	(3)	_____
Town house or equivalent	8	(4)	_____
Mid or high rise	8	(5)	_____
Other	8	(6)	_____
No Response/Don't Know	8	(9)	_____

c.
Under $100 monthly	(under $12,000)	9	(1)	_____
$100-135 monthly	($12-17,499)	9	(2)	_____
$136-175 monthly	($17,500-24,999)	9	(3)	_____
$176-249 monthly	($25-39,999)	9	(4)	_____
$250-399 monthly	($40-59,999)	9	(5)	_____
$400-599 monthly	($60-85,000)	9	(6)	_____
Over $600 monthly	(Over $85,000)	9	(7)	_____
Other		9	(8)	_____
No Response/Don't Know		9	(9)	_____

7. Did you find this housing available?

Yes (commonly)	10	(1)	_____
Yes, but not in desirable areas or preferred housing configurations	10	(2)	_____
No (skip to 8)	10	(3)	_____
No Response/Don't Know (skip to 8)	10	(9)	_____

8. Why have you chosen your current community or Princeton as your place of residence?

Housing value	11	(1)	_____
Environment	11	(2)	_____
Place of birth or early renting	11	(3)	_____
Good commuting distance	11	(4)	_____
Local schools	11	(5)	_____
Required to live there	11	(6)	_____
Other	11	(7)	_____
No Response/Don't Know	11	(9)	_____

9. Are you satisfied with your present accommodations?

Yes	12	(1)	_____
No	12	(2)	_____
No Response/Don't Know	12	(9)	_____

10. Do you currently own or rent?

Own	13	(1)	_____
Rent	13	(2)	_____
Other	13	(3)	_____
No Response/Don't Know	13	(9)	_____

11. What type of housing do you currently occupy?

Single family	14	(1)	_____
2-3-4 family	14	(2)	_____
Apartment	14	(3)	_____
No Response/Don't Know	14	(9)	_____

12. How many bedrooms do you have?

None	15	(1)	_____
One	15	(2)	_____
Two	15	(3)	_____
Three	15	(4)	_____
Four or more	15	(5)	_____
No Response/Don't Know	15	(9)	_____

Owners Only

13. What is your monthly mortgage payment, including taxes?

Less than $150	16	(1) _____
$151-200	16	(2) _____
$201-275	16	(3) _____
$276-400	16	(4) _____
$401-550	16	(5) _____
No Mortgage	16	(6) _____
No Response/Don't Know	16	(9) _____

14. Could you tell me what the present selling price of your home is? — I mean what it would bring if you sold it today?

Under $17,500	17	(1) _____
$17,500-24,999	17	(2) _____
$25-39,999	17	(3) _____
$40-59,999	17	(4) _____
$60-85,000	17	(5) _____
Over $85,000	17	(6) _____
No Response/Don't Know	17	(9) _____

Renters Only (Question 15)

15. How much is your monthly rent without utilities?

$10-99	18	(1) _____
$100-149	18	(2) _____
$150-199	18	(3) _____
$200-269	18	(4) _____
$270-349	18	(5) _____
$350-449	18	(6) _____
$450-999	18	(7) _____
No Response/Don't Know	18	(9) _____

16. Do you think municipal employees in general should live within the community in which they work?

Yes	19	(1) _____
No	19	(2) _____
Mixed feelings	19	(3) _____
No Response/Don't Know	19	(9) _____

16 (a). Do others in your profession generally hold this view?

Yes	20	(1)	_____
No	20	(2)	_____
No Response/Don't Know	20	(9)	_____

17. Do you in particular have any desire for initial or continued residence within Princeton?

Yes, initial	21	(1)	_____
Yes, continued	21	(2)	_____
No (skip to 19)	21	(3)	_____
No Response/Don't Know	21	(9)	_____

18. Would this supersede a vertical promotion of primary head of household?

Yes	22	(1)	_____
No	22	(2)	_____
Undecided	22	(3)	_____
No Response/Don't Know	22	(9)	_____

19. If more housing were available in the future, would you move to or remain in Princeton?

Yes	23	(1)	_____
No	23	(2)	_____
Undecided	23	(3)	_____
No Response/Don't Know	23	(9)	_____

20. As you envision the next five years, will your housing needs remain the same, increase, or decrease?

Remain the same (skip to 24)	24	(1)	_____
Increase	24	(2)	_____
Decrease	24	(3)	_____
No Response/Don't Know	24	(9)	_____

21. When would this happen?

Within a year	25	(1)	_____
1-5 years	25	(2)	_____

6-10 years		25	(3) _____
No Response/Don't Know		25	(9) _____

22. Would you require similar housing as you now inhabit?

Yes (skip to 23)		26	(1) _____
No		26	(2) _____
No Response/Don't Know		26	(9) _____

22 (a). If "No," list type (owner, renter, etc.) and price range.

a. Renter		27	(1) _____
Owner		27	(2) _____
Cooperative		27	(3) _____

b. Under $100 monthly	(Under $12,000)	28	(1) _____
$100-135 monthly	($12-17,499)	28	(2) _____
$136-175 monthly	($17,500-24,999)	28	(3) _____
$176-249 monthly	($25-39,999)	28	(4) _____
$250-399 monthly	($40-59,999)	28	(5) _____
$400-599 monthly	($60-85,000)	28	(6) _____
Over $600 monthly	(Over $85,000)	28	(7) _____
No Response/Don't Know		28	(9) _____

23. In view of future plans would this suffice for the next 5-10 years?

Yes		29	(1) _____
No		29	(2) _____
No Response/Don't Know		29	(9) _____

24. What is your specific relationship to Princeton as a community?

Employee 9-5		30	(1) _____
Employee with many extracurricular activities			
Professional		30	(2) _____
Non-professional		30	(3) _____
Both		30	(4) _____
Concerned yet inactive member of its working populace		30	(5) _____
An active aid to community leadership		30	(6) _____
Other		30	(7) _____
No Response/Don't Know		30	(9) _____

25. Do you think living outside Princeton hurts your job effectiveness?

Yes   31   (1) _____

No   31   (2) _____

Depends upon the individual (explain)

_____   31   (3) _____

Undecided   31   (4) _____

No Response/Don't Know   31   (9) _____

26. Do you believe that there should exist other responsibilities to the community by whom you are employed that extend beyond the 9 to 5 work period?

Yes   32   (1) _____

No   32   (2) _____

Depends upon the job   32   (3) _____

Undecided   32   (4) _____

Other   32   (5) _____

No Response/Don't Know   32   (9) _____

27. Does living outside the community hinder these responsibilities?

Yes   33   (1) _____

No   33   (2) _____

Undecided   33   (3) _____

No Response/Don't Know   33   (9) _____

28. What is your present marital status?

Single   34   (1) _____

Married   34   (2) _____

Separated   34   (3) _____

Divorced   34   (4) _____

Widowed   34   (5) _____

Other   34   (6) _____

No Response/Don't Know   34   (9) _____

29. How many children under age 18 do you have?   35   _____
    (If 0 skip to 33)

30. How many of these now attend public school locally?   36   _____

31. What is the age of your youngest child?   37   _____

32. What is the total size of your household?   38   _____

33. What is your total household income?

Under $10,000	40	(1) _____
$10-15,999	40	(2) _____
$16-20,999	40	(3) _____
$21-30,999	40	(4) _____
Over $31,000	40	(5) _____
Other	40	(6) _____
No Response/Don't Know	40	(9) _____

34. Do you think the Princeton populace is concerned about municipal workers housing/lack of housing within the community?

Yes, deeply	41	(1) _____
Yes, superficially	41	(2) _____
No	41	(3) _____
Undecided	41	(4) _____
No Response/Don't Know	41	(9) _____

35. What action do you think will come about as a result of this study?

More housing	42	(1) _____
Increased concern	42	(2) _____
Paperwork	42	(3) _____
Nothing	42	(4) _____
Other	42	(5) _____
No Response/Don't Know	42	(9) _____

36. What is Princeton's first most serious housing deficiency?

    a. People served

Low income	43	(1) _____
Middle income	43	(2) _____
Senior citizen	43	(3) _____
Singles	43	(4) _____

    b. Type of unit

Renter	44	(1) _____
Owner	44	(2) _____
No Response/Don't Know	44	(9) _____

37. Do you think Princeton is a good place to be a municipal employee?

Yes	45	(1) _____
No	45	(2) _____
No Response/Don't Know	45	(9) _____

38. Why?

Attitude of the populace	46	(1) _____
Facilities, equipment or working conditions	46	(2) _____
Education of the populace or talent of offspring	46	(3) _____
Attitude of co-workers	46	(4) _____
No Response/Don't Know	46	(9) _____

39. List the first thing which comes to mind when someone mentions the prestige of Princeton.

Affluence	47	(1) _____
Status	47	(2) _____
Education	47	(3) _____
Distaste non-existent	47	(4) _____
No Response/Don't Know	47	(9) _____

40. Are you the primary head of household?

Yes	48	(1) _____
No	48	(2) _____

41. What is your position in municipal government?

Senior administrator	49	(1) _____
Working professional	49	(2) _____
Subsidiary professional	49	(3) _____

42. What is your area of municipal specialty?

Education	50	(1) _____
Public Safety	50	(2) _____
Administration	50	(3) _____
Clerical	50	(4) _____
Engineering	50	(5) _____
Library Service	50	(6) _____